A Century of
Boston Sports

BOSTON CELTICS
MEDIA PASS

1980 NBA PLAYOFFS

GAME

D

1967
WORLD SERIES
AMERICAN LEAGUE vs.
NATIONAL LEAGUE
FENWAY PARK

BOX SEAT
$12.00

DO NOT
DETACH
THIS
COUPON
FROM
RAIN
CHECK

GAME
7

GEORGE

Boston College

HOME
SEPT. 28   WICHITA
OCT. 12   VILLANOVA
NOV. 2   VANDERBILT
NOV. 9   BUFFALO
NOV. 16   VIRGINIA

AWAY
SEPT. 21   SYRACUSE
OCT. 4   DETROIT
OCT. 26   AIR FORCE
NOV. 23   BOSTON UNIV.
NOV. 30   HOLY CROSS

1863   1963

1963

EAGLE FOOTBALL SCHEDULE

BOSTON BRUINS
75

vs

NEW YORK
RANGERS
GAME 27
FEBRUARY 7, 1999
SUNDAY, 3:00 PM
Premium Seating - Club

CLB117   E   11
Section   Row   Seat

B00307
0006

FleetCenter

PREMIUM
SEATING

BOSTON BRUINS
75

U.S. OPEN CHAMPIONSHIP
1988

U.S. OPEN
THE COUNTRY CLUB
Brookline, Massachusetts

GALLERY

This ticket must be displayed at all times.
NO COOLERS, RADIOS, LADDERS,
FOLDING CHAIRS, SIGNS PERMITTED ON COURSE.
NO EXCHANGE OR REFUND

$20.00

THIS TICKET VALID ONLY FOR

MONDAY
JUNE 13, 1988
No. 008256

SEC.
25

Price $2.00   Fed.Tax .40   Total $2.40
GRANDSTAND
FENWAY PARK

ROW
20

SEAT

HOLY CROSS
vs.
BOSTON COLLEGE

Nov. 26
1944
1:15 P.M.

ENTER
GATE
A

ENTER JERSEY STREET

SULLIVAN BROS.   LOWELL

A Century of Boston Sports

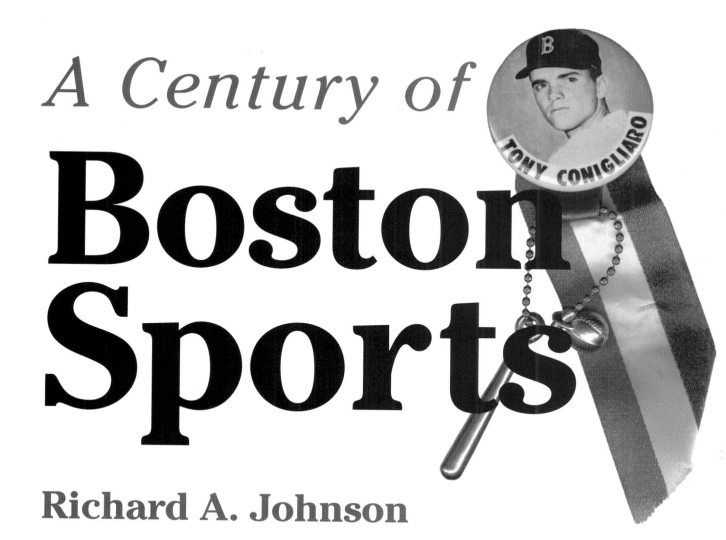

Richard A. Johnson

with a foreword by Bill Littlefield

and essays by Glenn Stout

Northeastern University Press

Boston

Dedicated to:
Dr. Robert Andrew Johnson and Minna Flynn Johnson
My Parents, My Friends

The Memory of Bob Walsh, Tom Stack, and Charlie O'Rourke
Friends and Sportsmen

Glenn Stout
Friend and Colleague

Library of Congress Cataloging-in-Publication Data

Johnson, Dick, 1955–
  A century of Boston sports / Richard A. Johnson ; foreword by Bill Littlefield.
    p.   cm.
    Includes index.
    ISBN 1-55553-456-2 (cloth : alk. paper)
  1. Sports—Massachusetts—Boston—History—20th century. I. Title: Boston sports. II. Title.

  GV584.5.B6 J64   2000
  796'.09744'610904—dc21   00-058227

Designed by Peter Blaiwas / Vernon Press, Inc.

Composed in Cheltenham and Helvetica Condensed by Stratford Publishing Services, Inc.,
Brattleboro, Vermont. Illustrations scanned by All Systems Colour, Inc., Lebanon, Ohio.
Printed and bound by Friesens, Altona, Manitoba.
The paper is Patina, an acid-free stock.

MANUFACTURED IN CANADA
04 03 02 01 00   5 4 3 2 1

Contents

Preface and Acknowledgments

This book is not meant to be a comprehensive history of sports in Boston over the past century. Instead, I have sought to capture something of the unmatched diversity, excellence, and character of America's greatest sports town. In selecting and writing about over 150 photographs, I have sought to document those athletes, teams, and events that collectively have defined Boston's identity as a world-renowned center of sports. Within these pages I have attempted to assemble a mosaic of words and pictures.

This volume should have been written and compiled by my longtime friend and mentor, the late Jerry Nason of the *Boston Globe.* As a reporter, columnist, editor, archivist, and historian he had no peer. His enthusiasm and wisdom inspire me to this day.

In the nearly twenty years I have served the Sports Museum of New England as curator, I've seen many thousands of photographs of Boston sports and listened to countless hours of stories and anecdotes. This volume attempts to convey much of the best of both.

I am especially grateful to my family—Mary, Robert, Elizabeth, Bob, Amy, and my parents—who provided great support for this project during what became a difficult year.

Among the clutch performers who helped in the creation of this book are Glenn Stout, the best writer and sports researcher I know; Bill Littlefield of NPR's "Only a Game"; Bob Ryan, Joe Sullivan, Donald Skwar, and Andy Dabilis of the *Boston Globe;* Luke Salisbury, Saul Wisnia, Jack Falla, R. R. Marshall, Frederick Lewis, Northeastern's own Jack Grinold, John Veneziano of Harvard University, Debbie Matson of the Red Sox, J. Harvey McKenney, Brian Codagnone, Matthew and Dennis Brearley, Marjorie Trenholm of the Stanley Museum, Sinclair Hitchings of the Boston Public Library, Pat Kelly of the National Baseball Hall of Fame, sportswriter extraordinaire George Sullivan, Zach Fleming of the Boston Athletic Association, and the invaluable and ever-cheerful John Cronin and Al Thibeault of the *Boston Herald* library.

As this book is the product of many years of work as curator of the Sports Museum of New England in Boston, I am compelled to mention the many museum officials and friends with whom it has been my privilege to work. I am grateful to people such as Vic and Charlie Caliri, Dave Cowens, Jan Volk, Richard Kreswick, Jim Bednarek, Jon Bonsall, Charlie O'Rourke, Richard Pond, Paul Dietrich, Bob Walsh, Kevin Aylward, Ted Harrison, Marjorie Harrison, Donald Reed, Andy Stern, Mary Duffy, Dorothy Duffy, Ira Jackson, Steve Belkin, Bob Margil, Richard Gold, Jim Davis, Bill Galatis, Lou Gorman, Joe Pellegrino, Mary Tierney, Al Coulthard, John McGrath, Fred Kirsch, Roger Clifton, Dr. Tenley Albright, Dr. Mike Foley, Tom Yewcic, Barry Morris, Jim Frisone, Tom Stack, Mal Graham, Steve Karp, Carl Chudnofsky, Peter Sollogub, Dick Lyons, Frank Zaremba, David Balfour, John Tighe, Sherwin Kapstein, Tony Lawrence, and Armand LaMontagne.

I am especially grateful to the staff and volunteers with whom I have served, including Brian Codagnone, Tina Anderson, Sheldon Brown, Mark Shreve, Fred Sawyer, Gene Valentine, Cynthia Atlas Goff, Charles Goff, Laurie Aronson Starr, Lisa Grundy, Kent Wian, Brian Delmore, June Ferestein, Ellen Johnson, Robin Dole, Jim Blake, Richard Malatesta, Joe Bertagna, Fred Hoskins, Mary McNiff, Margaret Santoro, Elizabeth Lunt, Jeff Liston, Jonathan Gerson, Harriet McGraw, Rita Tavilla, Lee Campbell, Michael LaVigne, P. J. Levin, Gordon Katz, Joe Dobrow, Steve Garabedian, Dennis Newman, Ronnie Freedman, Harvey Robbins, Linda Picard, and Albie Walton.

Also assisting with the research and production of this book were Bill Cleary, Mike Andersen, Michele L. Amundsen, Meg Cowe, John Sears, Bob Wood, Nick Tsiotis, Jeff Twiss, and John Hannah.

In addition, I am also appreciative of the support shown by Northeastern University Press, especially William A. Frohlich, John Weingartner, and Ann Twombly, and the talent and skill demonstrated by Chris Dall and Peter Blaiwas of Vernon Press.

—Richard A. Johnson, February 2000

Foreword

I've always been skeptical of claims that Boston is the greatest sports town. Willie Mays was born in Westfield, Alabama. He played ball in New York and San Francisco. Pele wasn't born in Boston, either, and when he finally brought his extraordinary game to the United States, he was employed by the team in New York.

On the other hand, in this remarkably thorough and entertaining volume, Richard Johnson makes a strong case for Boston as the very best place for the sports fan to visit via book. The historical currents of sports as varied as marathoning, baseball, basketball, football, and tennis all run deep in Boston, and thanks to the exemplary work of Johnson and essayist Glenn Stout, we can trace them with the aid of just one volume.

The details are here—the dates, the times, the sizes of the crowds— and the personalities of the champions as well. But Johnson and Stout have also included odd and engaging generalizations. Consider, for example: "If the sporting heart of Greater Boston could be seen, it would resemble a hockey puck."

My friend George Carter, who coaches not only midgets, mites, and squirts, but also germs and amoebas at the rink down Norwood there, would be pleased.

Johnson and Stout are both accomplished raconteurs and they recognize that the real point of our games is not records, money, or even championships. The real point is stories. If Boston is blessed to be the site of some of the most enduring and entertaining moments and memories of sports events and athletes, the town is doubly lucky for the presence of two such indefatigable sports chroniclers. As a fellow who's been batting around Boston's games like a moth around a lightbulb for years, I'm grateful for this book. I'd be grateful for it even if I wasn't dependent for a paycheck on these stories and the stories they have begotten and will beget. I think you will be, too.

—*Bill Littlefield*

Sports Town

Americans love sports because they represent the most conspicuous manifestation of our democratic ideals. In principle, America was founded partly on the notion of meritocracy; nowhere in our society has this ideal found better expression than in sports. This has been especially true in the years since Jackie Robinson broke baseball's color barrier and Title IX enabled women to compete in collegiate athletics. Although we still cherish the dream that anyone can rise from poverty to become president, it is far more likely that a millionaire governor with three names and a trust fund will claim that prize. But in the world of sports, the mantle of greatness will forever be granted to the unconnected among us with enough talent, courage, and perseverance to stake a claim.

Nowhere on Earth are sports a bigger deal—both from a business perspective and a fan interest level—than in America. And nowhere in America are sports a bigger deal than they are in Boston. For nearly two centuries, the city has been an unrivaled center of sports on all levels. Nowhere has the "American Dream" been better expressed through the games we play.

Boston is the Hollywood of sports. No city has a greater or more diverse sports history or embraces the sweaty endeavors of its teams and athletes with such unbridled passion. Some say that the one aspect of life that unites all Bostonians, apart from a rabid interest in politics, is sports. If you want to start a conversation in Boston, just mention the name Bill Buckner or even the name of more obscure sports figures such as Smead Jolley, Kathrine Switzer, Hambone Williams, or Billy Speer. It is guaranteed that at least one Bostonian, whether on the outbound Green Line train from Park Street to Kenmore or seated next to you at Durgin Park, will gladly share a personal memory or two.

Boston is blessed with a climate and geography that allow playing as wide a variety of sports as is possible anywhere on the planet. Within a two-hour drive of the city one could hypothetically ski in the White Mountains and surf the Atlantic on the same day.

Boston has been a sports mecca since renegade Puritans first raced horses south of the Shawmut Peninsula nearly four centuries ago. No

less a historic figure
than Ben Franklin was
recognized as one of
the best athletes in the
Massachusetts Bay
Colony in the early
eighteenth century.
The same British naval
officers who would
come to curse his
name in later years
gladly bet their
shillings and crowns
on the young appren-
tice boy as he chal-
lenged all comers to
swimming races in
Boston harbor. Today
the L Street Brownies
ply the same waters as
Franklin, and the bets
are more likely to be
placed on another
tribe of Patriots.

Throughout the century, Boston fans have shown their support for the hometown team.

Boston is the home of countless sports "firsts," such as the first base-ball dynasty (the Red Stockings, who won four of five National Associa-tion pennants from 1871 to 1875), the first American NHL franchise (the Boston Bruins), and the first World Series Champions (the 1903 Boston Americans) among others. It is also home to the oldest indoor ice arena in the world (Matthews Arena, c. 1910) and the oldest concrete sta-dium in America (Harvard Stadium, c. 1903).

Boston can also lay claim to one of the nation's first true sports super-stars—John L. Sullivan, the famed "Boston Strongboy"—not to mention such greats as Eleonora Sears, Cy Young, Bill Russell, Hazel Hotchkiss Wightman, Bobby Orr, and Nomar Garciaparra, among countless others.

But Boston is also a city that loves the role-player. Some of the loudest cheers have been reserved for muckers and working-class heroes such as Eddie Westfall, the quintessential Boston Bruin; any of the Celtics' sixth, seventh, or eighth men; Jim Lee Hunt and most any Boston Patriot; Bernie Carbo; and every last runner in the Boston Marathon. Heaven help the prima donna or highly remunerated superstar unwilling to get down and dirty for the paying customer.

Bostonians have been the kind of sports fans whose knowledge and respect for the game didn't allow them to boo future Hall of Famer Luis Aparicio when he went zero for forty after arriving via trade from the White Sox in 1971. Earlier generations tossed candy bars to Boston Braves right fielder Tommy Holmes from the Braves Field Jury Box and also inspired the Bruins from the "heavens" of the Boston Garden's second balcony. More recently, Bostonians opened their hearts to Boston University hockey player Travis Roy after he was paralyzed during his first-ever shift for the Terriers. Likewise, over fifty thousand attended the funeral of Harry Agganis, the finest local athlete of his or any generation.

Sports have also had a unifying effect on the city. Has Boston ever seen a day like that of the funeral of Celtics star Reggie Lewis? Over seven thousand gathered at Northeastern University's Matthews Arena in Boston's largest multiracial gathering in modern memory. On a day when color seemed irrelevant, sports once again unified in mourning this most racially troubled city.

Bostonians know their games the way Londoners know the theater. And, like theater, so much of the experience of attending a game involves that intangible quality called *atmosphere,* which depends in part upon the knowledge and involvement of the crowd. The Boston Garden had tremendous atmosphere. In fact, any big game at Boston Garden could have been graded on two very quantifiable scales: heat and noise. Never has there been an indoor arena where the emotional barometer of a crowd has fluctuated as wildly or had as great an impact on events. Similar atmosphere can be found at Fenway Park, Matthews Arena, Harvard Stadium for the Yale game, the Back Bay during the marathon, and the FleetCenter during the unmatched March carnival of high school championships. More than one grateful Boston athlete has noted the contribution of the crowd—the proverbial "extra player."

Some of the most unforgettable Boston crowd experiences have come when least expected. In 1979, New York Yankee pitcher Jim "Catfish" Hunter received an unlikely standing ovation from the Fenway Park crowd on the night of his last Boston appearance, which also happened to coincide with Carl Yastrzemski's three-thousandth hit. In 1982, Celtics fans paid homage to the essence of the game when, aware of their team's impending defeat by Philadelphia in the conference finals, they exhorted the hated Seventy-Sixers to "beat LA" in the NBA Finals.

Bostonians have been blessed not only with great teams and a plethora of great sporting events, but also with some of the best sports pages in the land. In the days when Boston boasted eight dailies, each paper included at least one sports story on either its back or front page. Nowadays, the Red Sox still possess the largest traveling cadre of beat reporters in the majors, and every team, even newcomers like the New England Revolution, receives comprehensive coverage. It is hardly surprising that the staffs of many national print and electronic outlets, such as ESPN and *Sports Illustrated,* are liberally staffed with former Boston writers and editors.

Sports radio has been with us for generations, having started with the "Voice of Sports" and the erudite presence of Eli Schliefer, Tim Horgan, Jake Liston, and George Sullivan; the acerbic cackling of Cliff and Claf; the understated wit of Guy Mainella; and the unforgettable antics of Eddie Andelman, Mark Witkin, and Jim McCarthy of "The Sports Huddle." These pioneers begat an industry that has spread to become nation-wide and now resides at several local stations, most prominently at WEEI, where fans have nearly limitless access to the airwaves and where some, such as "Butch from the Cape," have become radio personalities in their own right.

Bostonians have been and always will be connected by the games they watch and the teams they support. In a city where tradition is every-thing, Bostonians are willing to pay the highest ticket prices and endure the worst traffic for the genuine article. After witnessing an Impossible Dream pennant, sixteen Celtics world championships, two improbable Super Bowl teams, the Big Bad Bruins, and a host of memo-rable events like the marathon, the men's and women's World Cups, and a most unforgettable Ryder Cup, Bostonians always expect that some measure of magic resides in almost any game. For most of the past century, sports in Boston have delivered nothing less.

—*Richard A. Johnson*

the New Century

Jimmy Collins and
John L. Sullivan

By 1900 Boston had become the most Irish city outside Dublin, and never were two sports heroes more renowned or beloved in turn-of-the-century Boston than Irishmen John L. Sullivan and Jimmy Collins.

Sullivan, a boxer, was America's first sports superstar, the perfect athlete and personality for the budding republic. In an era when athletes lived at the same socioeconomic level as the working people who cheered them, the Roxbury native trained in a stable-turned-makeshift- gymnasium near the Allston stockyards. Legend has it that he availed himself of his surroundings by drinking a quart of freshly drawn beef blood each day. Confident in his abilities, Sullivan was also known to boast. It is hardly a stretch to imagine him walking into any drinking establishment in America and enhancing his reputation as the "Boston Strong Boy" by proclaiming, "I can lick any man in the house."

Following a world championship career in which he won thirty-eight fights and lost only one, Sullivan earned his living by selling his autograph at ten cents a signature before embracing sobriety and spreading the gospel of temperance via a lecture tour. Through it all he remained on the sports scene and, like many Boston baseball fans, quickly shifted his allegiance from the Boston Nationals (who became the Braves in 1910) to the Boston Americans (who became the Red Sox in 1908). Many fans jumped upon the rolling bandwagon of the fledgling team when Nationals third baseman Jimmy Collins jumped to the Americans in 1901. (The fact that the Americans charged half as much per ticket as their senior counterparts no doubt influenced team loyalties as well.) Like Sullivan before him, Jimmy Collins was viewed as a demigod in a city that valued tribal loyalties as much as success.

Collins was not only a superb third baseman but also the manager of the Americans squad that captured the first World Series, played against the Pittsburgh Pirates in 1903. In addition, Collins's defection to the Americans and the American League from the Nationals in 1901 helped the upstart league gain instant credibility. In his seven years with the Americans, Collins batted .296 with 25 home runs, 881 hits, 65 triples, and 102 stolen bases. Collins was elected to the National Baseball Hall of Fame in 1945.

Corinthians Football Club vs. Fore River Shipyard

At the time of their arrival in America, the Corinthians Football Club of England was the great amateur team of their generation. Not only had the Corinthians played most professional teams on equal terms, but they had once supplied the English National Team with nine of its starting eleven for a match in 1886. Although Corinthians FC never entered the Football Association (FA) Cup competition, it carried the banner of amateurism by defeating several defending FA Cup winners in challenge matches. So rigorous was their code of behavior that to receive a red card meant permanent expulsion from the team. Their appearance in Boston came at a time when most immigrants in the city would have recognized them as one of the world's great teams.

But on September 14, 1906, at the Locust Street Grounds, remembered now as the former incinerator site on the southeast expressway, Fore River Shipyard fought Corinthians FC to a 1–1 tie. Spectators agreed that

Corinthians Football Club of England versus Fore River Shipyard at Locust Street Grounds. In this photo a Corinthian player prepares to receive a pass.

the tie was a de facto victory for Fore River Shipyard, a team that comprised mostly immigrants from Britain. These men, who had first learned of their opponents' prowess as lads in the United Kingdom, had more than done themselves proud. The fact that the match was played at the Locust Street Grounds and not at a more prestigious location, such as the South End Grounds or Huntington Avenue Grounds, was due to the fact that both of Boston's major league baseball teams were still in season, as well as to the reluctance of Boston's mainstream sports fans to accept what was increasingly viewed as a "foreigner's game."

Aristocrat in Sneakers: Eleonora Randolph Sears

Hollywood missed a golden opportunity when it didn't film the life story of Eleonora Randolph Sears while Katherine Hepburn was in her prime. Sears, like Hepburn, was to the manor born and both stunningly handsome and lithe. An outspoken tomboy, she loved to play sports with a cadre of rugged relatives and adoring male friends. Nothing delighted her more than besting them at any number of games.

Eleonora Sears in polo attire, c. 1914

Born on September 28, 1881, Sears was a member of both the generation and social class that led the budding women's movement. Her father, Frederick, was heir to a shipping fortune, and her mother was a great-great-granddaughter of Thomas Jefferson. Growing up on suburban Boston's Gold Coast, Sears became skilled as a rider, tennis player, runner, walker, and swimmer. In an era when few men had ever flown an airplane or raced automobiles, Sears did both. In 1910, she became the first woman in Boston to fly an airplane. Likewise, she loved to race cars with her friend and alleged love interest, Harold Vanderbilt. She even organized her own teams in football and polo. Known as "Eleo" to her friends, Sears was simply "a piece of work," a woman possessed of astonishing talent and an indomitable spirit.

Although she excelled at many activities, Sears thrived at racquet sports, finishing as national runner-up in women's singles tennis in 1911, 1912, and 1916. She also managed to capture four national doubles tennis titles between 1911 and 1917, as well as a national mixed doubles title in 1916. As a senior player in 1939 she again captured a national title, winning the Women's Veteran Doubles Championship at age fifty-eight.

So talented was Sears that, after taking up squash at age thirty-seven, she won the first Women's National Singles Championship. She then helped found the U.S. Women's Squash Racquets Association in 1928. All this was accomplished after she ignored the signs barring women from the squash courts at the Harvard Club.

For six decades Bostonians knew Eleonora Sears as both character and competitor. Her exploits filled the society and sports pages of the more than half-dozen Boston dailies. Most notable among her feats was her famed annual fifty-six-mile walk from Newport, Rhode Island, to Boston. These treks usually included a local male athlete of note, such as the captain of the Harvard heavyweight crew, whom the middle-aged Sears would promptly walk into the macadam.

Sears was well ahead of her time in many ways. Not only did she challenge and surmount the athletic barriers that were erected against the women of her epoch, but she also achieved her success with an unmistakable grace and style. Her attire, masculine and contemporary in design, was beyond the proverbial cutting edge in the early twentieth century and often generated as much attention as her achievements.

Following her death at age eighty-six in 1968, Sears was honored with enshrinement in both the International Tennis Hall of Fame and the Horseman's Hall of Fame. Sears is remembered as a pioneer who helped set the stage for the social acceptance of women's sports and the era of Title IX. She was truly a woman for all seasons.

Eleonora Sears at Boston Arena, c. 1912

BAA Marathon Starts

The 1902 Boston Athletic Association (BAA) Marathon, the sixth running of the event, started in Ashland, Massachusetts, with a field of forty-nine runners. The length of the course was 24 miles, 1,232 yards, run over macadam of varying quality. The standard marathon distance of 26 miles, 885 yards would not be instituted until the 1908 Olympic Marathon, held in London.

Starting field, 1902 Boston Marathon

The 1902 BAA Marathon was won by New Yorker Sammy Mellor with a time of 2:43:12. Mellor, like most of his fellow competitors, was a blue-collar worker. He trained for the race by running under the gaslights of his hometown of Yonkers.

With the Boston Marathon field having increased tenfold since 1897, 164 runners started their journey to Boston on April 19, 1909, with temperatures in the nineties. Huge crowds gathered along the route both to enjoy the unseasonable weather and to witness what they knew would be a literal life and death struggle. So humid was the weather that the dye from many runners' singlets and shorts mixed with sweat and coated the runners' legs with rainbow hues.

Less than half the field would reach the finish in Boston's Back Bay. Hospitals along the marathon route were filled to capacity with runners and spectators stricken with heat and sunstroke.

Starting field, 1909 Boston Marathon

Nashua, New Hampshire, native Henri Renaud, a mill worker and son of a renowned ultra-marathoner, captured the race by nearly a mile over rivals Harry Jensen and Pat Grant. His winning time of 2:53:36 was the slowest since the third BAA Marathon, in 1899.

Denton True "Cy" Young

Cy Young
of the Red Sox, c. 1907

Cy Young's pitching career produced the most amazing, if not imponderable, statistics in baseball history. His 511 career victories will never be surpassed, nor will his 313 defeats. In eight seasons with the Boston Red Sox, Young established team career records in many categories, including victories (192), shutouts (39), and losses (112), while compiling an amazing 1.99 ERA. Most important, he lent credibility to both the fledgling American League and a franchise that instantaneously leapfrogged its National League counterparts—the Boston Nationals—in less than a season.

Young's first three seasons with the Red Sox were the stuff of legend, as he led the team with 33, 32, and 28 wins, respectively, from 1901 to 1903. He would go on to win twenty or more games per season with Boston for three more years and would average twenty-four wins per season with the Red Sox. Among his many achievements in a Boston uniform were leading the team to victory in the first World Series in 1903, pitching a perfect game in 1904, and tossing a no-hitter in 1908. Young also served the team as a player-manager in 1907. Among his pet projects was the development of a young player named Tris Speaker from a seldom-used substitute into the best all-around player in Red Sox history. Cy Young's name is immortalized by the annual award for pitching excellence that bears his name.

Blind Faith: The Battles of Sam Langford

"I have fought the good fight. I have finished my course. I have kept the faith."
2 Timothy 4:7

Sam Langford has been called the greatest non-champion in the history of boxing by such authorities as Bert Randolph Sugar and Nat Fleischer, two prominent boxing historians. Born in 1880 in Weymouth, Nova Scotia, Langford moved to Boston at an early age and began to box in 1902. Known to all by the racist nickname "Boston Tar Baby," Langford

In this poignant image, Sam Langford is shown wearing the glasses that allowed his scarred eyes to function. By the time this photo was taken, Langford was already blind in one eye and rapidly losing his sight in the other.

fought literally hundreds of bouts on the "chitlin circuit," where he would battle the best African American fighters, such as Joe Jeannette and Jack Blackburn, in settings as varied as saloons and railroad roundhouses. By his own account Langford fought in over 650 bouts, of which only 253 are officially recorded. Of these recorded fights, he won 139 and lost 25, with 31 draws and 58 no-decisions.

In Chelsea, in 1906, Langford lost to legendary champion Jack Johnson in a close fifteen-round decision, a fight that Johnson considered among his toughest. In fact, Johnson paid tribute to the five-foot seven-inch, 170-pound Langford by calling him "the toughest little son of a bitch that ever lived."

Langford's success came at a tremendous price. Partially blind as the result of a childhood accident, the diminutive fighter suffered further vision loss as the result of the thousands of blows he absorbed during a long and tortured career. In 1918, he lost one eye in a training accident. The other followed nearly a decade later as the result of cataracts. Upon his involuntary retirement, the gallant boxer was virtually blind. So poor was Langford's vision that he once suffered the embarrassment of knocking out a referee he had mistaken for an opponent.

In need of money, Langford continued to box even after full blindness had set in. He even boxed Joe Walcott in exhibition bouts staged at the infamous Old Howard burlesque theater in Scollay Square. In 1945, a benefit dinner raised eleven thousand dollars for Langford, but he nevertheless died penniless at age seventy-six in a Cambridge rooming house.

For years, Langford lay buried in an unmarked grave at Cambridge Cemetery until St. Louis filmmaker Tim Leone, a boxing historian and Langford expert, underwrote the expense of placing a headstone on Langford's grave. At the 1984 ceremony honoring the placing of the headstone, Leone remarked, "I thought it was a damn shame. . . . A man of his caliber and class should not be forgotten."

Sam Langford (left) and Bill Tate (right), c. 1917. Note the height difference between the two boxers, as well as Langford's extraordinary reach. In many bouts Langford was placed at a distinct disadvantage, as he was shorter and lighter than most of his opponents.

 ## *The Crowd Went Wild*

Music and Cheers Kept All in Good Humor Before, During and After the Great Struggle

At precisely 30 minutes of 5 o'clock yesterday afternoon, before a throng of 8,000 wildly excited "fans," the Boston Americans inscribed their names in baseball history as champions of the world, and the grand Pittsburgh team, three-time champions of the National League, went down to defeat after as plucky a fight as was ever seen on a ballfield. "Big Bill" Dineen wielded the pen hand that wrote "Victory" for Boston, and so well did he do the work that Pittsburgh's mighty efforts went for naught.

It fell to the great Honus Wagner, premier batsman of the National League, to make the last protest against Boston's claim to the world's championship, and as the mighty Dutchman came to the plate in the ninth, after two of his teammates had succumbed to Boston's play, the dramatic possibilities of the situation forced themselves on the mind of every excited "fan." Great big goose eggs hung from every one of the eight Pittsburgh frames on the score board and it was up to the greatest hitter of the National League to make his mark in the last one. From Boston's frames the three runs stood out in deep relief.

In the gathering gloom, "Big Bill" was shooting the new white ball over so fast that it looked like a will-o'-the-wisp. The big crowd hung on the moment in eager expectation and hardly a sound was heard. Then in a great stage whisper came "Strike Him Out!" as the stands realized no more artistic conclusion to the great series was possible. "Strike one!" called O'Day, and a hysterical yell broke out on the air and then subsided as quickly. "Strike two!" called O'Day, and the whispered "Strike him out" became a wild, incoherent, roaring demand.

Slowly the big pitcher gathered himself up for the effort, slowly he swung his arms above his head. Then the ball shot away like a flash toward the plate where the great Wagner stood, muscles drawn tense waiting for it. The big batsman's mighty shoulders heaved, the stands will swear that his very frame creaked, as he swung his bat with every ounce of power in his body, but the dull thud of the ball, as it nestled in Criger's waiting mitt, told the story.

The Huntington Avenue Grounds hosted the first World Series in 1903.

And then what a deafening roar rent the air as every one of the 8,000 "fans" realized that the game was over, that the dreaded Pittsburghs were beaten and that Boston's "own" had established their claim to the title of world champions. . . .

While some of the cooler, more matter-of-fact spectators started for home, the major part of the excited "fans" were still looking for an outlet for their excess of joy and flocked about the band, which was still keeping up its stirring music. After the voices had been laid away, the throng formed itself into a big procession with lines of ten and twelve front and behind the band began a march and war dance about the park. Around the field they went with the "Royal Rooters" leading the motley assemblage, and out of the park to Columbus Avenue.
—Boston Post, *October 14, 1903*

 ## The Fastest Man in the World

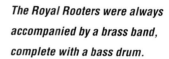

The Royal Rooters were always accompanied by a brass band, complete with a bass drum.

On January 25, 1907, in Ormand Beach, Florida, a sizable crowd of automobile enthusiasts gathered on the upper piazza of the racing clubhouse to watch Fred Marriott of Watertown, Massachusetts, attempt to break the world land speed record. Only one year earlier, Marriott had shattered the previous record by some thirteen miles per hour, racing a Stanley Steamer across a measured one-mile strip of sandy beach at 127.659 miles per hour. Returning in 1907 with a much improved machine, Marriott was confident he would obliterate his earlier mark.

Twice before that day Marriott had rocketed down the beach at less than full tilt, concerned about the cigar-shaped Steamer as it crossed a bothersome stretch of ripples in the sand. Satisfied with those tests, Marriott announced before his final run, "I'll hit those ripples so fast, I'll skim right over them without even feeling them."

On the piazza someone announced, "Here he comes!" The spectators strained to catch a glimpse of the Steamer struggling against the sand over a mile away. The crowd included F. E. Stanley, who designed the car with his twin brother, F. O., F. E.'s wife, Augusta, and their young son Ray. No sooner had the car come into view than disaster struck. Hitting the ripples, Marriott saw only a cloud of steam and then a stream of debris flying into the sea. Badly injured, Marriott survived, but his racing days were all but finished. Likewise, the Stanley Steamer, manufactured in Watertown, was withdrawn from competition, never to race again.

The Stanley Steamer

Later that day, Augusta Stanley was moved to write in her diary, "Truly this is black Friday. I can hardly write I am in such a nervous condition and it is all so dreadful. Oh! Why did we come down to this horrible place? . . . The car was dashed to atoms—and Fred inside. . . . Frank and I are just ready to collapse."

Over the ensuing decades, controversy has clouded the events of January 25, 1907. In his final, ill-fated run, how fast was Marriott going? Until his death in 1957, Marriott claimed to be traveling in excess of 190 miles per hour. But since that time others, including members of the Stanley family, have tried to debunk that claim. The race marked the beginning of the end for the steam automobile, but like the puff of steam that first announced Marriott's ill fortune to the crowd on the piazza, the questions surrounding the events of that day continue to cloud the legacy of the Stanley Steamer, once the world's fastest automobile.

—Glenn Stout

the
Teens

Francis Ouimet and the Democratization of Golf

In 1913, amateur golfer Francis Ouimet of Brookline, Massachusetts, changed the game of golf. A former caddie, Ouimet won the 1913 U.S. Open in a thrilling three-way playoff against English professionals Ted Ray and Harry Vardon. Ouimet's historic victory helped make golf, which had been viewed as a game for the upper classes, accessible to the public and did much to popularize it in the United States.

Reminiscing in his autobiography, *A Game of Golf,* Ouimet recalled his monumental playoff victory over Ray and Vardon at The Country Club in Brookline.

After taking a bath, I walked home and turned in for a real night's rest. I slept from nine-thirty until eight the next morning, and after a light break-fast, hustled over to the Country Club for my play-off with Vardon and Ray. I did not feel nervous or unduly excited. I slipped on my golf shoes, got hold of Eddie Lowery [Ouimet's caddie], and went out to the Polo Field to hit a few practice shots. There was nobody around. The shots I hit felt fine. Soon some people came along and watched me. After perhaps a half-hour's practice, I was told that Vardon and Ray were on the first tee waiting for the match to begin.

Johnny McDermott took my arm and said, "You are hitting the ball well; now go out and pay no attention whatsoever to Vardon or Ray. Play your own game." It was excellent advice and I promised Johnny I would do my best.

On the way to the tee my good friend Frank Hoyt (Stealthy Steve) asked me if I would not permit him to carry my clubs. I had played much golf with Steve and he was a master in the finer points of the game. I told him he must see Eddie Lowery. He made one or two offers of money, but they did not tempt Eddie in the least. It was interesting to see the reaction of Eddie as he definitely and positively refused to be bought off. Finally, Hoyt appealed to me. I looked at the ten-year-old Eddie, his eyes filled, and I think he was fearful I would turn him down. In any event, he seemed so sincere I did not have the heart to take the clubs away from him, and my final gesture was to tell Steve, Eddie was going to caddie for me.

It was raining, and the three of us were ushered into the tent near the tee to draw lots for the honor. I drew the longest straw and had to drive first. As I walked over to the sand box, and realized what I was up against and saw the crowd, I was terribly excited. If I could only get my tee shot away! Eddie stepped up as he handed me a driver and said, "Be sure and keep your eye on the ball." The opening salute was a drive well down the middle of the fairway and for good length. Vardon and Ray followed suit. Ray was the only one who was long enough to reach the green on his second, but he sliced a brassie to the right.

We all got on in three and took fives on the hole. I was left with a four-foot putt for my five, and I worried not a little over it. I tapped it in, and then almost instantly any feeling of awe and excitement left me completely. I seemed to go into a coma. Eddie kept telling me to keep my eye on the ball. He cautioned me to take my time. He encouraged me in any number of different ways. My first mistake was on the fifth hole where the slimy grip turned in my hand and my second shot went out of bounds. But Vardon and Ray both erred on the same hole, and I was safe for the time being. Ray had taken a five on the third to our fours, and that was the only difference in the scores up to that point.

Vardon made the sixth in three and went into the lead. Ray was now trailing Vardon by two strokes and me by one. The seventh hole at Brookline is a hard par three. Vardon was to the right of the green with his iron and needed four. I failed to lay a long approach putt dead, and took four. Ray was the only one to get a three and he pulled up on even terms with me.

The eighth hole was sensational. This hole measures three hundred and eighty yards and the view of the green is more or less restricted by a hill. You can see the flag, but no part of the green. We all had fine drives. A tremendous crowd had gathered around the green to see the balls come up. I played my second with a mashie straight for the pin. In a few seconds a mighty roar went up. As I handed the club to Eddie, he said, "Your ball is stone dead." I wanted to think it was, but I wished also to prepare myself in case it was not. Therefore I said to Eddie, "It is not stone dead, but I believe I shall have a putt for my three." You see I did not wish to be disappointed.

As we walked toward the green and came to the top of the hill, I saw a ball twelve inches from the hole. It was mine. Ray was forty feet away with a side hill putt and he tapped his ball as delicately as possible. It took the necessary turns and rolled right into the hole. Vardon had a four, and I got my three, which put us all even at the end of eight holes.

The next highlight was a short tenth. This green was so soggy that both Vardon and Ray, after pitching on, had to chip over the holes made by their balls as they bit into the soft turf and hopped back. I was fairly close in one. My opponents failed to make their threes, and I stepped into the lead by a stroke.

Francis Ouimet lines up his putt on the thirteenth green during the one-round playoff for the 1913 U.S. Open title.

I added another stroke on the twelfth, where I got my four to their fives. Vardon dropped a nice putt for a three on the thirteenth, one under par, which brought him within a stroke of me. The long fourteenth was important. Ray might reach the green in two, but it was beyond the range of Vardon and myself. Ray drove last, and I saw him hurl himself at his ball to get just a little added length. When he played his second from the fairway,

he put every bit of power into the shot, but his timing was poor and he hit the ball far to the right into a grove of chestnut trees. He recovered beautifully, and the hole was made in five by all.

I was paying as little attention as possible to the strokes of the others, because I did not wish to be unduly influenced by anything they did. I was simply carrying out McDermott's instructions and playing my own game. I could not help but notice, however, that Ray was struggling somewhat. I noticed, too, that Vardon, who seemed to be a master in mashie work, pulled his pitch to the green, which was not his natural way of playing such a stroke. Vardon normally played his pitches with a slight fade from left to right.

Ray got into all sorts of trouble on the fifteenth and he seemed out of the running. I never gave it a thought as he holed out in six. I still clung to my one stroke lead over Vardon through the sixteenth. Ray was now five strokes behind. Vardon had the honor on the seventeenth tee. This hole is a semi-dog-leg, and by driving to the right you eliminate all risk. On the other hand, if the player chooses to risk a trap on the left and gets away with it, he has a short pitch to the green. Vardon drove to the left. I saw his ball start, and that is all. I drove to the right. Ray tried to cut the trees on the left and hit a prodigious wallop that cleared everything, but his ball was in the long grass.

As we walked toward our balls, I saw that Vardon had caught the trap and his ball was so close to the bank he had no chance at all of reaching the green. He could just play out to the fairway. I knocked a jigger shot to the green, my ball stopping fifteen feet above the hole. Ray and Vardon took fives. As I studied my putt, I decided to take no liberties with the skiddy surface and simply tried to lay the ball dead for a sure four. I putted carefully and watched my ball roll quietly toward the hole. It went in for a three. With one hole left, I was now in the lead by three strokes over Vardon and seven over Ray.

The eighteenth hole was a hard two-shotter. The rains had turned the race track in front of the green into a bog, and my one thought was to get over the mud. All hit fine tee shots. I placed my second on the green. It did not enter my head that I was about to become the open champion until I stroked my first putt to within eight or nine inches of the hole. Then, as I stepped up to make that short putt, I became very nervous. A veil of something that seemed to have covered me dropped from *around my head and shoulders. I was in full control of my faculties for the first time since the match started, but terribly excited. I dropped the putt. Nothing but the most intense concentration brought me victory.*

I was fearful at the beginning that I should blow up, and I fought against this for all I was worth. The thought of winning never entered my head, and for that reason I was immune to emotions of any sort. My objective was to play eighteen holes as well I could and let the score stand for good or bad. I accomplished a feat that seemed so far beyond anything I ever hoped to do that, while I got a real thrill out of it, I felt I had been mighty lucky. Had I harbored the desire to win that championship or an open title of any kind, I might have been tickled beyond words. In sport one has to have the ambition to do things and that ambition in my case was to win the national amateur championship. Therefore, I honestly think I never got the "kick" out of winning the open title that I might have done if I had thought I could win it.

 ## The Duel: Joe Wood Bests Walter Johnson 1–0

In 1912, Red Sox right-hander Smoky Joe Wood enjoyed one of the greatest seasons ever had by a pitcher, winning thirty-four games and leading the club to its second world championship. The highlight of that season came when Wood pitched against Walter Johnson at Fenway Park, in a historic game that saw upstart Wood aim to match Johnson's record of sixteen consecutive victories, set earlier in the season.

Egged on by the media and Red Sox president James McAleer, manager Jake Stahl moved Wood up a day in the rotation for the duel with Johnson. Game-day headlines in Boston newspapers depicted the two starters in the manner of prizefighters, listing their height, weight, and reach. By the first pitch at 3:00 P.M., Fenway Park was filled beyond capacity. Fans crowded both dugouts, the roped-off portions of the outfield, and the entire foul section of the infield along the first-base and third-base lines.

The game lived up to its billing. Wood just barely outpitched Johnson for his twenty-eighth win, compiling nine strikeouts to his opponent's five and allowing five hits to Johnson's six. The Red Sox scored their lone run in the sixth inning, when Tris Speaker laced a two-strike pitch to left for a double and then scored on an opposite-field double by Duffy Lewis.

Red Sox officials bragged the next day that only one fan (a young boy) required medical attention as the result of an errant foul tip and that he insisted on rooting for the Red Sox after being treated. Only five fans complained about the tight seating arrangements, and their money was promptly refunded by team treasurer Bob McRoy.

Arm trouble prematurely ended what, for Wood, should have been a Hall of Fame pitching career at age twenty-five. His résumé included a no-hitter, 116 victories, 3 victories in the 1912 World Series, a .679 winning percentage, and a 1.99 ERA.

Smoky Joe Wood warms up amidst the Fenway Park crowd, September 6, 1912.

 ## *Tris Speaker: Red Sox' Greatest Player*

The greatest player in Red Sox history arrived in Boston in 1907 as a late-season spare part who played in seven games, hardly impressing anyone with his brash attitude and .158 batting average. In the off-season, the young Texan wrote to several teams asking for a chance to rekindle his major league dreams. Rejected by the likes of New York Giants manager John McGraw, Speaker returned to the Red Sox in 1908 via minor league stardom in Little Rock, Arkansas.

Once back in Boston, Speaker was taken under the wing of Cy Young, who recognized his extraordinary athleticism. Young, the elder statesman of the team, spent many hours hitting fungoes to Speaker. Soon teammates and fans alike were watching in wonder as Speaker played the shortest center field in baseball. In many ways he became a fifth infielder, a would-be revolutionary with no followers. His defensive prowess alone was reason to buy a ticket. Combining his remarkable defensive skills with superb hitting and superior speed, Speaker cut a dashing figure. His only American League peers were Ty Cobb and "Shoeless" Joe Jackson.

Nicknamed the "Gray Eagle" and "Spoke" by Boston sportswriters, Tris Speaker was considered baseball's greatest center fielder until Joe DiMaggio appeared on the scene in the thirties. As a batter, Speaker's lifetime batting average of .344 was matched only by Ted Williams. However, unlike Williams, Speaker was also known for his baserunning skills. His speed helped him reach a major league–leading career doubles total of 793. Old-timers swear that even the eccentric and gifted Jimmy Piersall never played as shallow a center field at Fenway as Speaker, who still holds the major league record for chances accepted by an outfielder with 7,244, as well as the career mark for unassisted double plays with four. Just imagining how he pulled off each of those four double plays conjures an image of a player with the flair of a Mays, the speed of a Mantle, and the baseball instincts of a Cool Papa Bell.

Tris Speaker batted .344 for his career and was the best defensive outfielder of his era.

Speaker's rifle arm was the forerunner of the likes of Roberto Clemente and Carl Furillo, and with it he established the single-season mark for assists with thirty-five in his rookie season of 1909 and again in 1912, the year he led the Red Sox to their greatest season of the century and their second World Series title in as many tries. His .383 batting average during the regular season and his World Series average of .300 helped pace the team that year.

In nine seasons with the Red Sox Speaker batted .336 with 793 doubles, 107 triples, and 266 stolen bases. Following a protracted contract dispute with the Red Sox, Speaker was sold to the Cleveland Indians. He enjoyed great success in Cleveland, leading the Tribe to their first world title as player-manager in 1920. Speaker was elected to the National Baseball Hall of Fame in 1937.

Fenway Park, c. 1917:
Home of Champions

The Fenway Park of 1917 was far different from the park we enjoy today. For one, the Dead Ball era ballpark was a defensive fortress. Because batters found it difficult just to hit balls off the wooden ancestor of the now famous "Green Monster," balls hit over the wall inspired bold sports page headlines. Fenway also possessed sun fields like no other park, which wreaked havoc with visiting players in an era when most games were played in the twilight of late afternoon.

The footprint of the playing field is virtually identical to that of the "new" park, but note the old wooden left-field wall and the slope of "Duffy's Cliff," just below the wall. It was here that left fielder Duffy Lewis scampered up his cliff to rob opponents of extra-base hits. Note also that the flagpole was placed prominently in fair territory in center field, the better to display the world championship banners that once graced the park in the days of Speaker, Hooper, and Ruth. The Boston Braves also captured their lone World Series here in 1914.

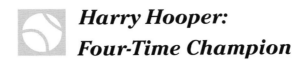

Harry Hooper:
Four-Time Champion

Harry Hooper was introduced to Boston as a budding young engineer out of Saint Mary's College in California. Red Sox owner John I. Taylor had learned of the talented student-athlete while visiting relatives in the San Francisco area. He asked Hooper to assist with the team of architects and engineers he had assembled to design his new ballyard in the Fenway neighborhood of Boston. It was strictly a bonus that the soft-spoken scholar was also a superb ballplayer with a smattering of minor league experience. Following an impressive spring-training showing, Hooper earned a starting position in 1909 and never sought to resume his engineering career.

Hooper had the great fortune to arrive in Boston in time to help lead the team to near dynasty status at the end of the Dead Ball era. However, he also arrived at nearly the same time as Tris Speaker, the greatest outfielder of his generation. Although overshadowed by his phenomenally talented teammate, Hooper was a superstar in his own right, winning games with his speed, glove, arm, and bat. Hooper, Speaker, and Duffy Lewis formed the famed "Million Dollar Outfield."

Harry Hooper was a brilliant right fielder with a potent bat and an impeccable reputation as a gentleman and sportsman. He mastered the sun and wind of right field at Fenway Park while gunning down 150 runners with his superb arm. Likewise, he was a particularly effective lead-off hitter, achieving a .403 on-base percentage while socking a franchise record 130 triples in twelve seasons with the Red Sox. Among other things, Hooper convinced Red Sox manager Ed Barrow to play a pitcher named Babe Ruth in the outfield on his off days!

During his dozen years with the Red Sox, Hooper was a mainstay on four world championship squads, batting .293 in twenty-four World Series games. He saved the Red Sox victory in the eighth and deciding game of the 1912 World Series (a best-of-nine series that year) with a dramatic, diving bare–handed catch of a ball hit by "Laughing" Larry Doyle of the New York Giants. In 1915, he became the first player in World Series history to hit two home runs in one game. The home runs came in dramatic fashion in the fifth and final game of the series. Facing future Hall of Famer Eppa Rixey in the eighth inning, Hooper tied the game with his first home run. He then hit the game-winning shot off Rixey in the ninth to secure the team's third world title.

Hooper was sold to the White Sox in 1921 following a salary dispute. He was the last of the superstars to depart the short-lived dynasty of the Dead Ball era. Hooper was elected to the National Baseball Hall of Fame in Cooperstown in 1971.

Harry Hooper, an outstanding fielder and hitter, was an integral part of the Red Sox dynasty.

"Bricklayer" Bill Kennedy, 1917 BAA Marathon Champion

For much of the century the Boston Marathon was strictly the domain of working-class athletes. The occupations of most marathon champions ranged from teacher to typesetter. Typically these men ran to and from work or on the borders of a forty-plus-hour week. Not only did they face this challenge, but they also dealt with primitive shoes and training conditions, as well as an amateur athletic establishment that forbade them any reward except for a medal and post-race bowl of beef stew.

This hard-bitten amateur tradition continued up through the first marathon triumphs by a special education teacher named Bill Rodgers in the mid-to-late seventies. It was a tradition perhaps best articulated in 1932 in a letter written by 1917 BAA Marathon winner "Bricklayer" Bill Kennedy to his friend John Halloran at the *Boston Globe*. Kennedy won what he considered the greatest marathon in America after hitchhiking to Boston from New York and sleeping on a pool table in the South End on the night before the race. The race would be the highlight of a life lived on the fringes of society.

Dear Johnnie:

I am well, but broke. Business is shit, but as long as I have my health that is the serious thing. I am looking forward to this year's race. I have been out of work so much this winter that I've had much time to run.

Speaking of Marathon runners, don't you ever wonder what is the lure of it all? What does a Marathon runner think of?

Well, Johnnie, I ran an average of 1,000 miles a year for the past 25 years, some do more, some do less, but that average is about 130 hours, along with your mind wandering here and there—building air castles—tragedy and comedy. He thinks and pictures so many things.

The lure of the Boston race, Johnnie, is far greater than any in the country and, to me, the world. I can only speak of my own thoughts; but I have been close enough to runners for 30 years that I also know their thoughts, hopes and chances—to win the Boston Marathon, that is the dream of every runner. Sometimes I hardly believe I realized that hope fifteen years ago; I am still dreaming, still building castles, and actually believe I am going to win again.

All Marathon runners are dreamers; we are not practical. The hours we spend every day every year! The strength we expend over long lonesome roads and the pot of gold we aspire to receive for it all! The end of the rainbow, Johnnie, is a survivor's medal.

Boston, to see the name in print, to hear it spoken, sends my blood racing as does the sound of "The Star Spangled Banner." I reached the heights in Boston and also I gazed down into the depths. I used to beat my way in these unnoticed, cold, and half-starved. Then I met Larry Sweeney of the old Globe *(Lord have mercy on him) and after that everyone seemed to be my friend.*

The 1917 race brings back memory of the ironworker who took me over to the public bath to clean up; the bricklayers who fed me and got me a job; Mr. & Mrs. John Brick, Jack Welsh, Jack Nason and Mrs. Nason and the children always to meet me at Coolidge Corner with a drink of hot tea; Rudy and Sam Allen, who put me to work; Jack Daily, who rode a bicycle for me and drank my brandy himself; Al Upham, his father and mother, George Brown, his boy Walter, yourself, McCabe and the most colorful bunch of newspapermen in the game are strong in my mind as I each year visit Boston.

And Edwin Geary of Hornblower and Weeks, whom I have not seen since winning, but his name and face are impressed in my heart. Chuck Mellor and I didn't have a dollar between us. I had won the Boston race two days before and Chuck finished sixth, but we couldn't eat those cups, nor cash them in and remain amateurs.

So the cheapest way to eat was to pay five cents for a glass of beer and fill up on the free lunch, which some were doing. Then a gentleman recognizing me from the pictures in the paper stepped up to me and asked me was I Bill Kennedy and was it true about my having two children, and gave me two ten dollar bills, one for each of them. Boy, I could have kissed him; a lucky thing, though, he didn't give a third for myself, or I would have automatically become a professional.

Well, John, meeting all these people gave me an incentive to show them I appreciated their interest, so I tried hard to win.

Do you know that I always loved the old way best when they had the bicycle riders with us? It seemed more colorful and seemed to make you feel you had a protector at your side.

The people up there appreciate the runners more than anywhere else; no slurs, no wisecracks. Just kind words and applause. Have you ever noticed how sympathetic the boys are? They are wild at times, but you can't help loving them. Some three or four years ago, the time I finished third, some little kid on a bike, he couldn't have been more than twelve, pulled alongside me at Coolidge Corner. To listen to that boy crooning to me, the words of sympathy his little heart was pouring out, my God, Johnnie, you wouldn't think I was fifty years old to his twelve. Seemed like he was the old warrior and I was the child.

"Bricklayer" Bill Kennedy continued to run the Boston Marathon long after his glory days had passed.

Johnnie, I better cut this short. I ran a Marathon in 1924, the hottest day of the year, and I won by over a mile and a half. The officials told me the prize was a beautiful bronze statue of a Marathon runner, six feet in height, too big to carry, and it would be shipped to me by express.

They gave me a receipt (one bronze statue, paid in full). Well, I still have the receipt. But the trophy never came, express or otherwise. Prizes don't mean that much to me anyhow. I won the race, which I think was satisfaction enough for me. I wouldn't give a damn if I fell dead across the line at Boston if I could just win that one more time.

The Olympic bait doesn't mean a thing to me. They wouldn't take me when I wanted to go. Hell, I can beat my way to Los Angeles anytime. But I want to beat the men they do send. There was never a time if I had six weeks to train and not work or worry over the wherewithal to run my home and family, I couldn't beat any man on earth.

Do you know that I have seldom come to Boston in any other race in the last fifteen years in shape. I dissipated last year before the race, and even the night before, but I ran the course, only to punish myself.

Another attraction in Boston is the old-time runners you meet. Who can help but love Monteverde, the biggest dreamer of us all, and probably the wealthiest; little Jimmy Henigan, and DeMar, with his honest but peculiar ways and short answers. A lot of old boys keep disappearing, but I try to keep in touch.

Can't you lean back, close your eyes and picture Tom Longboat and his funny teeth; Festus Madden, over whom I have had many a laugh; Fred Cameron, who became an amateur again in Chicago; great old Sid Hatch, lovable Chuck Mellor, Joe Forshaw, a millionaire. Mike Ryan and his red head leading the parade in '12.

Poor Harry Jensen, dying at home in New Jersey, wife and two kids penniless. Good old Johnny Hayes and a few of the old boys around New York visit Jensen and try to help. Jimmy Duffy, killed in France; youthful Johnny Miles, Linder, poor Sockalexis, and a host of others who have passed along the long, long trail. They all know "What Price Glory?" The handshakes and then oblivion. All we have are the good friends we make.

And that survivor's medal, well, I would rather have a pair of overalls.
*I can use them **if I get a job.** But I will be there Tuesday, glad to see the*
bunch. My feet will be blistered, my legs weary, every muscle aching, but
my heart will be happy at the cheers of the crowd. I will be giving them all
that's in me too and I look forward to that little thin string in front of the
BAA clubhouse, a cot to lie on, and get those damn shoes off my feet!
So long, old pal, I shall be in the prize winners.
—(Signed) Bricklayer Bill Kennedy

Well Played Harvard!
The 1920 Rose Bowl

Most of the players during 1919 had taken some part in the world war,
and many had taken part in the actual fighting, so it is little wonder that
we found an unsettled condition and spirit of unrest existing among the
players. Football to these men could never be made to look as important
as it did before the war.
—Robert T. Fisher, Harvard head football coach

In the thirty years that Yale legend Walter Camp selected the college
football All-America teams, he only once failed to name a Harvard
player to the team. Not only did Harvard lay claim to having played the
first genuine game of collegiate football in 1874, but the Crimson had
also ranked second in overall national success in the game to their
rivals at Yale. Prior to the 1919 season, Harvard had captured six
National Collegiate championships and seemed poised to challenge
for a seventh.

Having played (and crushed) such minnows as Bates, Tufts, and Springfield, Harvard finished the season unbeaten, with the only blemish
being a 10–10 tie with Princeton. Overall they scored 199 points to their
opponents' 13. As champions of the East, Harvard received an invitation soon after the Yale victory to play the University of Oregon
in the Rose Bowl on January 1, 1920.

Practice began on December 1 at Soldier's Field, in conditions so cold
that players complained of sore feet and their inability to grip the ball.
Permission was soon granted for the team to practice at the Common-

wealth Armory, where they trained until December 20. Their subsequent cross-country train trip provided Harvard alumni from around the nation an opportunity to greet the train as it stopped along the route. By the time they arrived in Pasadena, the Harvard players felt they had to win, both for their university and for the thousands who had feted them on the journey west.

Arriving tired in Pasadena after the long train trip, Harvard was viewed as just another Eastern patsy arriving for a New Year's Day beating from their Western counterparts. In the only two appearances by Eastern schools to date, both Brown and Penn had suffered one-sided shutout defeats. The Harvard players were representing not only the interests of the program but all of Eastern collegiate football as well. Needless to say, entering the game they were heavy underdogs.

The 1919 Harvard football team

Before a full house at Tournament Park, Harvard managed to emerge victorious by a score of 7–6 despite being outplayed in most depart-

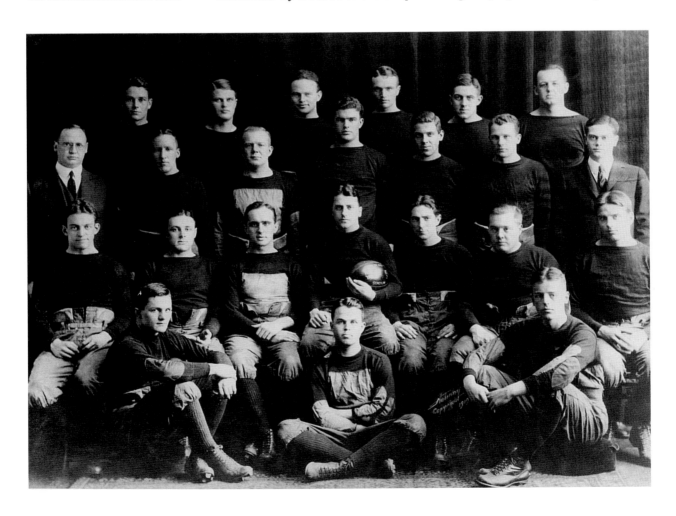

ments. Only the stalwart tackling of Arnold Horween and Eddie Casey thwarted an Oregon attack whose net yardage nearly doubled that of Harvard, with 272 yards to just 146 for the Crimson. Both teams would have two kicks blocked, with all four recoveries going to Oregon.

Harvard managed to win with the combination of a great run and a heady strategic maneuver at the end of the play. In the second quarter, Harvard substitute Freddie Church entered the game with his team in a kick formation. Taking Oregon by surprise, Harvard ran a play in which Church took the ball from center and ran straight through the line. One newspaper account likened his run to that of a mechanical rabbit being haplessly pursued by greyhounds. Church not only scored a touchdown on the run but also helped his team by downing the ball directly between the goal posts. He was aware that the rules called for the point after to be kicked from a point directly opposite from where the ball had been downed for the score. Arnie Horween, the defensive standout of the game, made the routine kick and Harvard held off Oregon for the next two-and-a-half quarters to capture the historic win.

The triumph marked the apex for Harvard football. The school that had created the game some forty-six years earlier has not won another National Championship since.

 ## *Babe Ruth of the Red Sox*

Babe Ruth joined us in the middle of 1914, a 19-year-old kid. He was a left-handed pitcher then, and a good one. He never had been anywhere, didn't know anything about manners or how to behave among people— just a big overgrown pea. . . . You know, I saw it all happen, from beginning to end. But sometimes I still can't believe what I saw: this 19-year-old kid, crude, poorly educated, only lightly brushed by the social veneer we call civilization, gradually transformed into the idol of American youth and a symbol of baseball the world over—a man loved by more people and with an intensity of feeling that perhaps has never been seen before or since. I saw a man transformed from a human being into something pretty close to a god. If somebody had predicted that back on the Red Sox in 1914 he would have been thrown into a lunatic asylum.
—Harry Hooper, Boston Red Sox, 1909–1920

When Babe Ruth stepped off the train at Back Bay Station on the morning of July 11, 1914, he had arrived in the capital of baseball in America. Ground zero. The Red Sox were the game's most celebrated team, with stars such as Tris Speaker, Harry Hooper, Duffy Lewis, and Smoky Joe Wood. Collectively, their nickname was the "Speedboys," and heaven help anyone who snickered at the sobriquet in the presence of their often inebriated fan clan, known as the Royal Rooters. In 1912, only two seasons prior to Ruth's arrival, the Red Sox had christened Fenway Park with a record-setting world championship season. Fans were hungry to see a repeat performance. This team won in as regular and consistent a manner as the Celtics teams of the sixties and possessed the sass and swagger of the Orr/Esposito–era Bruins. In short, the Speedboys owned both Boston and all of baseball.

Ruth arrived in the perfect city, with the perfect team for his major league apprenticeship. He was also fortunate to be managed by player-manager Bill Carrigan, also known by his well-earned nickname of "Rough." Not only would Carrigan start his newly acquired pitcher against the Cleveland Indians on his first day in Boston, but he would also room with him and teach him the fundamentals of the game from the ground up. In many ways Ruth found a surrogate father in Carrigan when he arrived in Boston.

Commenting on Ruth's victorious major league debut, *Boston Globe* sportswriter Tim Murnane wrote:

All eyes were turned on Ruth, the giant left-hander, who proved a natural ballplayer and went through his act like a veteran of many wars. He has a natural delivery, fine control and a curve ball that bothers the batsmen, but has room for improvement, and will, undoubtedly, become a fine pitcher under the care of Manager Carrigan. . . .

As the greenest of the young pitchers, Ruth became a project for Carrigan. The wily catcher picked up on many of Ruth's bad habits, such as allowing his tongue to hang out when he threw his curveball. Such a trait would have proved disastrous to the rookie if allowed to persist. Carrigan also paid his protégé on a daily basis after having learned of his wild partying and womanizing.

In six seasons with the Red Sox, Ruth became nothing less than the best left-hander in the American league, winning eighty-nine games and achieving a perfect 3–0 record in World Series play. His record for consecutive scoreless innings would last for over half a century before being broken by Yankee Hall of Famer Whitey Ford in the sixties.

In 1919, his final season with the Red Sox, Ruth alternated between pitching and playing outfield and socked a single-season record-shattering total of twenty-nine home runs. The best lefty in the league had suddenly become the best player and hottest property in the majors.

In six seasons with the Red Sox, Babe Ruth helped the team win three world championships.

The sale of Ruth to the New York Yankees for one hundred thousand dollars and a mortgage on Fenway Park was precipitated in part by his increasing volatility and temperamental nature. Although the controversial trade benefited the team financially, it is still considered one of the dark moments in the history of the Red Sox and Boston sports.

The 1914 Boston Braves: A Photo Album

In a most unlikely scenario, the Miracle Braves of 1914 came from ten and one-half games out at the end of July to capture the National League crown by the same margin over the heavily favored New York Giants. The Braves were led by the middle infield duo of future Hall of Famers Walter "Rabbit" Maranville and Johnny "Crab" Evers, as well as by the pitching trio of Lefty Tyler, Dick Rudolph, and Bill James. The underdog Braves won the World Series in an unprecedented four-game sweep of the Philadelphia Athletics.

Walter "Rabbit" Maranville

Arriving in Boston as a twenty-year-old shortstop in 1912, Rabbit Maranville brought with him a dazzling skill and a sense of showmanship. Within a season of his arrival in the majors, the Braves held a day in his honor at the South End Grounds. The stands were filled with friends and neighbors who had taken the train from his native Springfield.

Maranville was an entertainer in spikes, often amusing fans with a pre-game exhibition of skills in which he pegged strikes to home plate from a sitting position on the second-base bag. But his showmanship belied his fielding wizardry, as the five-foot five-inch dynamo led the league in putouts for four straight seasons. Although Maranville batted only .258 for his career, in eight World Series games divided equally between the Braves and the St. Louis Cardinals, he hit .308.

Known for his love of a good time, Maranville fought a lifelong battle with liquor while playing an astonishing twenty-three seasons in the big leagues. His Boston farewell in 1935, following a second broken leg, inspired as tearful an ovation as Boston had ever seen.

Johnny Evers had already forged his Hall of Fame credentials as a member of the famed Chicago Cub double-play combo of Tinker-to-Evers-to-Chance when he arrived in Boston in December 1913. Released by the Cubs because of a disagreement with ownership, Evers proved the keystone to manager George Stallings's improbable champions of 1914.

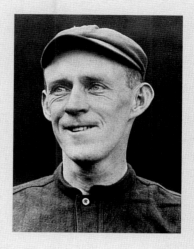

Johnny "Crab" Evers

Evers was nothing less than Stallings's alter ego, a player-coach on the diamond who exhorted his teammates to perform their best, even to the point of physical confrontation. His performance in 1914, which included a league-leading .976 fielding percentage and a .279 batting average, earned the second baseman the Chalmers Award as Most Valuable Player in the National League. But mere statistics hardly bear out Evers's value as a team builder and leader of men.

In the 1914 World Series, Evers batted .438 to help lead the four-game sweep of the heavily favored Philadelphia Athletics. His two-run single off Bob Shawkey in the fifth inning of game four sent Fenway Park into a frenzy, as the hit proved to be the series winner.

Boston Braves fan at Fenway Park, 1914 World Series

Fans of both the Braves and the Red Sox filled Fenway Park for the final two games of the 1914 World Series. Red Sox fans enjoyed the prospect of Philadelphia humiliating their fiercest rivals, while Braves fans, though still in disbelief at their team's miracle in progress, were hungry for a victory. It was an era when Boston's Royal Rooters marched to games from their unofficial headquarters, Nuf Ced McGreevey's Third Base Tavern, accompanied by a brass band. The ballpark atmosphere was entirely the creation of fans, free of marketing-driven manipulation and electronic noise.

Here, a loyal fan dressed in Pilgrim garb mocks Athletics manager Connie Mack. Note his bell, which probably denoted his status as "town crier" ringing a death knell for Mack and his team.

Hazel Hotchkiss Wightman:
First Lady of Tennis

In Mrs. Wightman's book, a champion, since she serves as a role model for thousands of impressionable girls, has many responsibilities, above and beyond performing with excellence. Her conduct must be exemplary in all respects, and this includes not confusing the tennis court with the stage and making too striking an appearance. This past season a contingent of fifteen year olds asked Mrs. Wightman what she thought of the black shorts which Gussie Moran, the game's current glamour girl, had worn in a tournament in Cairo. "I don't think there was really any need for it," Mrs. Wightman replied. "Didn't Gussie say that she had to wear those black shorts in the semifinals because she only had one pair of whites and was saving them for the final? Well, there was no reason in the world why she couldn't have worn the whites in the semifinals, washed and ironed them after the match, and had them ready for the next day."
—Herbert Warren Wind, sportswriter

Hazel Hotchkiss Wightman

Hazel Hotchkiss Wightman was one of the great builders, players, and teachers of tennis in the twentieth century. Her record as a player included a Wimbledon doubles title in 1924, an Olympic doubles championship in 1924, six U.S. Open doubles titles, six U.S. Open mixed doubles titles, two U.S. Open singles titles in 1909 and 1919, and countless U.S. indoor titles. She was also a great squash player, winning the national singles title in 1930.

Wightman's longevity was nothing short of astonishing. She won the national indoor doubles title with Pauline Betz in 1943, some thirty-four years after she had won the first of her countless national titles. She was held in such high esteem that her doubles and mixed doubles pairings read like a roster of the great players of the twenties and thirties, with the likes of Bill Tilden, Jean Borotra, René Lacoste, Helen Wills, Sarah Palfrey, and Pauline Betz asking to join her in countless Grand Slam tournaments.

Known as the Queen Mother of American Tennis, Wightman was originally from northern California but lived in Boston from 1912 onwards after marrying Bostonian George W. Wightman. Her boundless enthusiasm made her a perfect teacher. Whether demonstrating a serve or serving home-baked cookies in her Chestnut Hill home, Wightman inspired several generations of players. She was the epitome of the gracious amateur in an era when the game was still the province of country clubs and moneyed estates.

Wightman lived to see the professional game emerge, and with it the crop of superb female players who still play for the Wightman Cup, donated by her as the prize for teams comprising players from the United States and Great Britain. She remained an active player into her seventies, playing on the lawns of Longwood Cricket Club.

 ## *The Miracle Boston Braves*

Long before media mogul Ted Turner made the Braves America's team, they were Boston's team. In the summers that have passed since 1914, Boston has yet to witness a ball club achieve as improbable a victory and surmount such great odds as did the Miracle Braves. This team resurrected a moribund franchise that had averaged ninety losses per season since 1900, while finishing last five times and losing more than one hundred games on six separate occasions. The 1914 team appeared destined to follow the same path as they won only four of their first twenty-two games. However, before the season was over, they would put together an incredible streak of fifty-two victories in sixty-six games and climb from fifteen games behind to claim sole possession of first place, all in a span of less than three months.

The man behind the miracle was manager George Tweedy Stallings, the son of a Confederate war hero. He was a dapper gentleman who wore a three-piece suit, bow tie, and straw boater while directing his charges with the slogan, "You can win. You must win. You will win." As a former big-league catcher and dropout from Johns Hopkins Medical School, Stallings combined a tremendous intellect and knowledge of the game with intense motivational skills. He believed in utilizing every player in specific roles and was a pioneer in the art of platooning. During the 1913 season he used forty-six players in an attempt to find a winning combination. Finally, the catalyst Stallings needed arrived in the person of future Hall of Fame second baseman Johnny Evers, who was traded from the Chicago Cubs to the Braves in February 1914. Evers, a diminutive overachiever who had played for four National League champions and two world champions, exhorted and often browbeat his mates while setting an example as the league's best middle infielder. Without Stallings and Evers, the miracle season would never have happened.

In April 1914 the *Boston Post* advertised a seven-room house on a half acre in Weymouth for $2,300 and a man's suit at Filene's Basement for $7. The bottom line in Hub entertainment was presented at the Howard Theater in Scollay Square, where you could see "The Gordon Brothers and Their Boxing Kangaroo" and "Roser's Aerial Dogs, The Limit in Canine Intelligence!" The Boston Braves played their home opener on April 23 at their ramshackle bandbox of a park, the South End Grounds, situated on the corner of Walpole and Tremont. Playing to a capacity crowd of seventy-five hundred, they defeated the Brooklyn Dodgers 9–1 behind the pitching of Lefty Tyler in one of their few victories that month.

Tyler, along with fellow starting pitchers Dick Rudolph and Bill James, was also among the improbable stars of this team. Prior to 1914, Tyler had sported a mediocre 35–49 career record, while Rudolph at 14–14 and James at 6–10 were no better. The remaining six pitchers were even worse, with two rookies and four veterans having losing records. In the 120-year history of professional baseball, no pennant contender has started a season with such a lackluster pitching corps. Despite its apparent limitations, this staff, led by the efforts of its Big Three of Tyler, Rudolph, and James, would achieve astounding success. The trio alone won sixty-nine of the team's ninety-four victories, with Rudolph and James winning twenty-seven and twenty-six games, respectively, while Tyler chipped in with sixteen wins.

The Braves slogged through May and June in last place, playing before meager crowds of a few thousand at their sad, outdated ballpark. The team reached its lowest ebb on July 7, when it was beaten 10–2 in an exhibition game by the minor league Buffalo Bisons. In later years, Johnny Evers recalled the loss by saying that the Braves had been beaten by a "soap company team." He also said that the "miracle" was born on a train platform in Buffalo, where Stallings berated his troops by saying, "Big league ballplayers you call yourselves, Hah. . . . You're not even grade-A sandlotters. I'm ashamed of you." Whether out of shame or a desire to show up their manager, the Braves shuffled out of Buffalo and won five of their next six games. They left last place for good on July 19 by sweeping a doubleheader in Cincinnati. Entering the ninth inning of the nightcap, trailing 2–0, they scored three runs to win. As they left the field the players celebrated like schoolboys, throwing their caps and gloves in the air and mobbing Stallings.

By August 10 the Braves had moved into second place, and their feats were duly noted by the Boston press, which made their exploits front-page news along with the first battlefield reports of World War I and the daring exploits of Pancho Villa. In a crucial mid-August series at the Polo Grounds against the league-leading New York Giants, the Braves completed a three-game sweep as Lefty Tyler—the pride of Derry, New Hampshire—outdueled Christy Mathewson 2–0 in the third game, surviving a bases-loaded, no-out situation in the bottom of the tenth. By August 23 the Braves had tied the Giants and achieved the impossible by surging from last place to first in five weeks.

The 1914 Boston Braves

Coming into Labor Day the Braves were the toast of Boston. Red Sox owner Joseph Lannin seized a golden public relations and rental opportunity by allowing the Braves to use Fenway Park for all their remaining games, including the World Series. On September 7 the Braves would fill Fenway Park as it had never been filled before or since, with a morning/afternoon Labor Day doubleheader against the Giants that attracted a combined attendance of seventy-six thousand.

The crowds began gathering on Lansdowne Street at 7:30 A.M. for the 10:00 A.M. morning game. Ticket scalpers made easy money hawking $1.00 grandstand tickets for $5.00 and $.75 general admission tickets for $2.50. When the park was filled, the overflow crowd was allowed on the field spanning the outfield. Many perched themselves at the base of Duffy's Cliff and upwards, toward the base of the wooden left-field wall. The Braves won the first game in dramatic fashion by scoring two runs in the bottom of the ninth on a Johnny Evers double off Christy Mathewson to secure a 5–4 decision.

In between games of the doubleheader, Braves shortstop Rabbit Maranville entertained the crowd by sitting on the second-base bag while taking throws from catcher Hank Gowdy and outfielder Joe Connolly. The *Boston Post* reported that the roar of the crowd cheering both Maranville and the game could be heard miles away from the ball yard. "It was a typical Boston crowd. They yelled, they brought various noise-making implements along with them to show their allegiance to the Braves and they used them with unabated fury. . . . Their applause of good plays was deafening and came during practice sessions as well as the game."

In the second game the Braves fell by a score of 10–1, but not until Giants outfielder Fred Snodgrass nearly incited a riot. After being hit by a pitch from Lefty Tyler, Snodgrass stood on first and proceeded to thumb his nose at Tyler, the Braves, and the crowd. Tyler responded in kind by doing a perfect pantomime of the Snodgrass Muff, an infamous error that had cost the Giants a world championship in the final World Series game of 1912, which was also played at Fenway Park. During the inning the Giants scored four runs, rubbing salt into the wounds of the Braves and their fans. While trotting out to take his position in center field, Snodgrass was greeted by a barrage of bottles and garbage. Boston mayor James Michael Curley then jumped onto the diamond, where he attempted to persuade the police lieutenant and umpire Bob

Emske to throw Snodgrass out of the game for inciting a riot. While both men ignored the mayor's histrionics, Giants manager John McGraw removed his center fielder, feeling his star was of more value alive than dead. Despite the disappointing loss in the second game, the Braves had captured the heart and imagination of Boston in one dramatic day at Fenway Park.

On September 9 the Braves supplied more drama to Fenway when the park's first no-hitter was thrown by Braves righthander George "Iron" Davis in the second game of a doubleheader against the Philadelphia Phillies. Davis, a Williams College graduate and Harvard law student, allowed no hits while issuing five walks in a 7–0 triumph. In the fifth inning, Davis walked the first three batters and then proceeded to dig himself out of a hole by notching a strikeout and a double play to preserve his masterpiece. Such was the magic of the Miracle Braves, where the most unlikely players achieved remarkably under difficult circumstances.

By September 23 the Braves were well on the way to the pennant. Although a column in the *Boston Post* speculated—in a typically pessimistic Bostonian fashion—how the Braves could lose to the Giants, a cartoon in another section of the same newspaper depicted the pitching trio of Rudolph, Tyler, and James atop an onrushing steamroller, crushing the Giants on the road to the pennant. On September 29 the Braves clinched the pennant with a 3–2 victory over the Cubs at Fenway Park.

By season's end the Braves had opened a ten-and-a-half game margin over the second-place Giants. They had won fifty-two games and lost only fourteen during their unprecedented surge to the World Series. The performance of the team was epitomized by the achievement of spitballing pitcher Bill James, who won nineteen of his last twenty appearances while compiling a 1.90 ERA. Second baseman Evers won a narrow vote over teammate Rabbit Maranville for the Chalmers Award as MVP of the National League.

Entering the World Series against Connie Mack's Philadelphia Athletics, Stallings's team was listed as a two-to-one underdog, with many sportswriters predicting an Athletics victory in four straight games. Mack's team was a powerhouse that featured five future Hall of Famers in Eddie Collins, Frank Baker, Eddie Plank, Chief Bender, and Herb Pennock, who had helped the Athletics to victories in three of the previous four World Series.

The series opened at Shibe Park in Philadelphia on October 9. The Braves, cheered on by a rowdy contingent of three hundred Royal Rooters led by former Boston mayor John "Honey Fitz" Fitzgerald, defeated Chief Bender, the man Connie Mack had called the greatest money pitcher in baseball history, by a score of 7–1 in the first game. Catcher Hank Gowdy led the way for the Braves with a single, a double, and a triple.

Fans in Boston were treated to the action by attending one of several telegraph re-creations of the game. A large display board mounted on-stage at the Tremont Street Temple was outfitted with moveable tin players that were moved around the bases by attendants, who shouted the game's play-by-play—transmitted by wire to Boston—to a throng who had paid anywhere from twenty-five to seventy-five cents apiece to watch their Braves as baseball theater. Similar reenactments were shown at other Boston locations throughout the series. At the Braves' abandoned home, the South End Grounds, live players ran the bases in response to an announcer shouting through a megaphone!

In game two, Boston ace Bill James and Philadelphia hurler Eddie Plank engaged in a dramatic pitching duel. The Braves ended the scoreless tie in the ninth, when third baseman Charlie Deal stroked a one-out double, then took third on James's groundout, and scored on outfielder Les Mann's base hit. The Braves, surrounded by over five hundred Royal Rooters, clambered into their dugout at game's end as Stallings ordered his traveling secretary to ship all their equipment back to Boston. "We won't be coming back," he boldly proclaimed. "It'll be over after two games in Boston."

Game three, at Fenway Park, proved to be the most dramatic of the series. With ticket prices at $5.00 for box seats, $3.00 for grandstand, $2.00 for pavilion, and $1.50 for bleachers, the Boston faithful filled Fenway to inspire yet another miracle from the Braves. Hank Gowdy would again be the star, hitting two doubles and a homer while leading the Braves to a 5–4 victory in twelve innings—the longest series game ever played to that date. This would also be the only game in the series in which the Athletics held a lead. As the darkness of the late-autumn afternoon threatened to suspend play, Gowdy clouted his game-winning double into the roped-off crowd standing in the shadow of the left-field wall. Following the game Stallings said, "If we can win this game, we can't possibly lose tomorrow." With that emphatic statement he promptly canceled the team's train reservations to Philadelphia for the following night. That evening the Braves and their wives were the special guests of George M. Cohan, who treated them to a vaudeville show at the Plymouth Theater.

The Braves' World Series victory made the front page of the Boston Post.

BRAVES WIN FINAL 3 TO 1
NOW WORLD CHAMPIONS

Four Straight From Athletics Breaks All World's Series Records—Rudolph Holds Mackmen Safe, While His Mates Pound Shawkey and Pennock—Joyous Fans Turn Fenway Park Into Riot of Enthusiasm Over Wonderful Victories

The next day Dick Rudolph, pitching on three days' rest, set down the Athletics by a score of 3–1 before 34,365 spectators at Fenway Park to clinch the only World Series title in Boston Braves history. The fans celebrated by racing onto the field, where they gathered near the Braves' dugout and sang "America," led by the tenor voice of Mayor Curley, who stood atop a chair in the dugout. Each Brave took home $2,812.28 as a series share. The most acclaimed series hero was catcher Hank Gowdy, who batted .545 in helping the Braves secure the first sweep in World Series history and the last until the vaunted 1927 Yankees defeated the Pittsburgh Pirates.

On the day following the series, Stallings had his players hold an open practice at Fenway, where the team cavorted for the press and fans. Later that week the team was feted with a banquet thrown by Mayor Curley and the City Council at the Copley Plaza Hotel, where Stallings was quoted as saying, "There is only one thing lacking to make my business complete and that is to meet that big fat stiff Johnson [American League President Ban Johnson] and laugh in his face."

The 1914 world championship would be the last for the franchise until the 1957 title won by the Milwaukee incarnation of the team. During their seventy-six-year stay in Boston they left many memories, but the 1914 club provided the sweetest of them. In 1950, their World Series victory was selected by a nationwide poll of sportswriters as the greatest sports upset of the century. Perhaps John B. Foster, writing in the 1915 *Spalding Baseball Guide,* best summed up the spirit of the team and its era in the following passage: "It was hard to convince some of the seasoned baseball patrons that here was a team that actually seemed to be playing because the players liked it and were not confining their thoughts to their salaries or worrying for fear that they might work too hard in proportion to their reimbursement."

the Twenties

The Showman: Tex Rickard

George L. "Tex" Rickard's story seems like something out of the great American novel rather than the life of the man who built Boston Garden. He was a huckster, impresario, and visionary rolled into one.

Born in 1870 and orphaned at the age of ten, Rickard worked as a cowboy and town marshal, then went to the Klondike during the 1897 gold rush. After making and losing several fortunes in Alaska, he moved to the warmer but no less desolate environs of Nevada, where he became a part-time boxing promoter. So successful were his bouts—especially those featuring a heavyweight phenom named Jack Dempsey—that he eventually signed a ten-year lease to promote all events at New York's Madison Square Garden. In a short time he made the venue known simply as "the Garden" into the most famous indoor sports arena in the world.

Not satisfied with merely staging such events as six-day bicycle races, Rickard secured the backing to build a new Madison Square Garden in 1925. Among the tenants in his new building were the fledgling New York Rangers, a hockey team named after the famed Texas Rangers of Rickard's home state.

Tex Rickard (right), the original owner of the Boston Garden

Soon Rickard sought to expand his empire. He ultimately envisioned building a series of Madison Square Gardens around the country, in which he could promote his boxing matches and other events. He looked north to Boston as the location for the first in his series of Gardens. Long a boxing and hockey hotbed, Boston was a natural location for America's second great indoor arena.

On November 17, 1928, Rickard opened Boston Garden to an overflow crowd that watched hometown hero Honeyboy Finnegan defeat world welterweight champion André Routis in a charity boxing match benefitting the local chapter of the Veterans of Foreign Wars. Rickard lived only long enough to see the Garden celebrate the Bruins' first Stanley Cup victory in April 1929 before dying unexpectedly on June 5, 1929.

Boston Garden Opens

André Routis, the pride of France and the defending world welterweight champion, and Dick "Honeyboy" Finnegan, a native of Dorchester, fought the first boxing match ever held at Boston Garden before an overflow crowd of nearly twenty thousand on November 17, 1928. Cheered by a roaring crowd that rocked the new arena to its foundations, Finnegan defeated Routis in ten rounds in the non-title bout.

Among the preliminary events to the main bout was an exhibition of firearms assembly by local veterans, as well as a barbaric "battle royale" in which a blindfolded African American boxer was made to fight his way out of a ring filled with other fighters.

Boston Garden under construction, c. 1928

Boston Garden facade at night, c. 1929

André Routis (left) vs. Dick "Honeyboy" Finnegan (right), Boston Garden, November 17, 1928

The Beautiful Game: Early Professional Soccer in Boston

The beautiful game—aka soccer—flourished in Boston during the twenties as an influx of former professional and even a few national team players from England, Scotland, and Northern Ireland immigrated to America during the post–World War I depression. While these men arrived in Boston ostensibly to find work in local industry, their secondary purpose was to play "football" for one of the many professional and industrial league teams in the region.

1926 National Amateur Cup Championship

Boston Wonder Workers, c. 1927

Elite local clubs such as the Boston Wonder Workers of the American Soccer League fielded teams that more than held their own against touring British giants such as the Glasgow Rangers and Celtic. Such games were played at Fenway Park and attracted crowds that dwarfed the pitiful Red Sox attendance of the time. The Wonder Workers also played before overflow crowds at the Walpole Street Grounds in the South End.

James and John Ballantine,
Boston Wonder Workers

European club teams such as the Glasgow Rangers often toured the United States at the conclusion of their own domestic season. In June 1928, the Scottish League and Cup winners played in front of 10,000 fans at Fenway Park.

The quagmire in this picture (opposite page, top) is the Walpole Street Grounds, the former home of the Boston Braves, as seen during the 1926 Amateur Cup. Playing are the Revere Corinthians and Clan Robertson, a local collection of Scottish immigrants.

The 1927 Boston Wonder Workers (opposite page, bottom) boasted ten former Scottish players, including two previously on the Scottish National Team. James and John Ballantine (right) were among the Boston Wonder Workers' Scottish stars. Note the heavy socks, shin guards, and old-style boots.

George Owen:
A Man for All Seasons

In 1971, the Montreal Canadiens arrived at the Boston Garden for a mid-winter regular season game and watched with wonder the graceful moves of a lone skater as they prepared to dress for their traditional pre-game skate. Weymouth native Bobby Sheehan, a skater second only to the speedy Yvan Cournouyer of the Canadiens, asked a Garden maintenance worker about the identity of the skater, adding admiringly, "that old guy can sure as hell skate." When informed that the skater was Bruins alumnus George Owen, a member of the 1929 Stanley Cup champions and Eddie Shore's defense partner, several of the players waited respectfully for the sixty-nine-year-old to step off the ice before asking to shake his hand and inquire about the days of Shore and Howie Morenz.

George Owen's exploits on the hockey rink, football field, and baseball diamond made him a hero at Harvard.

Like F. Scott Fitzgerald's boyhood idol, Princeton star Hobey Baker, George Owen epitomized the ideal athlete and gentleman. The son of the head of the Naval Architecture Department at MIT, Owen first made his mark as a multisport athlete at Newton High School. As a child, Owen had been inspired to pursue athletics after having seen several historic sporting events. Among them were the Harvard Stadium debut of Jim Thorpe, the famous pitching duel between Walter Johnson and Smoky Joe Wood in 1912, and many a Boston Arena hockey game featuring the talents of the aforementioned Hobey Baker.

Owen competed in an era when the best athletes competed in a variety of sports, for the greater glory both of themselves and their school. At Harvard he became one of only four men to capture nine varsity letters; he would have won more had freshmen been eligible to do so. In football Owen played on both sides of the ball, as a rugged fullback and as a linebacker. His accomplishments secured him a place within the National Football Foundation Hall of Fame. In hockey he anchored the Harvard defense, often skating forty minutes per game. During the spring he played first base for the Harvard baseball team and, as a senior, outhit his Columbia University counterpart Lou Gehrig in inter-collegiate competition.

In 1921, Owen and his father dreamt up the concept of line changes in hockey. Interviewed in 1986, two months before his death at age eighty-four, Owen described the development:

We eventually came up with an idea based on comparing a hockey player to a boxer. We focused on the principle of the three-minute-round system being transferred from boxing to hockey in order to give players a suffi-cient rest. We figured a boxer could not box indefinitely without collapsing or losing much of his sharpness. Hence we devised a system where our players would alternate on a regular schedule during a game. Our locker room was located in close proximity to the bench area and our players would rest by lying down in the locker room between shifts, and our man-ager, using a stop watch, would alert the players to either get off the ice or get off their backs.

The multitalented Owen was also an accomplished tennis player.

During his senior year at Harvard, Owen nearly single-handedly defeated Yale in football, hockey, and baseball. His heroics prompted the Yale trea-surer to send a telegram to the president of Har-vard on the eve of Owen's graduation, asking that the multitalented Owen please be given his di-ploma and sent on his way for the good of Yale.

Following his graduation from Harvard in 1923, Owen continued to play hockey for Boston's University Club while also playing such sports as tennis and golf. During one memorable stay in Newport, Rhode Island, he was playing doubles in a tennis tournament at the famed Newport Casino when he was asked to join the singles rotation for a match against reigning world champion Bill Tilden. As Owen recalled in 1986:

The tournament director, who had given us a break by allowing us in the doubles draw, called me aside and asked me if I would do him a favor, and I said sure thing. It seemed that a local gentleman who played in the match each year had the misfortune of

drawing Bill Tilden as his opening match and refused to face the cham-
pion. The tournament director then asked me if I would be willing to take
the gentleman's place in the draw and thereby help the tournament by not
letting a large crowd be treated to the news of a default. I told him he had
to be kidding, here I was a decent doubles player and fair singles player
being asked to face the greatest player of his time. Finally I talked to
Tilden himself and he told me not to worry and that he would make a
good match of it. True to his word every game was a deuce game. During
the match he had learned which shots I could reach and make and was
playing to my strength. He could make any shot in the book and won 6–1,
6–1. I'll never forget that Tilden the athlete was also a great gentleman.

In 1928, the Boston Bruins finally persuaded Owen to turn pro. Flush
with cash as the result of the opening of the Boston Garden, the Bruins
signed the former Harvard star for what was then the highest bonus
(twenty-five thousand dollars) ever given a player. Bruins General Manager Art Ross outbid rival Conn Smythe of the Toronto Maple Leafs for
Owen's services, and the Bruins bolstered their defense for what
proved to be a successful campaign for the Stanley Cup.

The smooth-skating, hard-hitting defenseman was only the second
product of an American high school to make the NHL, after Melrose
native Myles Lane of the New York Rangers. Despite waiting five years
after his Harvard graduation to turn pro, Owen not only held his own
against the league's best forwards but was named Bruins captain in
1931. Unfortunately, his career was cut short that same season when he
suffered a bout of phlebitis following an appendectomy.

In later years Owen taught and coached at Vermont Academy and
Milton Academy while remaining active as an athlete. Owen, a skilled
designer of athletic equipment, even designed the heel cushion that
allowed Joe DiMaggio to play in the latter stages of the heated 1949
pennant race.

In 1986, the eighty-four-year-old Owen admitted that he had once spent
part of an afternoon in twenty-degree cold playing catch in his backyard
by throwing a baseball against a pitchback screen that he had recently
developed. Truly a man for all seasons.

Clarence DeMar

Clarence DeMar, the premier marathoner of the twenties, dominated the Boston Marathon during the decade, capturing five of his seven Boston titles between 1922 and 1928. His bronze-medal performance in the 1924 Olympic Marathon was the best American finish in the event until Frank Shorter's victory in 1972. In his autobiography, *Marathon,* DeMar reminisced about his running career and his experiences in Boston.

On Running. *From the first I decided that whatever else I might do I would become a marathon runner. I ran at the leisurely speed of seven or eight miles per hour, to and from work, usually carrying a dry undershirt. I also bought a small Spaulding book about distance running for ten cents, and studied it carefully. I felt that I could absorb the instruction I needed better from reading than from a coach, since I could cogitate each problem and reach a decision without prejudice. Also, I could make sure I understood the theory before trying to put it into practice. My experience with coaches and would-be coaches in distance running is that they try to tell me something when I'm very tense and excited from running and I misunderstand them and get rattled. While reading and studying this little book I greatly admired Shrub, Longboat, Mahoney, Forshaw and Hatch, but I felt a serene confidence that I could eventually do as well as any of them on a full marathon. And I had never run over eight or ten miles in my life!*

Clarence DeMar with members of Melrose Veterans of Foreign Wars. With seven victories, Clarence DeMar is the all-time Boston Marathon champion. His amazing record includes an eleven-year absence from the race because of suspect medical advice. An irregular heartbeat kept him from competing in the race until he sought a second opinion in the early twenties.

On the Boston Marathon. *At the crack of the gun on the stroke of twelve there was a scramble, but as usual by holding out my elbows, like a chicken about to fly, I protected myself. And, as always, I was fortunate enough not to have anyone step on my heel and pull my shoe off.*

In less than half a mile I began to feel very tense and somewhat like a foreman of a print shop with a lot of work piled up, or perhaps the editor with a scoop coming in ten minutes before the presses started. All my faculties were being concentrated on the race and it was about as natural for me to do this as it would be for a dog to walk on his hind legs or a college student to do some thinking. My physical distress at having my heart, lungs and legs work at abnormal speed and the mental difficulty of keeping my body at the task was such that the one thing I dreaded was interruption or distraction of any kind. Any word or deed aimed to get my attention would be like throwing a monkey wrench into a finely geared piece of machinery. Just a personal word like, "Step on it there" or "Get Going, Clarence" and I felt furious. But of course the impersonal yelling and cheering was a slight encouragement. . . .

With periods of tenseness and fear of distraction alternating with periods of comparative calm I continued, the pendulum of distress and ease swinging back and forth about a dozen times during the race. From this I can truthfully say that I got not only my second wind but also tenth and twelfth wind in most marathons. But whether I'm tense or calm it is not a time for reasoning things like mathematics. Sometimes minor problems of addition, subtraction, or division present themselves in figuring how I should run some stretch in comparison to other years considering my present condition. Sometimes it takes several miles to get an answer I could get in a minute at my desk; but I can get it and know when it is right. . . .

While I can't figure mathematics easily nor think deeply on most subjects while running with all my might, yet I always feel confident that I am very much master of my fate. Keyed up I am super-quick to dodge traffic and do broken-field running. I am extremely alert to grab the shortest curve in the road or to get out of a troublesome bunch of competitors by ducking around autos or sidewalks. "This one thing I'm doing" as Saint Paul said, only in this case it happens to be merely running a marathon race and not preaching or practicing a better life. As I put everything I am capable of into the contest, I sometimes feel that the whole world is divided, not only as Charles Lamb said, into those who borrow and those who lend, but also into those who pay attention and accomplish things and those who distract

attention and are infernal nuisances. The runners are paying attention
and the rest of the world is mostly trying to distract them.
—Clarence DeMar

 ## *Home Ice:*
The Bruins and Boston

If the sporting heart of Greater Boston could be seen, it would resemble a hockey puck. Not only has Boston embraced the Bruins through good times and bad, but the city and surrounding suburbs have also become one of the great hotbeds of the game. The multitude of young players inspired by the teams of the Bobby Orr era continue to fill the rosters of collegiate and professional teams. It seems as if everyone in the Boston area knows someone who has reached either the collegiate or professional level in the game, which certainly cannot be said about any other major sport in the city. The Boston Bruins, the very symbol of the hockey boom in the United States, are the team closest to the hearts of fans in America's greatest sports region.

For nine decades the Boston Bruins have served as the National Hockey League's flagship franchise in the United States. They were the first NHL team in the lower forty-eight, and they have enjoyed as storied and colorful a history as any franchise in the history of North American professional sports. They are a team whose roster has included the likes of the mercurial Eddie Shore, a virtual Ty Cobb on skates; Aubrey V. "Dit" Clapper, a hockey Iron Man who played forward and defense with equal skill; the Kraut Line of Milton Conrad Schmidt, Woody Dumart, and Bobby Bauer; and the greatest hockey player of all time, the incomparable Bobby Orr. No fewer than forty-two members of the Bruins are enshrined in the Hockey Hall of Fame. For teams based in the United States, the Bruins' five Stanley Cup championships are second only to the eight won by the Detroit Red Wings.

To recognize the significance of the Boston Bruins one must imagine the time in which they were founded. The national sports landscape was dominated by only one truly professional team sport, major league baseball, with boxing a distant second. In baseball, Bostonians rooted for teams in both the American and National leagues as well as countless local school and town teams. In amateur circles, Harvard's football team was Rose Bowl champion in 1920 and it regularly played before crowds of 60,000 at Harvard Stadium. At this time, the NFL and NBA would have been almost unimaginable to the Boston fan. It was in this context that the Bruins arrived at Boston Arena in the autumn of 1924.

By the time the Bruins played their first game, hockey was already a staple of the Boston sports scene. Teams from local prep schools and colleges formed the base of the first generation of American players. Stars such as Hobey Baker, George Owen, and Myles Lane dazzled capacity crowds at Boston Arena while playing for Princeton, Harvard, and Dartmouth, respectively. Boston was also home to the first inter-scholastic hockey league in the country. The NHL couldn't have selected a better American city in which to establish its first franchise.

The prospect of attracting the capacity crowds that supported Boston's local club and college teams lured local businessman Charles F. Adams to invest in the first American NHL franchise. In time the Bruins became such an attractive property that promoter extraordinaire Tex Rickard built them a home worthy of their fans. When Boston Garden opened for hockey on November 20, 1928, the first of thousands of sellout Bruins crowds arrived, only to witness a 1–0 loss to the Canadiens.

The Bruins were both an outgrowth of local tradition and a manifestation of the ambitions of the NHL. It was vital to the long-term growth of both the sport and the league for it to sink solid roots in American soil. Boston was the perfect place to start, and it has remained America's home ice for nearly a century.

Boston Garden opens for hockey, November 20, 1928

The Bruins' Big Three:
Adams, Ross, and Shore

Charles F. Adams

In the beginning the Bruins relied on the talents of three men to secure the franchise's place in sports-mad Boston and to establish the National Hockey League as a legitimate second "major league" team sport in the United States. It took the money and enthusiasm of Charles F. Adams, the resolve and inventive genius of Art Ross, and the sheer will and talent of Eddie Shore to make the Bruins a world-renowned franchise.

Legend has it that Adams selected the name *Bruins* because the team colors could then imitate the brown and gold used in the logo of his business, the First National Stores. The bruin, a creature with solid local roots, also made for an alliterative name for the newest franchise in town. Adams used his business acumen to find and hire the best available coach in Art Ross and then get someone else to fund the building of his home arena. The Adams family owned the team for six decades and were the stewards of all five Stanley Cup victories in the twentieth century.

Coach and General Manager Art Ross was the greatest innovator the game has ever seen. A great player in his own right, Ross developed the design of the puck and net that are still in use today. He also experimented with metal hockey sticks as far back as the thirties, roughly fifty years before such equipment became standard issue.

Ross, a ferocious competitor, was the alter ego of superstar defenseman Eddie Shore, allowing his star to dominate games with his rink-length rushes and savage checking. Ross's great Bruins teams of the twenties and thirties captured three Stanley Cups and did more to popularize hockey in the United States than any other NHL team.

Shore, a native of Fort Qu'Appele, Saskatchewan, broke into the NHL with the Bruins in 1926. In short order he was proclaimed the Babe Ruth of hockey and his appearances filled arenas across North America. Shore was the greatest player of his era, a defenseman who controlled the game with dramatic rushes and bone-crunching body checks. It was Shore's popularity that inspired the construction of major indoor arenas in several large North American cities. In the "Golden Age" of sports, he took his place alongside such athletes as Ruth, Red Grange, Helen Wills, Bill Tilden, and Jack Dempsey as a performer who guaranteed both box office and media appeal in equal measure.

Shore's rough and tumble style of play was the stuff of legends. In one 1929 game against the Montreal Maroons, Shore suffered a broken nose, three broken teeth, two black eyes, a gashed cheekbone, and a two-inch cut over his left eye. Nonetheless, that same year—their inaugural season at Boston Garden—Shore helped lead the Bruins to their first Stanley Cup championship.

Art Ross

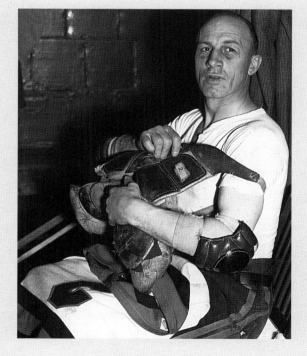

Eddie Shore

Eva Morrison, Marathon Swimmer

Nova Scotia native Eva Morrison moved to Boston as a young girl and soon became a local celebrity for her feats as a long distance swimmer. During the twenties and thirties, Morrison was virtually unbeatable. Her accomplishments made headlines and earned her countless trophies.

Eva Morrison was known around Boston for her famous cold-water swims. In March 1926, Morrison amazed onlookers as she swam for thirty-seven minutes in thirty-three-degree water in Boston Harbor. In April of that year Morrison swam for forty-three minutes in thirty-seven-degree water, and in 1928 she beat the famed L Street Brownies at their own game by swimming for twelve minutes in twenty-nine-degree water. *Boston Globe* writer Jerry Nason once referred to the Nova Scotia native as a "human seal."

Morrison is shown here at Revere Beach. One of her greatest feats was an epic swim that took her from Charlestown Bridge to Boston Light and Graves Light, and finally to Revere Beach on August 30, 1931.

Eva Morrison at Revere Beach, c. 1931

Judge Emil Fuchs:
Owner, Manager, Fan

*Baseball is my life—it has meant everything to me. If by chance I get back on my feet, I have an ambition to revive the National League in Boston.
—Judge Emil Fuchs in 1957*

In 1977, when Atlanta Braves owner Ted Turner attempted to serve as team manager, the experiment lasted only one day and one loss before Commissioner Bowie Kuhn informed the owner that henceforth he and all owners were banned from serving as managers of their teams. At the time, only one or two sportswriters mentioned in passing that Turner was not the first owner-manager in franchise history, much less the first in major league history.

For an entire season in 1929, the Boston Braves were led by none other than the team's owner, Judge Emil Fuchs. Fuchs, a New York native, had grown up playing youth baseball for a settlement house team that featured players such as future entertainers Al Jolson and Eddie Cantor, as well as future Supreme Court Justice Felix Frankfurter. The experience fostered a lifelong passion for the game. In his career as one of New York's most prominent attorneys, Fuchs served as counsel to the New York Giants, during which time he learned the business side of the game and plotted someday to own a team. When the Boston Braves became available for purchase in 1923, Fuchs's friend, composer George M. Cohan, suggested he buy the team.

Emil Fuchs (left) receiving an award at Braves Field, c. 1930

Fuchs quickly assembled the necessary backers, including team president Christy Mathewson, and assumed control in February 1923.

For the first six years that Fuchs owned them the Braves finished an average of seventh in the eight-team league. So in 1929 Fuchs took a leave of absence from the bench to become the team manager, figuring he knew as much as any fan about the game and couldn't do any worse than the managers who had led the Braves to countless second-division finishes. In his memoirs, Fuchs's son Robert recalls that when word of his father's hiring reached his old friend John McGraw, the New York Giants manager sent him a pair of pants with a reinforced leather seat, emphasizing that they could be a buffer for "squirming on the bench."

Assisted from the bench by a brain trust of future Hall of Famers such as Dave "Beauty" Bancroft, Rabbit Maranville, George Sisler, and Johnny Evers, the judge could only manage a last-place finish with a record of 56–98. In fact, for the remainder of his ownership, the well-intentioned fan saw his team finish in the first division only three times, capped by an overachieving third-place team in 1933.

In his dozen years as owner (and one as owner-manager), Fuchs lost money but accomplished a great deal for the franchise and for baseball in the city of Boston. Among the hallmarks of his ownership were keeping the Braves in Boston despite overtures from Henry Ford, who considered moving the team to Detroit to compete with the Tigers; introducing the first major league baseball game to be played on Sunday in Boston; establishing the Boston Baseball Writer's banquet, now a staple on the annual baseball calendar; and creating the concept of the Knot Hole Gang, which allowed a child to purchase tickets from local playground directors for only a nickel during the height of the Depression. The last concept was widely imitated by other major league teams, and was carried on by the Braves until their move to Milwaukee in 1953.

Always the loyal fan, Fuchs discussed with a reporter in 1957 his dream of one day striking it rich and bringing the team back to Boston. In 1960, he was one of a handful of baseball friends in the Red Sox clubhouse, both before and after Ted Williams sent the final home run of his career into the outer reaches of the right-center bleachers.

Fuchs died in 1961, never getting the chance to bring his Braves back to Boston. However, in his tenure as owner the team rapidly improved, with a lineup as eclectic and colorful as any that have worn the Braves uniform.

Twenty-year-old Johnny Miles startled the running world when he won the 1926 Boston Marathon with a time of 2:25:40, clipping an incredible four minutes off the course record. He would win again in 1929, with a time of 2:33:08.

The Prodigy: Johnny Miles

John Christopher Miles was the son of a miner from a part of Canada's Maritime Provinces seldom featured in travel brochures. His hometown of Sydney Mines, Nova Scotia, was just that—a coal pit, similar to those in West Virginia and Kentucky. Life in Sydney Mines at the beginning of the twentieth century was a hardscrabble proposition in which nearly all men went into the pits. In many ways life there was nearly identical to the existence the residents thought they had left behind when they emigrated to Canada from the northeast corner of England.

At an early age Miles dreamed of a life beyond the dreary mining town. His escape route followed almost precisely the streetcar tracks leading out of town. As a young man he became hooked on running after winning a ninety-eight-pound bag of flour in a local road race. During the long winters he ran along the only plowed path in town, the streetcar roadbed. Soon he was competing in races in Halifax and drawing the attention of the local press.

When Miles won a major ten-mile race in Halifax in 1925, his father promised to take him to Boston to run in the marathon. Legend has it that, prior to finalizing plans for the trip, Miles ran a solo twenty-six-mile time trial in a snowstorm in two hours and forty minutes. Not only was this a world-class clocking for the marathon, but the fact that he ran the distance in heavy sweats and tennis shoes made the feat all the more remarkable.

Arriving in Boston a week before the 1926 marathon, Miles and his father lived in a local boarding house while carefully preparing for the race. Miles would go on to shock the running world by winning the marathon and upstaging an anticipated duel between Clarence DeMar and 1924 Olympic Marathon champion Albin Stenroos. His victory made him a national hero in Canada.

the
Thirties

Off Track: The Story of Louise Stokes

The reports published by the American Olympic Committee (AOC) after the 1932 and 1936 Olympic Games include photos of the U.S. women's track-and-field teams. In each photo you can spot a young black woman—Louise Stokes of Malden, Massachusetts. Stokes and Tidye Pickett of Chicago were the first black female athletes to earn places on an American Olympic team. Yet Stokes was not allowed to compete, and she never received recognition for her pioneering exploits in women's track and field. Ironically, Jesse Owens, a black man, was the star of the 1936 games in Berlin. But being both black and female kept Louise Stokes out of Olympic competition.

Louise Stokes was the oldest of the six children of William Stokes, a gardener, and his wife, Mary Wesley Stokes, a housekeeper. Louise went to Malden High School, where she was a member of the girl's basketball team. A teammate introduced her to William Quayne, a postal worker who sponsored a women's track team called the Onteora Track Club. As Stokes's sister Emily Collins recalls, until Louise met Quayne, she "used to just run for the sport of it." But under Quayne's guidance, Stokes became serious about running. In her sophomore year she began to run competitively. Soon she was winning.

In the summer of 1931 Stokes collected her first significant award when she won the Curley Cup as the best all-around performer at the annual track meet sponsored by Boston mayor James Michael Curley. That day, she set the New England women's 100-yard-dash record with a time of 12.6 seconds, finished second in the 50-yard dash, and placed third in the standing broad jump.

On December 30, 1931, Stokes leapt into the record books. At a Young Men's Hebrew Association (YMHA) indoor meet in Roxbury, she tied the women's world record in the standing broad jump with a leap of 8 feet, 5¾ inches. The following month, she won the National Junior championship in the 40-yard dash and successfully defended her broad-jump mark against a national field at a meet in Princeton, New Jersey.

Today such spectacular success would attract widespread acclaim and a story in *Sports Illustrated.* But then, no one paid much attention to female track athletes. In fact, it was debated whether women should compete in track and field at all. So it's not surprising that Stokes's accomplishments were barely acknowledged, even in her hometown newspapers. Both the *Malden Evening News* and the black weekly the *Boston Chronicle* devoted only a paragraph or two to her performance. But William Quayne recognized Louise's talent. He brought the possibility of participating in the Olympics to her attention, and she began to train in earnest.

In June 1932, at a meet in the Fenway sponsored by the Boston Parks Department, Stokes captured the New England regional crown in the high jump and finished second in the 100-yard dash, ahead of 1928 Olympian Olive Hasenfus. A month later, she traveled to Northwestern University in Evanston, Illinois, for the Olympic trials.

The trials that year were dominated by Mildred "Babe" Didrikson, whose athletic abilities were matched by her arrogance and ego. Some said that Didrikson felt that the trials were held solely for her benefit. She attempted to enter all the events and complained bitterly when Fred Steers, manager of the women's track-and-field team, balked at changing schedules to suit her. Helen Woods, Didrikson's chaperone, claimed that Steers was conspiring against her charge and repeatedly raced from the stands to alert Didrikson to the start of another event. When the day ended, Didrikson had qualified in three events. This virtual one-woman team was the only female athlete who mattered to the national press.

Louise Stokes lacked Didrikson's entourage and arrogance. Competing only in the 100-meter dash, Stokes finished third, which earned her a place on the women's 4 × 100-meter relay team that would compete at the 1932 Los Angeles Olympics. But membership on the U.S. squad depended on more than just performance in the trials. Despite AOC president Avery Brundage's statement in a 1932 report that "there could be no charge of favoritism in the selection of the team," the committee was sensitive to public opinion.

By 1932 black athletes were pacing the American Olympic effort in track and field. Sprinters Eddie Tolan, a star at the University of Michigan, and Ralph Metcalfe of Marquette University, both black and both well known to track fans, performed brilliantly at the Los Angeles games, with Tolan collecting gold in the 100- and 200-meter dashes

Louise Stokes winning the 100-yard dash at the Mayor's Day Races, 1931.

and Metcalfe earning a silver and a bronze, respectively, in the same events. Edward Gordon, also black, won a gold in the long jump. Although these high-profile black athletes received full support from the AOC, some lesser-known blacks had been blocked from competition at the games.

Sensitive to the possibility that blacks might dominate the American team, the AOC maneuvered to keep several black athletes from competing. Sprinter James Johnson qualified for the men's 4 × 100-meter relay, but was removed from the team and replaced by a white runner, despite the objection of his coach. Chicago's Tidye Pickett was nearly bumped off the team at the tryouts. And performer Clarence Muse, who was supposed to take part in the entertainment, was dropped by the chairman of the Olympic entertainment committee because, according to the *Boston Chronicle,* "too many Negroes had already got too much glory from the Olympics."

It was in this climate that Stokes and Pickett arrived in Los Angeles expecting to run in the 4 × 100-meter relay. Little did they know that, at a meeting of AOC honchos, it had been decided that two white women from the West Coast were faster and would take Stokes's and Pickett's places in the relay. The pleas of team manager Fred Steers and others fell on deaf ears. Annette Rogers and Evelyn Furtsch joined the relay team and the American women set a new world record and won the gold. Stokes and Pickett returned to their homes without ever taking the track in Los Angeles.

The only person who could have seen that the black women athletes got their rightful place on the team was not disposed to take action. Avery Brundage hated controversy, was insensitive to racism, and felt that women had little place in track-and-field competition. Clearly, Stokes and Pickett had no ally in him.

It was up to Fred Steers to issue a veiled apology for the decision. In his contribution to the report on the 1932 games, Steers wrote: "I further recommend that all matters pertaining to the team be transacted and carried on through the manager only. This was not done in many cases and as a result considerable confusion was caused which might otherwise be avoided."

But Louise Stokes did not complain. That was not her way. Her sister Emily Collins says that Louise was simply "a very friendly person. You know—everybody was wonderful until she found out they weren't." In a brief story about Stokes, the *Boston Chronicle* praised Steers as "an enemy of prejudice" and hinted at a "row" between Tidye Pickett and Babe Didrickson that may have contributed to the removal of the two black women from the relay. At least publicly, Stokes refused to speculate about the decision. All Emily Collins remembers is that "Babe Didrikson never liked Louise and Tidye Pickett. Louise never told us it was racial problems. She [Didrikson] was from Texas. A lot of people didn't like her."

In 1935, Louise Stokes began competing again. That February she set a New England record in the 40-yard dash and became the New England Amateur Athletic Union (NEAAU) senior champion with a mark of 5.6 seconds. In July, at the national Amateur Athletic Union (AAU) meet at Chicago's Soldier's Field, she won the 50-meter championship in 6.6 seconds and captured second place for the Onteora Track Club, despite being the team's sole representative.

Over the next year, Stokes continued to win, retaining the 50-meter crown and adding NEAAU titles in the 100-meter dash, the 100-yard dash, the 200-meter dash, the broad jump, the high jump, and the 25-yard sprint. In 1936, she again looked toward the Olympics, which were to be held in Berlin. This time around, Louise Stokes appeared more aware, telling the *Chronicle,* "I feel I have more to fear from my own countrymen than from Nazi officials."

Not only Adolf Hitler cheered on the "master race" at the 1936 Olympic Games. An American newspaper cartoon suggested that the American team represented "Uncle Sambo," not "Uncle Sam." Women fared little better when Avery Brundage said: "I am fed up to the ears with women as track and field competitors. . . . [Their] charms sink to something less than zero. As swimmers and divers, girls are as beautiful and adroit, as they are ineffective and unpleasing on the track. . . . The ancient Greeks kept women out of their athletic games. I'm not so sure but they were right."

The trials for the 1936 Olympic team were held on July 4, 1936, at Brown University, in Providence, Rhode Island. Competing again in the 100-meter dash, Stokes won both the preliminary and semifinal heats to reach the finals. But in the most important race of her career, she faltered. Running third with only twenty meters remaining, she inexplicably glanced over her shoulder, broke stride, and finished a disappointing fifth. Helen Stephens won in a world record 11.7 seconds. Stokes still made the team but was again relegated to a spot on the 4 × 100-meter relay.

But getting to the Olympics in 1936 proved to be even more difficult than in 1932. The privately financed AOC, always struggling to raise money, decided to experiment in 1936 and, as Brundage wrote in the post-games report, required that "those interested in each sport on the program finance the team in that sport." The AOC thus instituted a quota system, whereby each athlete was responsible for a certain amount of money. For some athletes this was little or no hardship, as parents, sponsors, well-organized athletic clubs, or the athletes themselves had the cash on hand. But Louise Stokes lacked all of those resources. Her five hundred dollar quota might as well have been five million.

The citizens of Malden came to her aid. Even as Stokes was on her way to New York to catch the boat to Germany, Malden mayor James D. Devir was tapping residents for money. A testimonial on Stokes's behalf at the Eastern Avenue Baptist Church netted $243.15, and in only a few days the fund grew to $680.30. A $500 draft was wired to the AOC, and an additional $75 was sent to Stokes for personal expenses. The remaining money was put aside for a homecoming celebration.

Although the fund-raising effort was successful, the quota system itself helped keep Stokes out of the games once again. No one knows precisely why Louise Stokes was denied an opportunity to compete in these Olympics, but a suspicious and curious chain of events may point toward the truth.

According to Hitler's racist ideology, the athletes of the "master race," the Aryans, were destined to win the Olympics. But in 1936, as in 1932, black American track stars dominated. Jesse Owens alone won gold medals in the 100-meter dash, the 200-meter dash, and the long jump. After winning the three golds, Owen asked for a chance to try for a fourth in the men's 4×100-meter relay. Owens had not originally been selected for the relay squad, but the AOC and coach Lawson Robertson gave in to public sentiment and replaced two white athletes, Sam Stoller and Marty Glickman, with Owens and Ralph Metcalfe. But that decision may not have been made because of Owens's spectacular abilities. Stoller and Glickman were Jewish, and their presence in the games was an obvious affront to the anti-Semitic Hitler and the thousands of Nazis in attendance. With Owens and Metcalfe on board the men's team won, and Owens secured his fourth gold medal. (Brundage later vehemently denied that Stoller and Glickman were kicked off the team because of religion.)

The fallout from this episode may have cost Louise Stokes her last chance in the Olympics. Before the first race in the women's 4×100-meter relay began, neither Stokes nor Tidye Pickett had any reason to suspect anything was amiss. Several days before, Pickett had run and lost in the 80-meter hurdles. But as the two women approached the track, they were stunned to find two white runners in their places.

Although the motives remain unclear, both Pickett and Stokes had been replaced in a move that, intentionally or not, served two purposes. First, some backers of the American team felt that their contributions were to be earmarked for the participation of particular athletes and not for the team as a whole. The removal of Stoller and Glickman from the men's relay may have offended some of these backers, who may have demanded a veto in the women's 4×100-meter relay. Secondly, Owens's and Metcalfe's appearance in the men's relay still represented a significant affront to Hitler. By replacing Stokes and Pickett with two white runners, the AOC could not only mollify the offended American backers, but also perhaps appease Hitler. Stokes and Pickett were the perfect dupes for the scheme. They were, after all, just two black women. As Stokes herself commented in 1972:

I was just a cute little girl that hardly didn't know anything. It was a lot of fun. Traveling around Europe was a wonderful time. But when we went out to run, we found other runners in our places. We just had to stand there and I felt terrible. I really should have said something after it was done, but what could you do? The worst part of all is that they [the U.S. Olympic Committee] haven't said a word about it.

Without Stokes or Tidye Pickett, the U.S. women's 4×100-meter relay team still won a gold medal when the German team dropped the baton on the final pass. Again, it was Fred Steers's post-games report that hinted at what lay behind the starting line switch. Powerless to stop the injustice at the time, he later wrote: "A short time before sailing a mad scramble started. Contributions were made by towns, communities, clubs, friends, and relations of those who had qualified for the team, and in some cases substantial amounts were given by the athletes themselves. This caused complications, as certain persons felt they had a direct interest in individual athletes. . . . These conditions led to considerable embarrassment to the coach of our group particularly in the selection of a relay team. No athlete should be permitted to finance himself, nor should anyone be permitted to earmark his contribution for any particular athlete or athletes."

Louise Stokes returned to Malden to a hero's welcome. People there understood. A parade preceded a reception at Ferryway Park, where she displayed her mementos and gave a short speech before a crowd of more than six thousand. Although Stokes kept a stiff upper lip in public, she was deeply hurt. According to her sister Emily, "After she came home from Germany she never talked about it much. You'd have to sit down and almost pull the information out of her. We knew more about what happened in California than in Germany."

Yet Stokes never challenged her banishment from the games in 1936. As her sister recalls, "She was not that kind of person, she was a very nice, quiet person, humble, and just stayed to herself. But she was very disappointed they didn't compete."

Following her snub in 1936, Stokes "politely stopped running," her sister recalls. She worked as an elevator operator and, in 1941, founded the Colored Women's Bowling League. Three years later she married Wilfred Fraser, a cricket star from the Caribbean, and gave birth to a son, Wilfred Junior, who became a basketball star at Graham Junior College. She later worked for the Massachusetts Department of Corporations and Taxation and retired in 1975, three years before her death. Although she remained only a footnote in American Olympic history, her friends in and around Malden never forgot.

Louise Stokes winning the 220-yard dash at a 1931 meet.

In 1972, the City of Malden named a field house after Louise Stokes, and on September 13, 1987, a statue was dedicated in the courtyard of Malden High School in her honor. In one twenty-four-hour period, students at Malden High contributed $505 in her memory.

Asked if there is anything she wants people to know about her sister, Emily Collins softly says, "Just that I miss her, very, very much."

We should all miss Louise Stokes. Although she never competed, Stokes was still an Olympian. Because of indifference and prejudice, we will never know just how great an Olympian she might have become.

—*Glenn Stout*

The Boston Gob: World Heavyweight Champion Jack Sharkey

If I got bad decisions I'd go into a tantrum, might look like I was crying. They called me crybaby. They called me "The Lispin Lith," "The Garrulous Gob," "The Weeping Warrior," tack different titles on you. But it didn't matter to me as long as I got the old paycheck. Always deposited it before a fight in a Boston bank and when I returned home it was credited to my account.
—Jack Sharkey

Born in Binghamton, New York, on October 6, 1902, Josef Paul Zukauskas was reborn as Jack Sharkey in fight manager John Buckley's Friend Street Gym in Boston in 1923. Zukauskas, an ex-shoemaker and construction worker, joined the Navy as a teenager in 1919 and learned to box in the superb Navy program. His shipmate and boxing trainer Joe Lavelle felt his young protégé had the makings of a future champion and referred him to Buckley. After winning thirty-five of thirty-six naval bouts, the young fighter felt the time was right to explore the pro ranks.

Before long the ex-sailor had selected his new name, a combination of those of his boxing heroes, Jack Dempsey and Tom Sharkey. He soon went from making $30 a month to working toward the $100,000 paydays of his dreams. Sharkey fought everyone and anyone who would sharpen his skills while moving him closer to either a title bout or a date with a big name such as Jack Dempsey. To Sharkey's everlasting credit, he fought and defeated two of the best African American heavyweights of the era, Harry Wills and George Godfrey. This was in stark contrast to Dempsey, who made a career-long habit of ducking these and other African American challengers.

On July 21, 1927, Sharkey finally got his match with Dempsey, before seventy-five thousand fans at Yankee Stadium. Most of the crowd cheered Dempsey as the young challenger punished the champ through five rounds. Cheers turned to boos when Dempsey suddenly stunned Sharkey with a below-the-belt jab, quickly followed by a left hook to the stricken challenger's jaw. Before Sharkey could call the referee for the obvious foul, he'd violated the first rule of boxing— defend yourself. His schooling came at a price.

Below-the-belt punches would figure prominently in several other key Sharkey fights. In a bout with English contender Phil Scott in Miami on February 28, 1930, Sharkey fought for the right to be recognized as the chief claimant to Gene Tunney's recently vacated world heavyweight title. Scott cried foul as Sharkey quickly dispatched him with a low but legal punch. Despite the victory, press and public alike vilified Sharkey more than ever for the alleged "taint" of the Scott bout.

Jack Sharkey (right)
vs. Max Schmeling

While awaiting his title shot, Sharkey was described by boxing historian Stanley Westin as biding his time wearing fine tailored suits, hanging out in posh surroundings, and smoking "dollar" cigars. But life was about to get more complicated for the temperamental contender.

When German newcomer Max Schmeling was presented as an opponent, the cocksure Sharkey dismissed him by saying, "I'll knock him out, it may take a few rounds, but I'll take him out." Sharkey's cockiness turned to rage when Schmeling claimed a below-the-belt hit in their bout on June 12, 1930. Unlike the Scott fight, Sharkey this time came out on the wrong side of a decision by referee Dave Crowley, who believed Sharkey had landed the low blow. An immediate call for a rematch followed.

On the night of June 21, 1932, sailors in Havana on the cruiser USS *Denver,* Sharkey's old ship, were relayed telegraphed accounts of their old friend's title fight with Schmeling at New York's Long Island Bowl. After a hard-fought, fifteen-round bout, Schmeling all but raised his hands in triumph, only to see the referee raise Sharkey's hand in victory. The USS *Denver* erupted in drunken joy, as sailors celebrated the victory.

Sharkey would hold the title for 373 days before losing it to Italian giant Primo Carnera. To the day he died, Sharkey claimed he lost the title because of a vision of his friend and fellow boxer Ernie Schaf, who had been killed in the ring by Carnera. As Sharkey attempted to fight, his gaze fixed upon the dead boxer, who watched him from another corner of the ring.

Sharkey won only two of his final seven bouts, with one victory coming over a boxer with the unlikely name of "Unknown" Winston. On August 18, 1936, Sharkey's career ended in a bout with Joe Louis. The "Brown Bomber," as Louis was known, hit Sharkey so hard that ringside fans claimed you could see tears running down his cheeks even before the decisive knockout blow was landed.

Following his retirement, Sharkey owned and operated a Canal Street bar named Sharkeys and remained a fixture on the local sports scene. He loved to compete with Ted Williams and Jim Thorpe in an annual fly-casting competition at the old Mechanics Building. In countless interviews, he'd admit to only one regret: not being more aggressive with Jack Dempsey in 1927, when he had the legendary fighter on the ropes. He remains one of the great local heavyweights, along with John L. Sullivan and Rocky Marciano.

Blood on the Ice:
The Bailey-Shore Incident

On December 12, 1933, the Toronto Maple Leafs visited Boston Garden for a game against the Bruins. The Leafs were the Bruins' most hated rivals at the time. Bruins coach Art Ross expressed extreme personal contempt for Leafs president Conn Smythe, whose famous admonition to his players was, "If you can't beat them in the alley, you won't beat them on the ice."

Confusion reigns as Boston and Toronto players seek to assist their stricken teammates in the aftermath of one of the most notorious incidents in NHL history.

Games between Boston and Toronto in this era possessed that extra edge that makes a simple sporting event into a happening. But nobody could possibly have expected the depths to which this would sink on a night that marked one of hockey's darkest incidents.

The Boston press villified Shore following the Bailey incident.

In the second period of the game, Eddie Shore was tripped from behind during one of his patented end-to-end rushes. Shore fell hard, but play resumed up ice. As Toronto forward Ace Bailey dropped back to cover on defense, Shore rose and cut the legs out from under the Leafs' star. The collision between the ice and Bailey's skull could be heard in the loge. Stories varied as to what exactly took place, but Toronto goalie George Hainsworth, who had the best view, noted that Shore charged Bailey from behind.

Regardless, Bailey lay motionless on the ice as play ceased and a cry arose for a doctor to attend the stricken player. After seeing Bailey on the ice, Toronto's Red Horner, a bruiser in the mold of Shore, chased after the Bruins' defenseman. Horner caught up with Shore and the two exchanged harsh words before Horner proceeded to knock Shore out with an uppercut. The Bruins' defenseman also hit the ice skull-first.

Total confusion set in as both benches emptied onto the ice, with players not knowing whether to fight or simply attend to their mates. Both Shore and Bailey were carried off the ice on stretchers in a scene more appropriate to a battlefield than to a hockey game. Bailey suffered a fractured skull and needed two delicate operations to save his life. The Toronto star hovered near death for several days, with his condition updated on the front page of the many editions of Boston's seven daily newspapers. He remained in Boston for several weeks until fully recovered and able to return home to Toronto. After Bailey recovered and regained all his faculties, it was determined he would never play hockey again.

NHL president Frank Calder, who had carefully monitored Bailey's condition, was faced with a tremendous dilemma. Shore was the league's main drawing card and any lengthy suspension would harm the entire league. In the end, Calder decided that Shore would be assessed a sixteen-game suspension and that a benefit all-star game would be played, with all the funds going to Bailey and his family. Not only did Shore play in the game, but the two players met both publicly and privately to express their regret for the event. Both men reached a robust old age, with Bailey becoming one of the oldest living members of the Maple Leafs, along with his brother-in-arms Red Horner.

The Beast: Jimmie Foxx

It is ironic that one of the gentlest and kindest men ever to play in the majors was known to America as "The Beast." No doubt Jimmie Foxx was given this nickname by American League pitchers, who lived in fear of his crushing swing. Foxx, a man of average stature at just under six feet and two hundred pounds, might as well have been of Paul Bunyan proportions. He remains one of the greatest right-handed power hitters in American League history.

Jimmie Foxx arrived in Boston in 1936 from the Philadelphia Athletics, part of Red Sox owner Tom Yawkey's push to match the performance of the hated Yankees. His new first baseman produced immediate results.

Obtained by Red Sox owner Tom Yawkey from Connie Mack's Philadelphia Athletics in 1936 along with pitcher John "Footsie" Marcum, Foxx made an immediate impact in Boston, producing 41 home runs, 143 RBI, and a .338 batting average that year. In 1938 he enjoyed what is arguably the greatest season of any Red Sox player ever, as he swatted a team-record 50 home runs, knocked in a league-record 175 RBI, and batted .349 while capturing the American League MVP award.

Foxx saved his best for the hometown fans that season, batting .402 in games at Fenway, with 35 homers and 104 RBI as well. In all, Foxx socked 222 of his 534 career homers in Boston. Among his good friends was Ted Williams, who marveled at his hitting and proclaimed, "I love Foxx. What a hitter and what a gentleman."

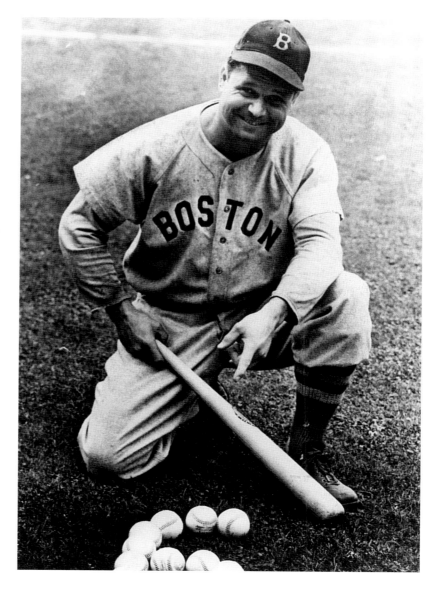

Pro Football in Boston

Until the Boston Patriots arrived on the scene in 1960, the fortunes of professional football in Boston had been dubious at best. Among the teams that got their start in Boston were the Redskins, who would relocate to Washington, D.C., in 1937. The Redskins' familiar logo first appeared in Boston on the uniforms of the Boston Braves football team. When Braves Field owners asked the football team to leave after their failure to pay back rent, Braves owner George Preston Marshall moved the team to Fenway Park. The practical and thrifty owner then changed the team's name to the Redskins in order to utilize the uniforms left over from their former home. Such were the origins of one of the most controversial and widely recognized team names in professional sports.

Among the other football teams to call Boston home in the thirties were the Boston Shamrocks (who played makeshift night games at Fenway Park under jury-rigged lighting), the Boston Yanks (who became the Baltimore Colts), and the Boston Bulldogs.

Fullback Ace Gutowski of the Portsmouth Spartans (below) is upended by Redskins defensive back Ike Frankiah in this 1933 game at Fenway Park. Number 57 is the helmetless Father Lumpkin, another well-known Portsmouth back.

Boston Redskins action, Fenway Park, c. 1933

Nine years before night baseball became a fixture at Fenway Park, the professional football team the Boston Shamrocks played the College All-Stars in a game that started at 8:00 P.M. None of the listed collegiate all-stars weighs over 210 pounds, or stands over six-feet three-inches.

George Kenneally made every attempt to make pro football a success in Boston. The former All-Pro defensive end first moved the NFL's Pottsville, Pennsylvania, franchise to Boston, where they played one season before going out of business. In 1936 he was named coach and general manager of the fledging Boston Shamrocks of the American Football League (AFL). In 1938 the franchise was literally swept away when a hurricane forced the cancellation of a game with the Pittsburgh Steelers, whose star running back, Byron "Whizzer" White, later became a U.S. Supreme Court justice.

Boston Shamrocks vs. College All-Stars, September 14, 1938. The teams played under makeshift lighting at Fenway Park.

George Kenneally (left)

The Long Good-bye:
The Babe Returns to Boston

Boston will forever be recognized in baseball lore as the town that lost Babe Ruth. As a star left-handed pitcher and budding slugger, Ruth played a central role on three Red Sox world champions, only to be sold in 1920 to the then pennantless New York Yankees for one hundred thousand dollars and a mortgage on Fenway Park. In New York Ruth became a national figure while leading his pinstriped teammates to seven pennants and four world championships.

Despite his move to greener pastures, Ruth maintained an off-season home at his Wayland digs, appropriately named "Home Run Farm." As much as Ruth remained loyal to Boston, the city that launched his career remained just as loyal to the colorful slugger. Fans who had jammed Fenway Park over the years to see Ruth in his periodic visits to Boston spilled from the stands onto the field in September 1934, for what most expected would be the Bambino's final Boston appearance. Little did they know their hero would soon reappear in one last and ironic curtain call.

In the winter of 1935, Ruth reached the milestone of his fortieth birthday with the physique and condition of a man ten years his senior. The Yankees, aware of his condition and unwilling to name him their manager, waived his contract and negotiated his transfer back to Boston. However, this time he would play across both a city and a league, in the flannels of the Boston Braves.

Braves owner Judge Emil Fuchs, a legal superstar of his era, skillfully negotiated a contract that made Ruth both team vice president and assistant manager to Bill McKechnie. In addition, Ruth was guaranteed a base salary of twenty-five thousand dollars and a share of gate receipts over a specified threshold. The judge badly needed a gate attraction to rival that of the newly renovated Fenway Park and the many high-priced acquisitions secured by his baseball neighbor, Tom Yawkey. Fuchs was certain that Ruth would prove to be an instant draw, even if he was relegated to performing batting practice for his legion of fans.

On February 28, 1935, Ruth and his wife, Claire, made a triumphant return to Back Bay Station, the same station at which the rawboned teenager had arrived from Baltimore more than twenty years earlier. Over three thousand fans greeted his return. Ruth was feted that evening with a banquet in his honor at the Copley Plaza Hotel.

It was the hope of two dreamers—Ruth and Fuchs—that each could revive the sagging fortunes of the other. Ruth's dream was to become manager of the Braves, and Fuchs desperately needed the cash Ruth could provide as his prime gate attraction. Such was the aura of optimism and delusion that pervaded the Braves organization at the beginning of what was to be the most dismal season for any team in the fifty-nine year history of the National League.

Though his skills had greatly deteriorated by 1935, Babe Ruth still drew the admiration of young Braves fans.

Opening Day gave no indication of the impending doom, as Ruth was honored in a raucous pregame ceremony that included an on-field bear hug from his pal, world wrestling champion Ed "Strangler" Lewis, the

Hulk Hogan of his generation. A less-than-capacity crowd wondered aloud if the pregame high jinks would inspire their loudest cheers. They soon received their answer when Ruth greeted Giants starter Carl Hubbell with a towering 420-foot, three-run homer to lead the Braves to victory.

For a period of hours it seemed as if Fuchs had scored a major coup. But after several more games, even fans perched in the outer reaches of Braves Field's Jury Box could see that their hero's skills had deteriorated to a shocking extent. Ruth, once majestic while striking out, now looked like a bloated impostor. For every game he won with his bat he lost two with his poor fielding and pitiable base running.

The end was near, and Ruth, a man of great pride, finally admitted to the press that baseball had become drudgery. His presence in the clubhouse soon became an irritant to his less famous teammates, who resented his lavish salary and felt it unbefitting of a .180 batting average. But no one had the heart to tell the most famous man in America that it was time to retire.

However, for one glorious day, Ruth recaptured a measure of the magic that had made him a legend. On the afternoon of May 25, in an otherwise meaningless game, Ruth cracked the final three home runs of his career in a prodigious hitting display against the Pittsburgh Pirates at Forbes Field. It was somehow appropriate that the last of his blasts was the longest home run in the history of the park. Following the memorable performance, Braves manager Bill McKechnie took Ruth aside and quietly asked the aging superstar to quit in the afterglow of his achievement.

Ruth agreed at first but later relented when Judge Fuchs begged him to complete the last few games of the road trip. The end finally arrived in Philadelphia, on May 30, 1935, when the haggard star, injured and demoralized, called a hasty press conference to draw the curtain on the most celebrated career in American sports.

The final record will show that Ruth batted .181 for the Braves—a full .161 below his career average—with six home runs in twenty-eight games. In the wake of his bittersweet return to Boston, fans can only wonder what Ruth might have accomplished had he remained in Boston for his entire career. It would seem as likely a scenario as Elvis remaining in Tupelo or the Beatles staying within the confines of the Cavern Club. While Ruth certainly would have remained the greatest double threat in baseball history, his talents demanded a larger stage than Fenway Park. His ascendance and subsequent sale to the Yankees came at a time when baseball—and America—needed him most.

So as far as any curse, real or imagined, can be associated with Ruth, such speculation is ridiculous. Instead, the facts bear out that Boston fans enjoyed the "blessing of the Bambino," insofar as the young Adonis-like lefty played an integral role on three world championship teams in his six seasons with the Red Sox. Later, the Falstaffian Ruth managed to close out his career with an equal measure of pathos and splendor in one final spring with the club forever known as Boston's "other team."

 ## *The 1936 All-Star Game: A National League Triumph amid Empty Seats*

On Tuesday, July 7, 1936, Boston played host to its first-ever All-Star Game at the newly renamed National League Park (aka Braves Field). It was the fourth playing of what has become the midsummer classic, which was created in 1933 by Chicago sportswriter Arch Ward as a benefit for the Association of Professional Baseball Players. That Boston was hosting the All-Star Game seemed only fitting, for it had been the Boston Nationals who played the first game in National League history some sixty years earlier, in 1876. The Nationals could also boast of the first dynasty in the majors with their dominant "Beaneater" teams, which had captured five pennants in the 1890s. In many ways Boston was and still is the historic and spiritual hometown of baseball in America.

Fans eagerly anticipated the first truly *big* baseball game in Boston since the Red Sox had captured their last World Series in 1918. They were even prepared for the prospect of a rainout, which would have moved the game to an 11:00 A.M. starting time the next day. Boston Police captain Archibald Campbell of Division 14 in Brighton readied his detail of thirty-five men, including five superior officers and six mounted officers, in preparation for what was then the largest baseball crowd in Boston history.

Much of the pregame press coverage centered on a train wreck that threatened to prevent Detroit Tigers outfielder Goose Goslin and pitcher Lynnwood "Schoolboy" Rowe from appearing in the game. Their train had crashed on its way from Cleveland, and the pair made headlines in each of the four daily editions of the *Boston Globe* before their status as uninjured had even been reported.

Also noted in the press was the presence of several Boston all-stars, led by the Red Sox trio of future Hall of Famers—catcher Rick Ferrell, first baseman Jimmie Foxx, and pitcher Lefty Grove. They would be accompanied by the Boston Bees' lone representative, slugging outfielder Wally Berger. (The Braves, in one of their more forgettable moves, changed their name to "Bees" in 1936.)

American League all-stars gather at Braves Field in 1936. Rookie Joe DiMaggio (top row, far right) had a nightmarish performance in the game.

Joining the Boston players in this game were thirty-eight colleagues, thirty-two of whom had been selected by fan balloting, with the rest having been selected by *The Sporting News* and the Baseball Writers Association of America. Included on the teams were future Hall of Famers Lou Gehrig, Mel Ott, Ducky Medwick, Charlie Gehringer, Lefty Gomez, Bill Dickey, Dizzy Dean, Billy Herman, Luke Appling, Earl Averill, Arky Vaughan, Ernie Lombardi, Carl Hubbell, Leo Durocher, and a rookie named Joe DiMaggio. The others happened to be near greats

such as Ripper Collins and Lon Warnecke. Rounding out the squads were assorted one- or two-season phenoms for whom an all-star selection represented the high-water mark of their career. Included in this category were such non-immortals as Cardinal second baseman Stu Martin, Cub pitcher Curt Davis, Cub outfielder Frank Demaree, and White Sox left fielder Ray Radcliff.

Managing the two teams were Charlie Grimm of the defending National League Champion Cubs and Joe McCarthy of the Yankees, who served as a last-minute replacement for Detroit Tiger player-manager Mickey Cochrane, who had taken ill. The nonchalant McCarthy would go as far as to arrive from New York on the morning train from Grand Central Station. And, in keeping with the informal nature of these early all-star games, McCarthy included himself among the American League players taking batting practice. Such were the pleasures a lifetime minor leaguer could enjoy as a stand-in all-star skipper.

Depending on which of the six daily Boston newspapers you read on the morning of the game, the contest was expected to attract a capacity crowd of between forty-two and fifty thousand spectators. With most tickets priced between $1.10 and $1.80, the game was affordable even by Depression standards.

But in a move he would forever regret, Boston Bees president Bob Quinn had placed twenty-five thousand of his nonreserved $1.10 tickets on sale for the day of the game. In the days leading up to the game, scalpers were already getting the unheard-of price of $15.00 a pair for box seats and $3.00 apiece for the uncovered seats in the distant reaches of the Jury Box. However, as the first group of fans entered the park for batting practice, many of these same tickets changed hands for as little as eighty-five cents. Scalpers soon discovered what the nation would learn in the following day's headlines. A multitude of fans, unable to buy the tickets prior to the game, remained at home with the mistaken impression, relayed by press and radio reports, that the game had already been sold out! In holding back so many tickets for the day of the game, Quinn had ensured that almost twenty thousand seats remained empty. Sportswriters from across the continent made the ticket snafu the lead paragraph in their game stories.

Despite the embarrassing ticket mess, the game itself was superb. National League starter Dizzy Dean pitched three perfect innings, while rookie Joe DiMaggio suffered the most miserable afternoon of his otherwise brilliant career. As the first rookie ever to start in the All-Star Game, DiMaggio not only misplayed a Gabby Hartnett liner into a run-scoring triple, but also made a crucial fifth-inning error on a hit by Billy Herman, which eventually allowed the Cub second baseman to score the National League's winning run. His nightmare continued at the plate as he went zero for five, socking a bases-loaded drive at Leo Durocher to end the seventh and popping up to Herman to end the game.

The 1936 All-Star Game program

The National League won its first All-Star Game 4–3, behind the shutout pitching of Dean and Carl Hubbell and the timely hitting of Hartnett, Herman, Augie Galan, and Joe Medwick, who hit the game-winning single off Schoolboy Rowe. The American League opened its account in the eighth, when Lou Gehrig socked his first All-Star Game home run off Cub right-hander Curt Davis. Before the inning was over, Davis had loaded the bases for White Sox shortstop Luke Appling, who shot a single into right to bring the American League its final two runs.

In his analysis of the game, *Boston Globe* sports editor Vic Jones awarded his daily "knock" to National League manager Grimm for not playing Boston Bees outfielder Wally Berger. He would also comment:

As one who enjoyed yesterday's ballgame as much as any he has ever seen, barring possibly the knockdown drag-out World Series contests between The Gas House Gang (Cardinals) and the snarling Tigers in 1934—it comes as something of a shock to realize that yesterday's affair was pretty much a flop.

There's no getting away from the fact that all "big" sporting events depend on their setting for much of their glamour and if there's anything less glamourous and more depressing than empty seats, I don't know what it is. Yesterday there were barely 25,000 persons in a park which seats 42,000 comfortably and which once held 55,000.

The 1936 All-Star Game, the only one ever held at old Braves Field, will forever be remembered as the game where the great Joe DiMaggio was booed by a crowd nearly equaled by empty seats. Such was the almost surreal atmosphere in which this game was played.

 ## *The Origin of Heartbreak Hill*

Heartbreak Hill: the last of three arduous inclines on the twenty-six-mile route of the world-renowned Boston Marathon. Most believe or assume it is dubbed Heartbreak Hill because it lies just past the twenty-mile mark, where most runners' bodies begin to betray them. A perfectly plausible explanation, but it's incorrect. So how did this near-mythic stretch of running real estate get its name?

The year was 1936. The Boston Marathon was the first of two Olympic trials that year. The favorite that Patriot's Day afternoon was hometown hero Johnny Kelley. The plucky little plodder from Arlington was the defending champion and seemed poised for a repeat victory and a trip to the Berlin Games. Most Boston newspapers favored Kelley or listed him as co-favorite with Pat Dengis of Baltimore, the 1935 national champion. The *Globe*'s Jerry Nason, however, picked neither, instead opting for a long shot named Ellison "Tarzan" Brown. A Narragansett Indian from Rhode Island, Brown had won a pair of national championships at shorter distances but had yet to distinguish himself in the marathon. Just twenty-two years old, Brown had run Boston the previous year wearing a jersey made by his sisters and cut from the cloth of a dress that belonged to his mother, who had died two weeks earlier. The sneakers he wore that day fell apart, and he ran the last five miles barefoot, placing thirteenth.

Johnny Kelley runs Heartbreak Hill in his victorious effort in 1935.

Nicknamed Tarzan by his boyhood friends because of his love for climbing trees and hollering like vine-swinger Johnny Weissmuller, Ellison Brown was at that time the greatest physical specimen ever to compete in the Boston Marathon. Blessed with outstanding speed and strength, he lived in rural poverty his entire life and trained erratically, often substituting wood chopping for distance work. Jerry Nason came upon him once, minutes before the start of the marathon, wolfing down several hot dogs. "I didn't have any breakfast," Brown explained, washing down the dogs with soda pop. Brown was also known to hold back in a race if the second or third prize was more salable. "You can't eat trophies," he said.

When the pistol reported, Tarzan Brown flew away from the start as if he were running a dash. His pace was so outrageous that the press cars followed the wrong runners for five miles, mistaking them for the leaders. Shattering checkpoint records, Brown amassed a nine-hundred-yard lead heading into the infamous Newton hills. But he was beginning to pay for his foolish frontrunning. Not wanting to take the chance that Brown might fade and come back to him, Johnny Kelley gave chase. Erasing a half-mile lead with a furious run through the hills, Kelley finally pulled even with Brown at the top of the last hill, near the gothic spires of Boston College. As he passed, Kelley gave the flagging Brown a friendly pat on the shoulder, as if to say, "Nice try, kid, I'll take it from here."

But Johnny Kelley's lead was short-lived. Tarzan Brown, incited by the well-meaning tap, suddenly summoned enough strength to speed past the local favorite, who was now feeling the effects of his mad pursuit through the hills. The pair came down off that final hill with Brown back in the lead. Between Lake Street and Cleveland Circle, Johnny Kelley made one last desperate surge past Brown, who remained expressionless through it all, head down as if running in a trance. But Kelley was utterly spent. Brown eventually passed him for a second and final time. Both runners began weaving like punch drunk prizefighters.

On Beacon Street, William "Biddie" McMahon of Worcester overtook Johnny Kelley. A mile and a half from the finish, Brown began walking, so disoriented that he was nearly struck by an oncoming car. McMahon was within seventy-five yards of Tarzan when he, too, began to walk, depleted by his efforts to catch the staggering leaders. Two hundred yards back, Kelley was also walking, unable to muster a final challenge.

After being doused with water by one of his handlers, Brown began to run again. He stopped once more and then hobbled home in 2:33:40, suddenly assured of a trip to Berlin. McMahon, with a weak trot, held on to second place. Johnny Kelley gutted out the last mile but was overtaken by two more runners before he crossed the line in 2:38:49 and was carried away to the dressing room.

"All I had to do was run a minute slower than I was going," Johnny Kelley says, looking back, still somewhat haunted by an error he made six decades ago. "I would've gone right by Tarzan at the end. But he was so far ahead—I used very, very poor judgment and I'm man enough to admit that."

Ellison "Tarzan" Brown broke Johnny Kelley's heart in the Newton hills in 1936.

To this day, the disappointment is still evident in Johnny Kelley's blue-green eyes. It was that same crestfallen gaze that Jerry Nason, riding in the *Globe's* press car, saw in Johnny's eyes on that final hill, which prompted Nason to name the hill "Heartbreak." Though many hearts and soles have been battered on that brae before and since, it was named in honor of one relentless little man, Johnny Kelley, whose heart was indeed broken there—but not his indomitable spirit.

Kelley would go on to amass a staggering record at Boston. In addition to his two wins and seven second-place finishes, he would complete the course fifty-eight times in sixty-one attempts! A statue of Johnny Kelley now greets modern-day marathoners as they struggle through the hills. Nason, who was covering just his second Boston race in 1936, became a legendary scribe and editor and helped popularize the marathon by giving it ample coverage in the *Globe.* He reported the race fifty times before retiring. Tarzan Brown failed to finish the Olympic Marathon in Berlin, and, except for a record-breaking run at Boston in 1939, never realized his boundless potential. In 1975, he was struck down and killed by a van in the parking lot of a bar in Westerly, Rhode Island.

Sadly, Ellison Brown is now recalled more for his unpredictable antics than his unbridled running prowess. Though the last Newton hill memorializes the ever-popular Kelley, it should not be forgotten that it was this impoverished Narragansett Indian's own huge heart that broke Johnny's and equally inspired Nason's naming of distance running's most legendary landmark.

—*Frederick Lewis*

# Brothers-in-Arms:
The Kraut Line

The National Hockey League of the prewar seven- and eight-team era was as exclusive a club as has existed in professional sports anywhere in the world at any time. Only slightly more than a hundred men skated in a league where job openings were as rare as they were in the real world during the Great Depression. So it is nothing short of a miracle, pure serendipity, that three linemates would join together on one team after having grown up in the same moderately sized town in Canada.

Bobby Bauer, Milt Schmidt, and Woody Dumart arrived in Boston in the mid-thirties from their hometown of Kitchener, Ontario. At the time, the franchise was dominated by tough guys such as Eddie Shore and Aubrey "Dit" Clapper. Not only did the trio prove tough enough to pass muster with these future Hall of Famers, they soon combined to form one of the most prolific forward lines in hockey history. The triumvirate, all of German heritage (described euphemistically as "Dutch" by a press corps sensitive to the events in Nazi Germany), were instantly dubbed the "Kitchener Kids" or "the Kraut Line."

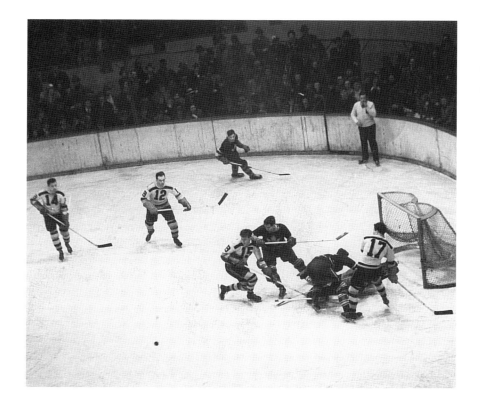

The Kraut Line in action:
Woody Dumart (#14),
Milt Schmidt (#15), and
Bobby Bauer (#17)

Assembled as a line in Boston by coach Art Ross, Bauer, Schmidt, and Dumart led the Black and Gold to four regular season crowns and two Stanley Cups. In the 1939–40 season, the trio finished 1-2-3 in the NHL scoring race, with Schmidt capturing the title with fifty-two points. They are the only line in NHL history to accomplish that achievement. The three players also signed identical contracts until Bauer retired in 1947. Both Schmidt and Dumart continued to play into the mid-fifties, and both collected over two hundred goals in their careers.

Following his playing career, Schmidt coached and later served as general manager of the Bruins, winning two Stanley Cups in the process. He is still a fixture at many Bruins games, where he often meets Woody Dumart, a longtime sporting-goods distributor in Greater Boston. Bauer, who followed his Bruins career working for his family's Bauer Sporting Goods Company in Toronto, died at the age of 49 in 1964.

 ## Sudden Death: The 1939 Stanley Cup Champions

The 1938–39 Bruins were considered by many to be the best team of their era. Led by veterans such as four-time NHL MVP Eddie Shore, Dit Clapper, and team captain Cooney Weiland, the team also featured a nucleus of talented forwards such as Bill Cowley and Roy Conacher, along with the Kraut Line of Milt Schmidt, Woody Dumart, and Bobby Bauer. The Bruins finished the regular season with a record of 36 wins, 10 losses, and 2 ties.

However, their success was hardly a foregone conclusion at the start of the season. Shortly after it began they faced a major transition when all-star goalie Tiny Thompson was sold to the Detroit Red Wings on November 26 for fifteen thousand dollars. The transaction unleashed a firestorm of fan reaction unseen since the sale of Babe Ruth to the Yankees.

Thompson's replacement was Frank Brimsek, a Minnesota native ten years younger than his predecessor. When he arrived from the minor-league Providence Reds, he was one of the few Americans in the American Hockey League, much less the NHL, to which he had now been promoted.

The soft-spoken newcomer was largely an unknown quantity who at first was viewed with skepticism by fans and teammates alike. Skepticism escalated to boos when he lost his first game at Boston Garden.

The boos turned to standing ovations in short time. In his first month with the team, Brimsek secured six shutouts in twelve wins. He earned three straight shutouts on two separate occasions and set an NHL record for consecutive shutout minutes, going 231 minutes and 54 seconds without giving up a goal. He was soon known by a newly minted nickname of "Mr. Zero," and General Manager–Coach Art Ross was once again hailed as a genius when Brimsek won the unprecedented honor of receiving the Vezina (top goalie) and Calder (rookie of the year) trophies in the same season.

The Bruins' march to the Stanley Cup began with a hard-fought semifinal series against the New York Rangers, a series that many historians and eyewitnesses have called the greatest playoff series in league history. The first game, played at Madison Square Garden, was decided with seconds remaining in the third overtime period when winger Mel

In the classic Leslie Jones photo shown here, the Bruins are captured in the locker room following their historic 1939 Stanley Cup victory. Front row, left to right: Roy Conacher, Mel Hill, Charlie Sands, Cooney Weiland, Milt Schmidt, Gordon Pettinger, and Flash Hollett. Back row, left to right; Frank Brimsek, Jack Crawford, Eddie Shore, Woody Dumart, Bobby Bauer, Dit Clapper, Bill Cowley, Jack Portland, and Ray Getliffe.

Hill, an ex-Ranger, converted a perfect pass from center Bill Cowley to clinch the 2–1 decision. Game two in Boston ended in similar fashion, as Cowley once again fed Hill for the winning goal in overtime. In game three the Bruins won easily by a 4–1 margin and contemplated a series sweep.

But the series was far from finished. The Rangers stormed back to even the series at three-all with two wins at Madison Square Garden and a tough 2–1 overtime victory at Boston Garden. The series was eventually decided after forty-eight minutes of overtime in game seven at Boston Garden, when Mel "Sudden Death" Hill scored his third overtime goal of the series.

The Bruins went on to meet Toronto in the finals, in a far less dramatic series. They dropped the only overtime game of the finals against the Leafs at Boston Garden, but it was their only loss of the series. Their 3–1 victory at Boston Garden in game five marked the first time the Bruins had ever won the Stanley Cup on home ice. Following the game, the Garden crowd beckoned Eddie Shore to the ice to take part in NHL president Frank Calder's presentation of the Stanley Cup.

As the rugged stoic was removing his uniform in the locker room, several writer friends pleaded with Shore to make a final triumphant return. One writer was said to have remarked, "C'mon Eddie, these people helped make you, the least you can do is acknowledge their ovation." Within minutes the half-dressed superstar appeared on the ice, and the crowd rewarded him with a ten-minute standing ovation. The cheers were said to have rocked the building to the extent that pedestrians on Causeway Street could hear the cheering within a block of the arena.

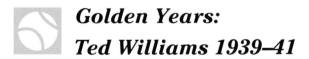

Golden Years: Ted Williams 1939–41

I want to walk down the street someday and have people say, "There goes the greatest hitter that ever lived."
—*Ted Williams, Boston Red Sox, 1939–60*

When Ted Williams arrived at his first Red Sox spring training camp in 1938, he was greeted by manager Joe Cronin, who told the teenaged slugger that he ought to watch Jimmie Foxx hit. Williams's cocky and oft-repeated reply was, "Oh hell, Foxx should watch *me* hit." Within a month Williams was headed to Minneapolis for seasoning, but the Red Sox camp buzzed about the kid who was surely the future of the franchise.

Starting his career as Boston's right fielder in 1939, Williams became an immediate fan favorite, doffing his cap with regularity after great plays. He was so obsessed with hitting that he even practiced his swing during pauses in outfield play. Boston hadn't seen his like since Babe Ruth occupied the same position in 1919. By 1941 Ted Williams had already achieved cult status. Each of Boston's seven daily newspapers, as well as countless regional dailies, included stories about him every day of the 154-game season. Ted's fans included a female bobby-sox contingent that was matched only by the legion of long-suffering diehards who remembered Babe Ruth and Tris Speaker and prayed that Williams would someday match their stardom and championship output.

The Red Sox faithful had ample reason to believe. Williams batted .327 and .344, respectively, in his first two seasons. As a rookie in 1939 he led the American League with 145 RBI, and his slugging percentage of .600 placed him at the level of hitters such as Hank Greenberg and teammate Jimmie Foxx.

Despite suffering a bone chip in his ankle in spring training, Williams started the 1941 season in fine fashion, batting .389 for the month of April, followed by an incredible .436 clip in May. It was during May that Williams and Joe DiMaggio began to capture the imagination of the nation, as the Yankee began his famed consecutive-game hitting streak and Williams embarked on his quest to become the youngest hitter ever to reach the .400 mark. By the end of the season DiMaggio had gained immortality with his fifty-six-game streak, and with two games remaining in the season, Williams's average was .400 when rounded off.

Faced with a season-ending doubleheader in Philadelphia and the prospect of losing his .400 average, Williams was asked by manager Joe Cronin if he wanted to sit out. Williams's characteristic reply was to play both games, a decision he had come to after having nervously walked the streets of Philadelphia the night before with equipment manager Johnny Orlando. His six-for-eight performance, which is now central to his legend, boosted his average to .406. He was the youngest batter ever to reach .400 and the last major leaguer of the century to do so.

 ## *Mystery Season*

Two talented pro football teams called Boston home in 1936: the NFL Redskins and the upstart AFL Shamrocks. And late that year it seemed as if each club was charging toward the championship of its respective league. But something happened. Neither team brought a trophy back to Boston, and within a year professional football in the city was merely a memory. In the seasons that have passed since then, no professional football team from New England has ever come closer to winning a championship than did the Redskins and Shamrocks in 1936. Indeed, the Shamrocks did become champions—after a fashion.

The 1936 season should have been a benchmark year for professional football in Boston, a year fondly remembered as when the pro game came to stay and gave the city its first in a long line of subsequent championships. But today, the Redskins and Shamrocks have been largely forgotten. The turmoil of that season is now compressed into a few dry paragraphs in contemporary histories of the pro game.

Those few paragraphs report that late in the 1936 season, just prior to the playoffs, the Boston Redskins were abandoned by their fans and hounded out of town by a hostile press. They also report that the Boston Shamrocks players, angry at not receiving several paychecks, refused to travel to Cleveland to play in the AFL Championship game. Implicit in these reports is the assumption that Boston simply did not yet deserve professional football. But the story is far more complex.

Professional football had had a couple of false starts in Boston before arriving, presumably to stay, in 1932. It was then that a group of investors, led by a showy impresario named George Preston Marshall, secured a Boston entry in the fledgling National Football League. The team signed a lease to play at Braves Field and adopted the Braves' name. They struggled through their first season and finished with a respectable 4–4–2 record, but the franchise still lost forty-six thousand dollars. Marshall's partners bailed out and left the club under his sole direction.

Prior to the 1933 season, Marshall and Chicago Bears owner George Halas persuaded the other league owners to adopt several innovative organizational and rule changes that were designed to distinguish the pro game from its more conservative collegiate counterpart. These changes led to divisional play and allowed for the more wide-open, pass-oriented game that still characterizes the NFL.

Not that the Braves were able to take advantage of those changes. When baseball's Braves threatened to raise the rent for Braves Field in 1933, Marshall moved his team to Fenway Park. He dropped the Braves name but retained the Native American motif, calling the team the Redskins. Always the showman, Marshall hired a Native American, Lone Star Dietz, as coach and recruited several Native American football players. Before the Redskins home opener, he even had his men dress up in war paint, feathers, and full headdress. But Marshall's sense of theatrics was no more effective on the field than at the gate. The next three years, the last one under coach Eddie Casey, were marked by losses on the gridiron as well as in the ledger.

In other cities the NFL was starting to prosper. The forward pass became an increasingly important offensive weapon. Most teams used the single-wing formation, which featured a triple-threat "deep back," who took the long snap from the center and then either passed the ball downfield, handed it to another back, ran, placekicked, or punted. Uniforms resembled those of today, with the exception of the felt-and-leather helmet, which lacked a face mask but even so was eschewed by some veterans as a sign of weakness. The squad of twenty or so football players earned between $100 and $200 apiece for each Sunday of work, and each man was expected to play both offense and defense. Rougher and freer than college football, the pro game began to attract its own constituency.

But in Boston, where Harvard, Boston College, and a host of other area schools played football, Hub fans had no time for professional football. They attended college games on Saturday and went to Mass—or the racetrack—on Sunday. During the week, the semi-pro Park League had its own aficionados. As a result, the Redskins generally played their Sunday games before only 5,000 to 6,000 fans at Fenway Park, and the club continued to lose between $10,000 and $15,000 a year.

Determined to turn the team around, Marshall made several moves before the 1936 season. Following the New York Giants' playoff loss to Detroit, in 1935, Marshall hired the Giants' assistant coach Ray Flaherty to be his head coach. The savvy, strong-willed Flaherty was more than a match for the flamboyant Marshall. Redskins fans had grown accustomed to Marshall's visits to the Redskins' bench, during which he berated players and officials, offered coaching advice, and generally behaved like a buffoon. Flaherty stood for none of that.

Flaherty recalls how he dealt with Marshall. "The only time he came down to the bench I ran him off and told him to go sit in the stands." This prototypical George Steinbrenner "used to have a phone down to the bench. . . . I made him take that out. I wouldn't answer it. I'd put the clubhouse boy on."

Operating without Marshall's interference, Flaherty was able to help the Redskins concentrate on winning football games. Yet even as the team found the leadership it needed, another obstacle popped up. In the summer of 1936, the new American Football League sprang into being and Paul Thurlow, of the Cape Cod Steamship Company, placed an AFL team in Boston. The Shamrocks, as the club was called, worked out a deal to play at Braves Field and hired George Kenneally as coach.

Kenneally had coached the NFL Boston Bulldogs in 1929 and was familiar with local players. He built the Shamrocks around Providence College star Hank Soar, who eventually became a major league baseball umpire. According to Soar, the Shamrocks squad was made up primarily of New Englanders, "a bunch of old football players that were all through in the NFL and a bunch of young guys that were coming up like myself and wanted to play. . . . I was the ball carrier, I was the passer, punter, placekicker, everything. The whole damn works." Although the Shamrocks and the Redskins never met on the field, or even played in Boston on the same day, the new team had a sobering effect on the Redskins. It became even more important for them to win.

The Redskins opened training camp in Framingham late in the summer of 1936. They were experienced, strong, and talented. Three members of the team—fullback Cliff Battles, tackle Turk Edwards, and rookie end Wayne Millner— are now enshrined in pro football's Hall of Fame. The offense centered around Battles, a tremendous open-field runner who was perennially among the league leaders in rushing. Edwards, who, at 260 pounds, was one of the strongest men in the league, opened holes for Battles on offense and anchored the defense.

Turk Edwards anchored the Redskins' offensive and defensive lines.

Despite the Redskins' obvious talent, the 1936 season opened with a loss on September 13, in Pittsburgh's Forbes Field, versus the football Pirates. Despite outgaining Pittsburgh 213 yards to 129, the Redskins struggled with Ray Flaherty's new offense and fumbled the game away, losing 10–0. But the team righted itself the following week before twenty thousand fans in Philadelphia. Cliff Battles, whom the *Boston Herald* was moved to call the "high stepping phantom in moleskins," scored two touchdowns (one covering sixty-seven yards) to lead the Redskins to a 26–3 victory. One week later, in Ebbets Field, versus the Brooklyn Dodgers, Battles scored on a sixty-eight-yard run, and the Redskins won 14–3. Poised to open the home season against the New

York Giants, their Eastern Division rivals, the Redskins carried the look of a winning team. Hopes for both the game and the gate ran high.

Meanwhile, the Shamrocks had begun their own convincing march through the AFL. Their season opened on September 20 with a 14–3 win over the Syracuse Braves. Playing at home on September 29, the Shams profited from a blocked punt to score a 7–0 victory in the first night game ever played in Boston by a professional football team. A steady drizzle, however, kept the crowd down to five thousand.

A crowd of seventeen thousand, huge by Boston standards, turned up at Fenway Park on October 4 to watch the Redskins play the New York Giants. With Battles carrying the ball on nearly every play, the Redskins pushed close to the goal line several times. But fumbles once again stymied their efforts. A twenty-nine-yard, second-quarter run by Giants rookie Tuffy Leemans provided the game's only score, and the Redskins went down to a narrow 7–0 defeat. But the real story was in the stands, where the presence of a large crowd suggested that Boston was finally willing to give the Redskins the kind of support George Marshall desired. The crowd had just witnessed a Redskins team that, even in defeat, had proven itself to be competitive, and six of the team's next

The Boston Redskins vs. the Detroit Lions

seven games would be played in Fenway Park. October 4, 1936, should have been the day that sold Boston on professional football. But those seventeen thousand fans who entered Fenway Park flush with anticipation left it in a sour and bitter mood.

George Preston Marshall had forsaken his meddling on the field of play, but he couldn't resist a similar impulse behind the scenes. As Marshall saw the bleachers beginning to fill with people before the ball game, he took advantage of the growing crowd and doubled the price of bleacher tickets from $.55 to $1.10. In an economy still suffering from the Depression, late arrivers who had come to the game prepared to pay $.55 were either turned away or forced to dig deeper into their pockets.

Redskins owner George Preston Marshall and wife Corrine Griffith watch their team scrimmage in Chelsea.

The ticket incident was just one of many that added to Marshall's reputation. George Preston Marshall, born in Grafton, West Virginia, was the son of a newspaper publisher. When George was still a child, the family moved to Washington, D.C., where his father opened a laundry business. Marshall attended private schools, had little success in athletics, dabbled in vaudeville, and joined the army during World War I. By the time he was discharged, the elder Marshall had died and the laundry business was struggling. George took over.

In the next decade Marshall's promotional flair turned the family business into a chain of fifty laundry stores, all successfully operated under the slogan Long Live Linen. He left his mark on all aspects of his laundry business, even to the point of dressing his employees in blue-and-gold uniforms that matched the paint on the laundry's buildings. Marshall's success in the laundry business earned him the nickname "Wetwash."

After Boston's pro football fans were taken to the cleaners, they may have wished that Wetwash had remained in the laundry room. But by the roaring twenties Marshall, whom *Newsweek* later described as having "washed his way up the ladder," had already begun the ambitious social and entrepreneurial career that eventually led him to the virgin grounds of the NFL. During a few short years, Marshall bought a basketball team, poked around in politics, carried on in nightclubs, tried to buy the Boston Braves baseball team and the *Boston Transcript,* married a Ziegfeld girl, worked as publisher of William Randolph Hearst's *Washington Times,* lost the job by interfering in the city room, divorced the Ziegfeld girl, bought the Redskins, and married silent film star Corinne Griffith (who, according to *Newsweek,* once had a reputation for "the most graceful back in Hollywood").

The press often had a field day with the "luxurious laundryman." *Time* viewed him as "convivial, impudent and gregarious," a man of "genuine, if harmless, eccentricity" who "sleeps until noon, takes a nap before dinner, and stays up most of the night." And *Newsweek* reported, in that era of tight money, the thirties, that he spent "an average of $10 a day lunching at high-priced spots."

Boston Shamrocks star Hank Soar poses for a publicity still at Braves Field in 1936.

The Depression offered great opportunity to those who remained wealthy, and Marshall moved freely, if not always delicately, among the most powerful men and women in America. Owning a football team gave the flamboyant Marshall ready access to the press and fed his need for attention, which he craved more than money.

Marshall had long been critical of some local sportswriters for not doing enough to publicize the Redskins. He expected the sporting press to take his directions and didn't always understand when he was refused. Yet oddly, in the days following the Giants game at Fenway Park, the press made no mention of the ticket price increase. The public, however, did not forget.

One week later, in Green Bay, Wisconsin, the Redskins were drubbed 31–2 by the Western Division–leading Green Bay Packers, whose offensive attack the *Boston Herald* described as consisting of "passes to the right of them, passes to the left of them, and passes all around them." That same day, in Boston, the Shamrocks entertained Brooklyn at Braves Field, and Hank Soar led the team to a 10–6 victory. Ten thousand fans showed up for the game, more than double the Shamrocks' previous crowd at Braves Field. Apparently, the Shams, whose ticket prices remained at fifty cents, were the beneficiaries of Marshall's insensitivity.

On October 19, when the Redskins returned to Boston, Marshall's mistake was further evident. The Redskins beat Philadelphia 17–7, but only five thousand fans bothered to show up. The following Sunday, as the Redskins played an exhibition in Providence, the Shamrocks hosted the Syracuse Braves. Although the winless Braves handed the Shams their first loss (16–7), fourteen thousand fans had streamed into Braves Field to watch.

One week later, on November 1, the Redskins faced the Chicago Cardinals at Fenway. In a contest the *Boston American* was moved to call the "wildest, most breath-taking combat between helmetted and cleated warriors since herculean hulks first tangled limbs for a living in Boston," the Redskins hung on in semi-darkness to defeat the Cards 13–10. Inexplicably, Marshall had scheduled the game for a 2:30 P.M. start, and by the last period it was so dark that it was nearly impossible to tell the two teams apart. A hapless referee paid for Marshall's failure to check the almanac; he was attacked by Cardinals players and a few partisan fans following an out-of-bounds call late in the fourth quarter. The referee emerged from beneath the center-field bleachers unhurt, but his shirt hung in tatters around his waist. Only seventy-five hundred fans witnessed the spectacle. The Shamrocks' home season had already ended, and it appeared that as far as Boston fans were concerned, the Redskins no longer mattered.

However, this may have been precisely the reaction that George Marshall wanted. Even though he had lost $80,000 to $100,000 on the Redskins in five years, it is hard to imagine that the laundryman's business acumen was so poor that the dwindling crowds came as a surprise to him. It is possible that Marshall, sensing an early-season turnaround, raised prices in order to alienate Redskins fans and possibly drive the team from Boston. A suddenly successful Redskins team could then be free to choose a city that offered Marshall a better deal, both in the stands and in the press. The scenario that was played out over the next several weeks may have been what Marshall had in mind all along.

On November 8, with the Redskins in the thick of the Eastern Division race, the mighty Green Bay Packers came to Boston. The Redskins mustered their best defensive effort of the season, but the Packers scored on a risky fourth-down pass in the third quarter and hung on to win by a score of 7–3. With twelve thousand fans turning out for the game, it looked as if the locals might still give the Redskins a chance. But Marshall stopped all that.

After the game, the one-time newspaper publisher went into a well-timed diatribe against Boston's fans for the benefit of certain members of the press. "The nice thing about owning a pro football team," the *Herald* reported Marshall as saying, "is that all you have to do to move is pack your trunks. . . . Why, the Packers would draw more people in Paterson, N.J., than they did here." He then lambasted the press for its poor coverage of the team, although in truth the newspapers had been more than generous in the amount of space they allotted to the club. Marshall dismissed the idea that his ticket-price increase was a reason for the poor showing at the gate.

In that Tuesday's *Boston American,* sportswriter Austin Lake reacted to Marshall's outburst predictably. He wrote a blistering column entitled "George Marshall, or Portrait of a Man in a Complaining Mood," and indicted the Redskins' owner for his greed, his insensitivity, and his attempts to influence members of the press.

Boston fans responded to being put through the wringer much as the laundryman had probably expected they would. Attendance held steady for the Redskins' 26–0 loss to the popular Chicago Bears on November 15, but after that fell off badly. Only 4,197 fans paid their way into Fenway Park on November 23 to see the Redskins swamp Brooklyn 30–6; only a handful more turned out on November 30, when the Redskins took over first place for the first time in the franchise's history with a 30–0 whitewashing of Pittsburgh. When workers began removing Fenway Park's temporary bleachers on December 3, it became apparent to most observers that the Redskins—needing only a tie against New York on December 6 to win the Eastern Division title and earn the right to play for the NFL title on their home field—would never again return to Boston. Throughout this period the Redskins players, to their credit, stayed away from the controversy. Their minds remained on football.

At the same time the poor Shamrocks, who had last played in Boston on October 26, were beginning to fall apart. Games in other AFL cities drew poorly and the team began to have trouble making its payroll. "I still think they owe me something like $396," says Hank Soar. "If you were fourth in line to get your paycheck, you better run like hell to the bank and cash it because the fifth guy didn't get any money."

The Shamrocks ended their season in first place, but a scheduled championship game against the second-place Cleveland Rams in Cleveland was canceled. Soar claims that the Shamrocks players never refused to play the game, but that the Shamrocks simply "didn't have enough money to ship us out there." Indeed, what was left of the team would soon embark on an exhibition tour of the south—for the magnificent pay of between $20 and $30 a game, says Soar, who adds, "We had nothing else to do anyway."

Even without playing a championship game, the Shamrocks, who ended the season with a record of 8–3, compared with Cleveland's 5–2–2 mark, were named AFL champions by default. They would return to Boston in 1937, but by then Soar had jumped to the New York Giants of the NFL, and the AFL did not survive its second season.

It remained for the irrepressible George Preston Marshall to write the final chapter to the 1936 season. The Redskins, now sometimes referred to in the press as the "Lost Tribe," surprised the experts by upsetting the Giants 14–0, thus winning the Eastern Division title. Cliff Battles, who later called the team the "foreign legion of football," splashed seventy-five yards through ankle-deep mud to secure the final score.

The championship game against Green Bay was scheduled to be played on the home field of the Eastern Division winners, but the champion Redskins no longer had a hometown, not to mention a home field. Marshall absolutely refused to stage the game in Boston and, after a meeting with league officials, had the site changed to New York's Polo Grounds. The players, who stood to benefit from a larger gate, accepted the decision. The game took place on December 13, 1936. Cliff Battles went down early with a knee injury, and although the Redskins trailed only

7–6 at the half, Green Bay's vaunted passing attack eventually took its toll on Boston's secondary. The Redskins went down to defeat, 21–6. It was just as well: what's a championship without a city to celebrate it?

Three days later, George Marshall made it official and moved the Redskins to Washington, D.C. He began his campaign by signing the team's number one draft pick, "Slingin'" Sammy Baugh of Texas Christian University. True to form, Marshall had Baugh make his first appearance in the nation's capital dressed as a cowboy. The talented Texan led the Redskins back to the 1937 title game, this time played in Chicago against the Bears. The Redskins won, 28–21, but Boston fans understandably didn't pay much attention. The Redskins, after all, belonged to somebody else.

—*Glenn Stout*

the Forties

The 1940 Boston College Eagles: Sugar Bowl Champions

It will be a long time before any football crowd will see a game like this one. [It was] the greatest all-around exhibition of power, skill, and flaming spirit that I have ever seen.
—*Sportswriter Grantland Rice on the 1940 BC–Georgetown football game*

The Golden Era of Boston College football began in early January 1939, when the BC administration surprised everyone by naming Frank Leahy, an obscure thirty-year-old line coach from Fordham, as the school's new head football coach. Dubbed "Unknown Leahy" by the Boston press, Frank Leahy was a self-confessed perfectionist who demanded the same persevering standards from his players. With talent such as Chet Gladchuck, Mike Holovak, and Malden native Charlie O'Rourke on his roster, Leahy wasted little time turning Boston College football into a big-time football program.

In 1939, Leahy led the Eagles to a 9–1 record and a berth in the Cotton Bowl, where they lost to Clemson 6–3. By the following season the normally staid city of Boston had become crazed over college football, with crowds of fifteen thousand coming out to watch spring-practice scrimmages. Under Leahy's firm, guiding hand, Boston College ripped through the first seven opponents on their 1940 schedule by a combined margin of 261–27, setting up a match with undefeated Georgetown for supremacy in the East. Georgetown, under head coach Jack Hagerty, boasted a twenty-three-game unbeaten streak and played a tough, physical game that wore down their opponents.

On November 16, 1940, over forty thousand spectators squeezed into Fenway Park on a cold, damp, and overcast Saturday afternoon to watch the two undefeated combatants square off. Boston College quickly fell behind 10–0, then rallied for two scores to take a 13–10 lead at halftime. The teams traded touchdowns in the third quarter, but with the game winding down, BC still clung to a scant three-point lead.

Late in the game, the Eagles faced a fourth-and-long situation deep in their own territory. Leahy sent in the call to take an intentional safety. O'Rourke took the snap and backpedaled into his own end zone. Momentarily confused, the Georgetown players first paused and then swarmed after O'Rourke en masse. The diminutive O'Rourke managed to swerve, duck, and otherwise elude the entire Georgetown team for a full twenty-three seconds before he was brought down by a host of Hoyas. The safety narrowed BC's lead to 19–18, but the precious seconds that O'Rourke managed to take off the clock helped secure BC's greatest victory. The Eagles finished the season undefeated and received an invitation to play in the Sugar Bowl on New Year's Day.

Their opponent was the University of Tennessee Volunteers, a team that had lost only one game in three years. Facing a tough, bowl-tested opponent, Leahy was determined to prepare his charges properly for the task ahead of them. He drilled his team for two weeks at St. Stanislaus College in St. Louis, Missouri, in preparation for the showdown with Tennessee in New Orleans.

Boston College Eagles coach Frank Leahy (center, holding the ball) with (from left to right) Tom Moran, John Gill, Walter Dubzanski, Charlie O'Rourke, Robert Jauron

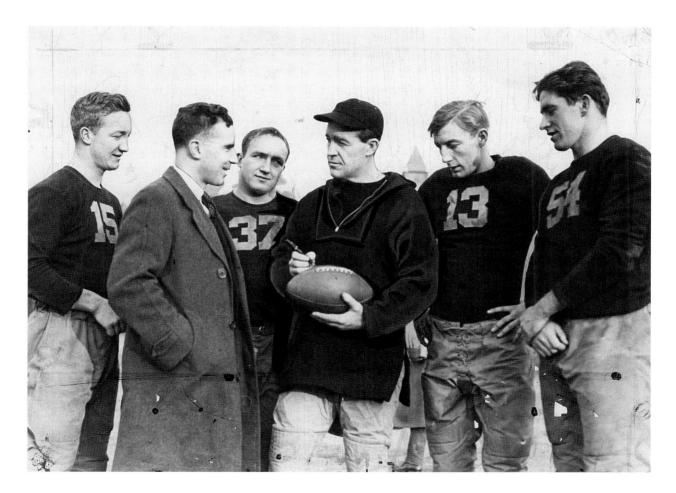

One member of the squad who would not see action in the game was BC's star halfback Lou Montgomery. As had been the case the previous year with the Cotton Bowl in Dallas, Jim Crow laws in the South prohibited the Eagles' lone black player from participating in the Sugar Bowl. These incidents remained with Leahy throughout his life and made a deep impression on him. He vowed never to let racial prejudice humiliate one of his players again.

The Eagles got off to a slow start in New Orleans, falling behind Tennessee 7–0 early in the game but rallying to tie the score in the third quarter. After the Volunteers drove fifty-five yards to retake the lead, the Eagles answered when Mike Holovak scored on a short plunge to knot the score at 13–13. With time winding down, O'Rourke drove the Eagles fifty-six yards to the Tennessee twenty-four-yard line.

The crowd of seventy-three thousand was now whipped into a frenzy, and the stage was set for what still stands as the most famous run from scrimmage in BC football history. O'Rourke took the snap and dropped back to pass. The Volunteers' defense scattered to defend against what appeared to be another O'Rourke aerial, but the shifty halfback had other intentions. O'Rourke faked a throw and cut back to his right, then reversed his field once he hit the secondary and deftly sidestepped and eluded several tacklers for a spectacular twenty-four-yard touchdown run. The amazing display of broken-field running put the Eagles in front for the first time all afternoon, 19–13.

The stunned Volunteers had no reply and could offer only a desperation pass from deep inside their own territory as the clock ticked down. Fittingly, it was O'Rourke who intercepted the aerial and was clutching the ball as the gun sounded.

In the locker room, a breathless Leahy offered his thoughts on his team's accomplishments: "I feel this team will always be dear to my heart for what it has done for Boston College and for me. . . . The boys came from behind whenever they had to. This ability paid off in the end as our players out-lasted the Vols."

Three days later, even a New England snowstorm couldn't prevent a crowd of over one hundred thousand from jamming the streets near South Station to greet their conquering heroes. The cheering throng lifted O'Rourke onto their shoulders and carried him to a waiting car. "My feet didn't touch the ground from the moment we arrived at the train station until I got home," O'Rourke fondly recalls.

Sadly, the triumph in New Orleans marked the end of the Frank Leahy era at the Heights. Shortly after signing a new five-year contract with Boston College, Leahy exercised the alma mater clause in his contract to take the vacant head-coaching position at his beloved Notre Dame. Boston College's football fortunes would sour for some forty years.

Despite staying only two years at the Heights, Frank Leahy left an indelible mark on the BC football program, leaving behind a legacy that future generations would strive to emulate. As for the man himself, Charlie O'Rourke offers this assessment: "That man took a group of individuals at Boston College and turned them into the greatest athletic team New England has ever seen. . . . There certainly wasn't anything like the 1940 Eagles before he got there . . . [and] there hasn't been a mortal I've respected more. He was a man to look up to. You don't meet many of them. Just one will do for your whole lifetime."
—R. R. Marshall

 ## *The Little Professor: Dom DiMaggio*

Who's better than his brother Joe?
Dom-in-ic Di-Mag-gio
—Popular song lyric, c. 1948

Long before the question of race dogged the Red Sox, Boston fans wondered why the team had taken so long to sign a prominent Italian American. Boston's large Italian American population seemingly made the Sox the perfect fit for the right player. Invariably, comparisons were made with the Yankees, who had won consistently with lineups featuring names like Bodi, Lazzeri, and Crosetti. To this day, many Italian American fans in Boston, Providence, Worcester, and Springfield continue a generations-long pledge of allegiance to the Yankees. When the Red Sox finally did sign an Italian American star, it typically raised further comparisons with New York, since it was

Joe DiMaggio's younger brother Dominic who was tabbed as Boston's center fielder of the future.

Dominic DiMaggio was the youngest of three brothers to play major league baseball. Dominic, Vince, and future Hall of Famer Joe all saw All-Star Game action during their careers. Although he toiled in the shadow of his illustrious brother Joe, Dominic was nonetheless a superb fielder and hitter. He was named to five all-star teams and helped lead the Red

Dominic DiMaggio at spring training. DiMaggio is shown posing in a manner typical of publicity photos of the period. His fielding rated comparisons with his brother Joe and legendary Red Sox center fielder Tris Speaker.

Sox to the 1946 American League Championship with a .316 batting average. Nicknamed the "Little Professor" because of his distinctive wire-rim glasses, DiMaggio soon became a fan favorite and was considered the best center fielder for the Red Sox since Tris Speaker.

During his eleven-year career with the Red Sox, DiMaggio batted .298 with 1,680 hits. Following his career, DiMaggio became a successful Boston-area businessman. In the late seventies he even put together an unsuccessful bid to purchase the Red Sox from the estate of Thomas A. Yawkey. DiMaggio is a perennial candidate for election to the National Baseball Hall of Fame.

Johnny Pesky: Heart and Soul

Johnny Pesky has spent nearly his entire professional career as the living embodiment of the Boston Red Sox. He has served the team as an all-star-caliber player, broadcaster, coach, scout, manager, and executive with portfolio (but sadly out of uniform since 1997). More than any player or executive associated with the team, Pesky is the very heart and soul of the storied franchise.

Johnny Pesky rubs his bat against a cattle bone, which is used by players to tighten the grain of the wood in their bats. Hitters still "bone" their bats to harden their hitting surfaces.

During his first three major league seasons, Johnny Pesky achieved a batting feat that eluded the great Ted Williams his entire career. Pesky collected at least two hundred hits in each of those seasons while establishing himself as one of baseball's slickest-fielding shortstops. More than one sportswriter has made the appropriate comparison with Nomar Garciaparra, the team's current all-star shortstop, by remarking that Pesky was "Nomar before Nomar." No higher praise could be afforded either player.

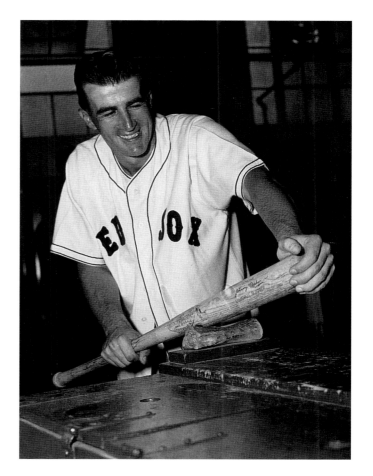

Alternating between shortstop and third base during an eight-year career with the Red Sox, Pesky batted .313 for Boston and served as table-setter deluxe for the RBI bat of Ted Williams. It is no surprise that Pesky scored one hundred or more runs in six of his eight years with the team. His career statistics might have been even more impressive had he not served in the armed forces during World War II.

Johnny Pesky (left) with Milt Schmidt of the Boston Bruins. In another era, Johnny Pesky would have faced the prospects of choosing between a career in hockey and one in baseball. As a boy in Portland, Oregon, Pesky served as stickboy for the local minor league hockey team. During his playing career he often skated with his friends on the Bruins and was good enough to be confused with members of the team on occasion.

Following his playing career, Pesky managed in the minors before becoming Red Sox manager in 1962. He later served the team as a broadcaster and coach. It was as a coach that Pesky seemed perfectly placed. His easy manner helped him explain the intricacies of the game to pupils such as Mo Vaughn and the aforementioned Nomar Garcia-parra, to name but two.

Like many players of his era, Pesky was, and continues to be, as regular and approachable a person as any who has ever worn the uniform. In his perpetual role as a goodwill ambassador for the team, he has addressed countless Little League banquets and community groups. Always a classy presence, he is quick to discuss the towering achievements of teammates such as Ted Williams, Bobby Doerr, and Dom DiMaggio while rarely mentioning his own substantial career.

Pesky remains among that rare breed whose enthusiasm has remained undiminished over seven decades of undying loyalty to his team and his game. In that time he has become a beloved figure in New England, a Boston original whose talent, generous spirit, and character have endured, enriching and inspiring all who make his acquaintance.

 ## Thomas Austin Yawkey

With his Yale education and large inheritance, Tom Yawkey could have lived a quiet, anonymous life of luxury. Instead, Yawkey chose to live every Boston fan's dream as sportsman-owner of the Red Sox. Fans related to Yawkey in basic, human terms because his love for and devotion to the team equaled and exceeded their own.

Tom Yawkey not only began rebuilding the Red Sox when he bought the team on his thirtieth birthday, but also rebuilt Fenway Park into the architectural gem it is today. Yawkey became an immediate hero in Boston when, at the height of the Depression, he hired hundreds of union laborers to rebuild Fenway between the 1933 and 1934 seasons. He soon also began making a full-scale attempt to purchase as many players as seemed necessary to challenge the New York Yankees, Washington Senators, and Detroit Tigers for American League supremacy. Although fans were rewarded with superstars such as Lefty Grove and Jimmie Foxx, they rarely experienced the thrill of a pennant race.

However, Yawkey's postwar team, which consisted primarily of homegrown talent, jelled perfectly to capture the 1946 pennant. Alas, their crushing game-seven World Series defeat at the hands of the St. Louis Cardinals seemed to augur future heartbreak.

Both in 1948 and 1949, the Red Sox just missed winning pennants on the final day of the season. The 1948 team even forced the first onegame playoff in league history, a debacle discussed to this day for manager Joe McCarthy's decision to pitch journeyman Denny Galehouse against the Indians. In 1949, McCarthy again baffled fans by removing Ellis Kinder in the pennant-deciding game at Yankee Stadium. Superfan Tom Yawkey endured both defeats.

In retrospect, Yawkey suffered more from allowing friendship to usurp common sense in the running of his team. Player-manager Joe Cronin was a particular favorite, and he exerted much influence over his friend and boss. What else explains the firing of Farm Director Billy Evans after he had set up the team with prospects such as Dom DiMaggio and two potential successors to Cronin in Johnny Pesky and Pee Wee Reese? Likewise, such managerial hires as Steve O'Neil, Lou Boudreau, Pinky Higgins, Billy Jurges, and Billy Herman proved disastrous. Never was a Boston team owner more adamant about doing things his way.

However, Yawkey's way also included resisting the many trade offers made for the services of Ted Williams, as well as maintaining Fenway Park as an understated masterpiece. In 1965, he made his best move by appointing longtime team executive Dick O'Connell as general manager.

Jean R. and Thomas A. Yawkey watch their team from Fenway Park's auxiliary press box, which was created in preparation for the 1946 All-Star Game. The 1946 Red Sox brought the Yawkeys their first pennant but lost to the Cardinals in a tense seven-game World Series.

It was O'Connell who, as architect of the Impossible Dream pennant of 1967, reversed the fortunes of the team and established it as a contender for years to come.

Yawkey was often a quiet presence within the ballpark. He loved to don khakis and a windbreaker and play pepper with Luis Aparicio's son or some of the batboys. More than one embarrassed player reportedly mistook him for a member of the grounds crew.

His regard for players and their families was typical of the man. Less than a year before his death from leukemia, Yawkey gave up his enclosed seats at Cincinnati's Riverfront Stadium for the 1975 World Series so that Carl Yastrzemski's mother, herself cancer-stricken and infirm, could watch the games in comfort. Yawkey viewed the games from the chilly confines of the grandstand, just like the fifty thousand fans surrounding him.

Perhaps Yawkey's greatest legacy is as philanthropist. In 1953, he willingly accepted the stewardship of the Jimmy Fund of the Dana Farber Cancer Institute following the move of the fund's original sponsors, the Boston Braves, to Milwaukee. Since then the Red Sox have raised millions of dollars for the Jimmy Fund, and both Tom and, later, Jean Yawkey made considerable donations to the cause as well. To this day, the Yawkey Foundation continues this tradition of giving to the Jimmy Fund, among many other charities.

 ## *Win or Die: Stylianos Kyriakides and the 1946 Boston Marathon*

The 1946 Boston Marathon was the event's golden anniversary run, and the first marathon after the World War II years. It was such a dramatic race that *Boston Globe* Sports Editor Jerry Nason dubbed it "the only Boston Marathon that mattered." That's because this was a run for the human race. Defending champion Johnny A. Kelley, a two-time winner, was hoping for a repeat victory but faced a friend he hadn't seen for eight years, a man who had barely escaped execution in Greece during the war.

Johnny Kelley had met Stylianos Kyriakides at the 1936 Olympics in Berlin, where the two became fast friends. Kelley invited him to run Boston, and Kyriakides came over in 1938 as the champion of the Balkans. He was given the number 1—and a new pair of running shoes that would be his undoing. Deep into the race, Kyriakides—who had finished every run he had ever started—developed bleeding blisters that forced him to drop out and take a bus and a cab to the finish line. His head bowed in shame, Kyriakides told Jerry Nason, "Someday I will come back and win your race."

Eight years later, Kyriakides showed up at Nason's office, emaciated and unrecognizable. He sat down and told a stunned Nason how a German patrol in Athens had spared him during a roundup because they found his Berlin Olympic credentials in his pocket. He told Nason he had come back to Boston to run the marathon and to let the world know that Greeks were dying of starvation by the thousands in the aftermath of World War II and because of the ongoing civil war.

Just before the race, a Greek American legislator named George Demeter handed Kyriakides a note. On the front it had a Greek phrase that meant "Win or Die," the ancient credo uttered by Spartan mothers to their sons before battle. There was writing on the back of the note as well, but Demeter told him to wait until the end before reading it.

At Heartbreak Hill, Kyriakides and Kelley broke away from the pack. With about a mile to go, Kelley took the lead. But Kyriakides, spurred by visions of the Greek flag and his starving family, tore past his friend to win. After his victory, he turned over the note and found it carried the words of the unknown Greek runner who had rushed from the Battle of Marathon to Athens in 490 B.C. to announce, "We are victorious," signifying that the Greeks had defeated the Persians.

A month later, having made the world aware of what was happening in Greece, Kyriakides returned to Athens with boatloads of food and medicine. He was greeted by a million people.

—Andy Dabilis

Stylianos Kyriakides's 1946 Boston Marathon victory was underscored by the attention he brought to the starvation in his homeland of Greece. His children had given up a portion of their food so that he could properly train for Boston.

"Hiya Son": John "Snooks" Kelley and Boston College Hockey

For Boston, for Boston
We sing our proud refrain!
For Boston, for Boston
"Til the echoes ring again."
—Thomas J. Hurley, Boston College, Class of 1888

John "Snooks" Kelley is most apt to be remembered as the first college hockey coach to record five hundred victories: actually, he won 501 victories over a thirty-six-year career that lasted from 1936 to 1972, with four seasons missed to navy service in World War II. The achievement is all the more remarkable in that Kelley spent his entire coaching career at the same college, and for thirty-four years he also taught in the Cambridge school system. Along with his records for victories and career longevity are other glittering, if less well remembered, achievements.

Kelley took Boston College teams to the NCAA hockey finals nine times—the most championship appearances of any team in the East. In 1949 Kelley coached Boston College to the first NCAA tournament win by any eastern team, a 4–3 victory over Dartmouth at Colorado Springs. He also coached Boston College to eight New England championships, nine appearances in the Eastern College Athletic Conference (ECAC) Division One postseason play, and the 1965 ECAC championship.

Kelley's natural persuasiveness and honest love of Boston College made him one of the best recruiters in the country. "Snooks Kelley could talk a dog off a meat wagon," says former player Paul Schilling. Kelley also had an eye for talent. He recruited a dozen players who earned All-American honors, including such luminaries as Ed "Butch" Songin, Warren Lewis, Len Ceglarski, Bob Kiley, Joe Jangro, Tom "Red" Martin, Billy Hogan, Jack Leetch, John Cuniff, Jerry York, Paul Hurley, and Tim Sheehy.

"But the thing I coached for and that I love so much to see," said Kelley, "was a young player who would mature, make a contribution to his team, and grow to love Boston College."

Following his retirement in 1972, Kelley served as a special assistant to athletic director Bill Flynn, with particular responsibility for administration of the National Youth Sports Program at Boston College, a summer sports program for inner-city youths. Kelley ran the program from his small, windowless office at the entrance to McHugh Forum, whence thousands of Boston College students and passersby would hear his familiar booming greeting, "Hiya son," or, for women, "How'r'ya, dear."

To the disbelief of many in the Boston College community—and to Kelley when he first heard of it—the National Hockey League came calling. In the summer of 1982, the seventy-five-year-old Kelley got an offer from the NHL's newly relocated New Jersey Devils to join the team as a special assistant to the team's owners. Responsible for evaluating players in New England and the Midwest, Kelley advised most would-be pros to get their college education before trying the professional ranks.

John "Snooks" Kelley (right) was Boston College hockey for six decades as both a player and coach. He led the 1949 team to the NCAA Championship with a 4–3 win over Dartmouth. BC's hockey arena in Conte Forum is named in memory of Kelley, who died in 1986.

"At first I couldn't believe a pro team would want a guy my age," said Kelley. But it was experience that the pros were buying. Kelley had built his college career around the development of American hockey players, a group that has lately made a progressively bigger impact in

the once entirely Canadian NHL. "The day is coming" observed Kelley, "when American players will be the equal of any in the world. Somewhere in this country there's going to be a Wayne Gretzky or a Bobby Orr."
—*Jack Falla*

Walter Brown: Sportsman

He was the most professional amateur
I ever knew.
—*Will Cloney, former BAA Marathon director*

Walter Brown would never have approved of the Boston Celtics' retiring the number 1 in his honor. Boston's greatest sportsman was simply a model of modesty, competence, and gentility in a profession filled with self-promotion, greed, and envy. He treated those around him with respect and rarely took on any project with more than a handshake and his good word.

Brown was that rarest of Boston men, neither defined nor restricted by the tribal culture that rules the city to this day. His name made it difficult for people to peg him as either Yankee or Irish, and his education extended to neither of the Hub's two tribal incubators, Harvard and Boston College. For nearly five decades, Brown floated above such nonsense while forging a reputation as a man to be trusted. Only on occasion did his temper reveal his proud Irish heritage.

Walter Brown, c. 1940

Following his graduation from Phillips Exeter Academy, Brown gradually found his way into the service of his father, Boston Garden manager George V. Brown. While serving this apprenticeship, Walter helped manage both the bronze medal–winning 1936 United States Olympic hockey team and the Boston Olympics, a semi-pro team that played their home games at the Garden. Following the death of his father in 1937, he became president of both Boston Garden and Boston Arena.

As president of Boston Garden, Brown promoted such events as indoor track meets, a winter carnival complete with ski jump, and a hockey tournament called the Beanpot, which attracted fewer than five hundred spectators in its first year at the Garden. In fact, in an ironic twist, the greatest owner in basketball history was a hockey man first and foremost. The Celtics, as well as professional ice shows such as "The Ice Capades" (which he co-founded), were created principally by Brown as attractions to fill open dates on the hockey calendar.

It was Walter Brown, businessman and arena operator, who founded the Boston Celtics in 1946. But it was Walter Brown, sportsman, who decided to remortgage his home and borrow against his life insurance to meet payroll. Among his loyal Celtics players was star guard Frank Ramsey, who routinely mailed his signed contract back to Brown with this note attached: "Please fill in the amount, Mr. Brown."

By the early fifties Brown ran both the Celtics and Bruins and served with Will Cloney as co-director of the Boston Marathon. Cloney recalls that when Brown put him in charge of the old Boston Athletic Association indoor track meet, his only request was "that the event not lose money." Each year the first thousand to fifteen-hundred dollars of meet revenue went toward funding the marathon.

Brown was involved in many sports at many levels. As president of the Boston Celtics, he presided over a team that won seven NBA world championships. While president of the Bruins, in the fifties and early sixties he helped rebuild a franchise that had sunk to a point where it attracted less than half-capacity crowds. Before he was finished, they had made two consecutive Stanley Cup appearances (1957 and 1958). In his spare time he chaired the Basketball Hall of Fame Corporation, was president of the International Ice Hockey Federation, and a member of the Hockey Hall of Fame Governing Committee. To date, Brown is the only man enshrined in both the basketball and hockey halls of fame.

Upon his sudden death of a heart attack at age fifty-nine, in 1964, Brown's widow, Marjorie, and his partner, Lou Pieri, were forced to sell the Celtics in order to pay the inheritance tax on his estate. Although he could—and should—have died a millionaire, his legacy was, instead, one of unsurpassed success and humanity. Walter Brown, a Boston original, will forever set the standard by which all other owners in professional sports should be judged.

 ## Steve "Crusher" Casey: Rower, Wrestler, Character

I never met a man I was afraid of, in or out of the ring.
—Steve Casey

Steve Casey's American dream began when Boston wrestling promoter Paul Bowser offered the twenty-six-year-old athlete one hundred thousand dollars to emigrate to America and participate in a series of wrestling matches. Casey's arrival in America in 1936 was much heralded, and before long many sportswriters were raving about the "Irish Adonis." Bowser himself called Casey the greatest athlete he'd ever seen. Irish American Boston welcomed Casey with open arms, and soon his powerful presence was a fixture in the sports section.

Steve "Crusher" Casey was a superb wrestler in an era in which the sport was closer to its amateur namesake. In the era before television, Casey was instant box office at local venues such as Fenway Park, Boston Garden, Boston Arena, and Braves Field. His appeal went beyond Boston. According to his *Boston Globe* obituary, Casey wrestled in every state except Florida. Facing opponents such as Ed "Strangler" Lewis, "The Hooded Terror," and "The French Angel," Casey won his first world title in 1937. Among the many crowd-pleasing holds of the theatrical giant were the "Kerry Crush" and the "Killarney Flip." Casey was one of the first pro wrestlers to combine a dramatic presence with superb athletic ability. However, he didn't limit his showmanship solely to the ring.

Steve Casey also was an Olympic-caliber oarsman. In fact, he had missed a chance at Olympic gold in the single sculls at the 1932 Los Angeles summer games as the result of having made fifty dollars in a wrestling exhibition. Casey had learned to row while living near the water in his native County Kerry. Legend has it that, every day, he rowed to school

In 1940, the Casey brothers of Boston (via Ireland) issued a challenge through the Boston Globe *to row against any competition. Russell Codman, an amateur singles champion, accepted their challenge. He was given a lead of over one mile at the start but still lost the race to each of the three brothers.*

across Kenmare Bay as well as to Mass and back on Sundays. He beat all comers in races on Lake Killarney and surrounding lakes while competing against his seven brothers. His apprenticeship as an athlete came naturally in an environment of constant competition. If he could beat his brothers, then he felt he could beat any man.

In the forties, Casey's annual races against Harvard rowers were a media event. And in 1940, Casey, along with brothers Jim and Tom, made front-page headlines when all three won a handicap challenge race on the Charles River against Boston fire commissioner Russell Codman, a famed oarsman who had been given a mile headstart in a race from Boston University Bridge to Harvard Bridge. For their efforts they received a silver cup and a prize of one thousand dollars. Casey later reflected, "Codman was a real gentleman. He never thought three clucks from Ireland could beat him."

A true working-class hero, Casey opened a bar named Crusher Casey's in the Back Bay following his wrestling career. It was here that he was shot in a 1968 mêlée in which a patron was killed. Casey survived his life-threatening wounds and remained active by teaching children rowing at Straits Pond in Cohasset. In 1987, he died of cancer at age seventy-eight.

More Popular Than the Celtics: Somerville's Champions

I played a third of my high school basketball career, roughly eighteen games, at Boston Garden. We'd open for the Celtics and boost their attendance from three thousand to nearly seven thousand. It was quite a thrill.
—*Ron Perry, Sr., Somerville High School, 1950*

In the days of the old Tech Tourney, a schoolboy basketball tournament, Somerville High School rocked Boston Garden to its rafters with epic battles against the likes of Waltham, Durfee, and Lynn Classical. In the pre-TV era, they captured the imagination of most of Somerville. Legions of Somerville fans marched to and from the games led by the school's pep band. Former Somerville star Ron Perry, Sr., described it as "being like the scenes in the film *Hoosiers,* where the fans travel in convoys to away games. However, we differed from the school in the movie in one major respect. We were expected to win."

The 1949 Somerville High Tech Tourney champs bask in their glory. This team included Ron Perry, Sr. (#14), who became the only athlete ever to win both a College World Series ring and the NIT Championship while at Holy Cross.

Perry and his Somerville High teammates were almost all first-generation immigrant kids who had played with and against each other for years on the city playgrounds and at Somerville's five junior high schools. By the time they reached high school, they had jelled to become a remarkably cohesive unit. In the late forties they made major headlines while winning the Tech Tourney three times in five years, in addition to winning state and regional championships. Somerville High was so popular that the team even served as an opening act on occasion for the Boston Celtics, who welcomed the extra three to four thousand Somerville fans.

The drums went bang and the cymbals clanged and Henry McCarthy's 24th annual basketball circus thrilled the 12,073 spectators who witnessed the 1949 Tech Tourney Finals at the Garden. . . . The Garden nearly burst at the seams from the undisciplined energy released by the teen-aged youngsters who composed most of last night's audience and the 46,704 persons in all who watched the three-day tourney. This total didn't break the all-time record of 46,845 set in 1948 but the noise must have broken some eardrums. . . .

There probably isn't a loose telephone book to be found in Somerville this morning but there were hundreds on the Garden floor—torn into thousands of shreds—when the cleanup crew began its task of removing the debris. The Somerville contingent literally "threw the book at 'em" before, during and after Vin Cronin's five had annexed its third tournament championship in five years.
—Boston Post, *March 12, 1949*

 ## *Before He Was a Genius: Casey Stengel and the Boston Braves*

The passing decades have left baseball fans with two vivid images of Casey Stengel as a major league manager. He was both the crafty "Old Professor," who produced ten pennants and seven World Series titles in just twelve years while piloting the mighty New York Yankees, and the wise-cracking older professor who led the lowly, but beloved, New York Mets through their first few laughable seasons.

Before Casey ever donned these famous franchises' uniforms, however, the future Hall of Famer was just another struggling skipper on a far less glamorous—and far less beloved—team. The Boston Braves of the late thirties and early forties were a perennial second-division club, a team so desperate for fans that its front office thought a name change to "Bees" might be of help. When manager Bill McKechnie quit following the 1937 season, Braves president Bob Quinn replaced him with the forty-seven-year-old Stengel, in a much-questioned move. Casey, known as a crowd-pleasing jokester during his playing days, had fared no better than fifth place in three seasons managing the Brooklyn Dodgers. But Quinn hoped his clowning might draw bigger crowds.

This optimism went unfulfilled. While Boston's sportswriters enjoyed dealing with the ever-quotable Casey, the city's fans were not as responsive. The grandstands at Braves Field (also known as National League Park, or worse yet, the "Beehive") remained largely empty, primarily because the ball club remained largely bad. Stengel worked well with young players, but not enough of them produced. In his six

Casey Stengel argues a point at Braves Field, c. 1941.

seasons at the helm, in an eight-team league, Boston finished fifth once, sixth once, and seventh four times. Attendance actually fell during Stengel's first inglorious summer and remained under three hundred thousand per season for his last five campaigns. A name change back to "Braves" in 1941 failed to alter the team's fortunes.

By 1943, Stengel's act had worn thin even with reporters. When the manager was hit by a cab just before the season and a badly broken leg forced him to the sidelines for two months, columnist Dave Egan quipped that the driver should be rewarded for doing a great service to Boston baseball. A new ownership group dismissed Casey following that 1943 season, but not before he had banished a young pitcher named Warren Spahn to the minors. Spahn, who would wrap up his own Hall of Fame career with Stengel's last-place Mets in 1965, summed up the Old Professor's Boston tenure with a single telling quote: "I'm probably the only guy who worked for Stengel before and after he was a genius."

—*Saul Wisnia*

the *Fifties*

The Handshake, April 8, 1952

This is the photograph that best captures the hardscrabble essence and competitive spirit of the then six-team National Hockey League. It is only fitting that it depicts the tribal tong war between the Boston Bruins and Montreal Canadiens.

Jim Henry (left) and Maurice Richard at the Montreal Forum, April 8, 1952.

Game seven of the hard-fought 1952 Stanley Cup semifinals between Boston and Montreal appeared to be headed into overtime, with the score knotted at 1–1. As a dazed and bleeding Maurice "Rocket" Richard took his shift for the Canadiens, he jumped to the ice, received

a pass in his own end, and burst down the right wing in one of his patented rushes—which more than one goalie described as comparable to staring down an express train from center track. Richard then stick-handled around a couple of Bruins and rocketed a shot past Bruins goalie "Sugar" Jim Henry. Despite being in a semiconscious daze, the Rocket literally broke the game open, leading the Canadiens to a 3–1 victory and a berth in the Stanley Cup Finals.

The Bruins, several of whom had sipped from their last Stanley Cup in 1941, lingered at center ice following the final horn, numb with disbelief at the game's sudden climax. Then Henry, sporting two black eyes from a broken nose suffered in game six, offered his hand to Richard, who earlier in the game had been cut above the eye and knocked unconscious. The Rocket, ever the sportsman, accepted the offer of his equally game rival.

 Walter "Killer" Kowalski

A native of Windsor, Ontario, and a five-decade resident of suburban Boston, "Killer" Kowalski (shown on page 129) began wrestling as a teenager. In 1956, he defeated Buddy Rogers to claim the National Wrestling Association (NWA) world heavyweight championship. He won the title again in a Boston bout in 1958. In Sydney, Australia, in 1965, Kowalski took the championship a third time in a competition with wrestlers from forty countries. A gentle giant, the six-foot seven-inch, 260-pound Kowalski is a nondrinking, nonsmoking vegetarian who today teaches wrestling at his own school on Boston's North Shore and preaches the benefits of a healthy lifestyle. For nearly twenty years Kowalski was a staple of Boston Garden wrestling matches.

I AM A PROFESSIONAL WRESTLER

I am a professional wrestler,
a world champion wrestler!
I am tough, I play rough,
money is my bread,
I want to get ahead!
I could tear your heart out,
My life is one big clout!

I could give you a clothesline,
which would make me feel just fine!
I do it all—just for love!

I am a professional wrestler,
a world champion wrestler!
You fans are great!

You love and hate:
Take sides—boo; or cheer,
but it's me you always fear!
I make the people wild . . .
I get them all up-riled!
Some people call me crazy,
but I sure as hell ain't lazy!
I do it all—just for love!

I am a professional wrestler,
a world champion wrestler!
I would grab and twist your arm,
but I'd mean you no harm,
I'd give you a leg dive—
your head to the mat I'll drive!
My next one is a suplex,
our bodies will be a duplex!
Another hold is the Boston crab—
with your feet your head you'll grab!
I do it all—just for love!

I am a professional wrestler,
a world champion wrestler!
I would grab you with a claw hold,
and the pain will make you fold!
I could put you in a headlock,
then it's time for you to drop!
Another is a sleeper,
when you'll meet the grim reaper!
I could drop kick you in the face,
which could get you out of pace!
I do it all—just for love!

I am a professional wrestler,
a world champion wrestler!
I will throw you with a slam—
you go down, "bam, bam, bam!"
All these actions I do play,
I mold your body like it's clay!
If your body is all flab,
I will flatten it into a slab!

All the girls call me 'honey',
'cause they know I'm worth the money!
I do it all—just for love!

I am a professional wrestler,
a world champion wrestler!
Many friends I met along the way,
which made me happy, I should say!
All the world has seen me go,
from country to country I would flow!
I did it all just for glory,
but, now, I say, "I am sorry."
They all thought that I was bad,
which made me very sad.
I did it all—just for love!

I was a professional wrestler,
a world champion wrestler!
When I was billed as the main event,
you found your money was well-spent.
All the arenas were always packed,
this was a well-known fact.
My autograph to everyone I would give,
this was worth it—just to live!
You always recognized who I was,
because my future had a cause.
I did it all—just for love!

I was a professional wrestler,
a world champion wrestler!
Time now marches on,
where have all the memories gone?
Everything I did was in the past,
but here "I am"—at last!
The legend is still living,
my love, "I am" always giving!
My star will always be—in the sky!
Killer Kowalski "am I."
I did it all—just for love!

—Walter "Killer" Kowalski

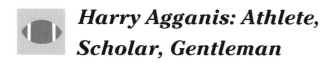

Harry Agganis: Athlete, Scholar, Gentleman

Harry Agganis is the best schoolboy football prospect I have ever seen.
—Frank Leahy, Notre Dame head football coach, 1941–53

At the age of fifteen Harry Agganis was a star on the Lynn Frasers, a boy among men blessed with a talent, physique, and poise way beyond his years.
—Al Coulthard, member of the Lynn Classical Frasers

Forty years after his premature death at age twenty-six in 1955, Harry Agganis was still the most heroic figure in the lives of countless New Englanders. Thousands gathered in his honor in church halls and community centers across the region to raise money to commission a life-size wooden sculpture of Agganis by artist Armand LaMontagne. Over a two-year period, more than $140,000 was raised for the sculpture, in increments ranging from 25 cents to $25,000. A banquet in Lowell alone raised over $70,000.

When the sculpture was finally unveiled at the Sports Museum of New England in July 1995, Ken Coleman and Curt Gowdy, both of whom had broadcast games featuring the man known forever as "the Golden Greek," were emcees for the ceremony. Both men, and most of the overflow audience, brushed aside a tear as the veil was lifted on a sculpture whose pose was described as "Zeus hurling a thunderbolt from the heavens." Such hyperbole would seem extreme in the description of any athlete. But Harry Agganis was most certainly a figure defined more by the values he brought to his achievements than the mere achievements themselves.

Time has not diminished the emotion caused by the tragic passing of Harry Agganis. He was an athlete whose accomplishments were so diverse and monumental they now seem the stuff of boys' fiction. And friends and teammates claim that as great as he was on the field, he was an even better person off it.

Family was always first to everyone's All-American. In order to stay close to his widowed mother in Lynn, Agganis rejected scholarship offers to schools such as Notre Dame and instead elected to play both football and baseball at Boston University. At Boston University, as a superb two-way quarterback and defensive back, Agganis set sixteen individual football records. He was also an excellent kicker, and was rated as the best all-around pro-football prospect by the legendary Paul Brown.

After finishing his All-American collegiate football career, Agganis again opted to remain close to his family and rejected Paul Brown's one-hundred-dred-thousand-dollar offer to join the powerhouse Cleveland Browns as successor to all-pro quarterback Otto Graham.

Instead, Agganis went against the flow, opting to embrace the challenge of becoming a major leaguer in baseball, his second sport. It was only right that the hometown Red Sox secure his services. General Manager Joe Cronin felt he would blossom with the club after some seasoning in the minors. Both Cronin and owner Tom Yawkey were well aware of the tremendous box office potential of the man who had filled Fenway Park for BU football games.

In 1949, BU sophomore Harry Agganis (center) threw 15 touchdowns, averaged 5.4 yards per carry, punted for a superb 46.5-yard average, and played 50 minutes per game on both sides of the ball. At the 1952 Senior Bowl, he threw for two touchdowns and was named the game's MVP.

Typical of Agganis was the story of his graduation from Boston University. At the time that he was finishing up college, Agganis was also playing with the Red Sox. On the Sunday afternoon in June 1954 that he was scheduled to graduate, he was playing in a tie game between the Red Sox and the Tigers. There was a question as to whether he'd make the ceremony he had worked six long years to reach. But Agganis socked a game-winning, two-run home run to clinch the victory for the Red Sox before quickly changing into his cap and gown and roaring up Commonwealth Avenue in his 1953 Mercury to receive his diploma.

Headline writers had a field day with the story, writing "BU Star Bags Horsehide & Sheepskin." Harold Kease, writing in the *Boston Globe,* speculated that it was the first time a home run hit at Fenway Park ended up being celebrated at Braves Field, the site of the graduation.

After playing with the Red Sox for two seasons, Agganis died in June 1955 from a blood clot. His funeral, one of the largest in Massachusetts history, was reported on the front pages of newspapers across the world, including Athens, Greece. Some fifty thousand mourners lined the route from St. George's Church to his resting place. He is buried within sight of the Manning Bowl, where he once attracted crowds of twenty thousand to watch Lynn Classical. To this day, visitors leave flowers, baseballs, and religious paraphernalia on his grave.

World Champions: Tony DeMarco and Paul Pender

To say that Boston and Brookline have never been considered boxing hotbeds in the same way Philadelphia and Detroit are is a major understatement. However, during the fifties and early sixties, welterweight Tony DeMarco from Boston's North End and middleweight Paul Pender of Brookline both captured world championships.

Born Leonardo Liotta, Tony DeMarco adopted the name of an older local boy in order to secure permission to box. His career reached its zenith on April 1, 1955, when the twenty-three-year-old welterweight won the world welterweight championship in Boston Garden with a fourteenth-round knockout of Johnny Saxton, placing him among the few Boston fighters ever to win a championship belt in any class. DeMarco defended and lost his title to Carmen Basilio in Syracuse, New York, on June 10, 1955.

Tony DeMarco is shown with trainer Sammy Fuller after he won the world welterweight championship on April 1, 1955.

On January 22, 1960, Paul Pender defeated Sugar Ray Robinson at Boston Garden in a close decision to capture the world middleweight championship.

Brookline native Paul Pender suffered from brittle hands, which delayed his rise to championship class. But Pender joined an exclusive club of local boxers on January 22, 1960, when he won the world middleweight boxing title against the immortal Sugar Ray Robinson at Boston Garden. Five months later, on June 10, Pender defended his title against Robinson, again defeating the former champion in a fifteen-round decision. In his last four bouts, Pender successfully defended his title against Terry Downes and Carmen Basilio before losing the title to Downes and then regaining it from him on April 7, 1962. Pender retired from boxing in 1963.

Amazing Grace: Tenley Albright

Long before Title IX opened up collegiate athletics to women, Tenley Albright represented the ideal of the female student-athlete. Born into a family of physicians in Newton, Albright aspired to follow in the footsteps of her father by becoming a surgeon. She also emerged as the most graceful and successful figure skater of her generation.

Albright ascended the ranks of national figure skating in a remarkably short period of time. She first learned the art of figure skating at the age of nine, on the pond at The Country Club in Brookline. Within three years she had won the Eastern Regional figure skating title for juniors twelve and under. This success was soon followed by a national novice championship and a national junior title. What made her climb astonishing was that she was battling nonparalytic polio at the same time.

After remaining inactive for five months because of the disease, Albright returned to skating as therapy for her weakened back and leg muscles. In 1952, at the age of sixteen, she won the first of five consecutive senior national championships. Competing for the United States at the Oslo Winter Olympics that same year, Albright captured a silver medal.

The following year, Albright inched closer to Olympic gold when she became the first American woman to capture the world figure skating championship. Soon she added the American and North American titles for an unprecedented triple crown.

Albright did not let skating get in the way of her medical pursuits. While a pre-med student at Radcliffe, she endured a grueling schedule that included ballet lessons, studies, and morning skating sessions that lasted from four to six A.M. But her rigorous training paid off when she won yet another world title in 1955. She then took a leave of absence from Harvard to pursue her dream of Olympic gold.

While training for the 1956 Olympics in Cortina d'Ampezzo, Italy, Albright suffered a deep laceration in her right ankle after a fall forced the blade of her left skate into the right skate boot. Not only was she cut to the bone, but she also severed a vein. Within two days after the fall her father, Dr. Hollis Albright, arrived in Italy to treat his daughter.

The injury did not prevent Albright from skating. Suffering intense pain, Albright nonetheless skated the performance of her life and secured the first place votes of ten of the eleven judges, becoming the first American woman ever to capture the gold medal in figure skating.

Within a year of winning her gold medal, Albright graduated from Radcliffe at age twenty-one. She soon joined five other women in a class of 130 first-year medical students at Harvard Medical School. She has since worked as an orthopedic surgeon and has advised and supported a generation of local skaters, including Nancy Kerrigan.

At the age of twelve, Tenley Albright contracted nonparalytic polio, but was told to continue skating to help her minimize the muscle loss in her legs.

Red Auerbach and Bob Cousy: Celtic Pride

*Red would never let things get very far out of focus. He thought about win-
ning more than I thought about eating when I was little. He ached when
we didn't win; his whole body would be thrown out of whack when we
lost. He didn't care about any player's statistics or reputation in the newspapers; all he thought about was the final score and who had helped put it
on the board. He was our gyroscope, programmed solely for winning, and
it was difficult for any of us to deviate from the course he set for us.*
—Bill Russell, Boston Celtics, 1956–69

Bob Cousy is the Boston Celtics
—Walter Brown, Boston Celtics founder and president, 1946–64

Red Auerbach

Arnold "Red" Auerbach and Robert Cousy both came to Boston via
the mean streets and playgrounds of New York—Auerbach from
Brooklyn, Cousy from Queens. Both were among the most doggedly
tough and competitive men ever to grace American sports. They
arrived in Boston within weeks of each other in 1950 and not only
saved the Boston Celtics but changed the face of the NBA and
basketball forever.

At first, they were an odd couple. The outspoken Auerbach made a
point of not selecting Cousy from Holy Cross in the 1950 NBA draft,
even going as far as to describe the fan favorite as a "local yokel" and

"Fancy Dan." Within weeks of the draft, Cousy, whose rights had been secured by the fledgling Chicago Gears, became property of the Celtics by default. When the Chicago franchise dissolved, its draft choices were released to other teams. Cousy's name was written on a slip of paper and included with others to be drawn from a hat. As luck would have it, the Celtics chose Cousy. Such was the serendipitous delivery to Boston of the player known as both the "Babe Ruth of basketball" and the "Houdini of the hardwood."

Only weeks earlier Red Auerbach had been told in no uncertain terms that the future of the Celtics lay in his hands. He was given a single season to achieve success. If he didn't, the team would likely be sold or go out of business entirely. Walter Brown simply hired the best man available for the job of head coach and general manager, then, wisely, stood aside and let him run the show. Within days the franchise made history as Auerbach, with Brown's backing, drafted Chuck Cooper, the first African American player in NBA history. Soon Cooper was joined by Cousy and Ed Macauley, yet another refugee drafted from a defunct team (the St. Louis Bombers). Although the Celtics lost their first three games under Auerbach, they went on to win their next seven and make the playoffs for only the second time in club history. They ended the season with a 39–30 record—good for a second-place regular season finish.

Auerbach had not only steered the team to its best-ever record but had also saved the franchise. Attendance rose by forty percent as fans flocked to see the artistry of Cousy, whose slick no-look passes and behind-the-back dribbling brought the street game to America. Flashy as it was, Cousy's game was based on team play, with assists counting as much as points. He set a superb example, as did Auerbach, who selected his team as much on the basis of character and intelligence as pure talent.

In thirteen seasons together, Cousy and Auerbach never missed the playoffs and helped lead the Celtics to six NBA world championships, including five in a row from 1959 to 1963. Never was their partnership more important as when new players came to the team. Cousy and Auerbach taught them the meaning of Celtic Pride both on and off the court. It is therefore no surprise that both helped establish the most successful franchise in Boston and basketball history.

 ## *The Agony and Ecstasy of Tommy Heinsohn*

What a show Tommy put on. I never saw anyone play like that under pressure, let alone a rookie.
—Bill Sharman describing teammate Tommy Heinsohn's seventh-game performance in the 1957 NBA Finals.

As an undergraduate at Worcester's College of the Holy Cross, Celtics rookie Tommy Heinsohn got used to playing in pressure games at Boston Garden. Arriving in Boston in the autumn of 1956 as the Celtics' territorial draft pick, Heinsohn joined fellow Holy Cross alums Bob Cousy and

Togo Palazzi on the team. Before long he was overshadowed by the presence of another rookie, named Bill Russell, who arrived in town with an Olympic gold medal and a raft of press clippings. But in time the talkative Heinsohn generated plenty of copy in his own right, with none more significant than that of his game of games on April 13, 1957.

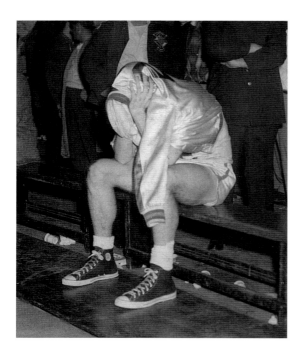

On this date the Celtics played the St. Louis Hawks at Boston Garden in the seventh game of their first NBA Finals appearance. The series was particularly hard fought, both figuratively and literally. In game three at St. Louis, Celtics coach Red Auerbach complained that Hawks owner Ben Kerner had supplied the team with substandard basketballs for their pregame warmups and had also set the basket height above ten feet. As officials measured the basket, Auerbach continued his verbal sparring with Kerner until he finally rushed toward the Hawks' owner and punched him in the nose. Auerbach claimed Kerner had cussed him out using particularly foul language, thus forcing the Boston coach to retaliate. Four games and a three-hundred-dollar fine later, the two teams were tied at three games apiece.

Tommy Heinsohn shows his frustration after fouling out with two minutes to go in the second overtime of game seven of the 1957 NBA Finals. His teammates are huddled away from the bench during a time-out.

On the morning of the seventh game, $1.50 tickets for second-balcony seats were still available at the Boston Garden box office. Fans lucky and smart enough to invest their hard-earned pocket change in tickets were treated to one of the greatest games in NBA history.

It was a game of odd twists, as veteran guards Bob Cousy and Bill Sharman picked the worst time to go cold. The two combined for only 21 points and 4 rebounds, although Cousy led both teams with 11 assists. The Celtics instead relied on rookies Tom Heinsohn (37 points, 23 rebounds) and Bill Russell (19 points, 32 rebounds) to lead the way. Russell also blocked five shots and was particularly effective in restricting the Hawks' shot selection as a result.

With two minutes remaining in the second overtime and the Hawks leading by one point, Heinsohn fouled out of the game. The rookie sensation wept on the bench while covering his head with his warm-up jacket, feeling that his foul-out might have cost his team the title.

During the ten minutes it took to play the final seventy-two seconds of the game, the Celtics gained the lead on a Frank Ramsey jump shot. A Jim Loscutoff free throw increased their lead to 125–123.

But the game was hardly over. With one second remaining, Hawks player-coach Alex Hannum took advantage of the rule that stated that the game clock didn't start until a player on the court touches the ball. He lofted the ball like a quarterback in a full-court heave that caromed off the backboard and into the waiting hands of all-star forward Bob Pettit. But Pettit's forced shot was errant, and the Celtics captured their first-ever championship in dramatic fashion.

Heinsohn was rescued from his tears by a crowd that quickly hoisted him onto their shoulders, as the city of Boston celebrated its first world championship since the Bruins' Stanley Cup victory sixteen years earlier. Heinsohn was later named NBA Rookie of the Year for the season. In his nine years as a Celtics player, Heinsohn would help win eight world championships. As head coach, he captured titles in 1973–74 and 1975–76.

After the Celtics' victory, Tommy Heinsohn is carried off the court by fans celebrating the team's win and Heinsohn's superb 37-point, 23-rebound performance.

Boston, First and Last: Chuck Cooper, Willie O'Ree, and Pumpsie Green

Willie O'Ree (left), Boston Bruins 1957–58, 1960–61

It seemed only fitting that Boston, the city where the death of Crispus Attucks was one factor leading to the Revolutionary War and the writing and oratory of abolitionist William Lloyd Garrison helped fuel the Union cause in the Civil War, would be the setting for the integration of at least one major league sport. One can only imagine the change in Boston's racial climate and the fate of several near-miss Red Sox teams of the late forties if Jackie Robinson had signed with the Red Sox after his 1945 Fenway Park tryout. Despite claims that the team could never have placed him with their Louisville affiliate, there is more than ample evidence that the future Hall of Famer would have served the club well in 1946, when a total of eight players manned a "revolving door" at third base. In due time, the Red Sox and the fourteen other major league teams that failed to sign Robinson were forced to reconsider the wrong and repugnant practice of excluding players of color.

As hard to believe as it seems, the National Basketball Association didn't integrate until 1950, when Boston Celtics owner Walter Brown authorized Red Auerbach to draft forward Chuck Cooper of Duquesne University. At the time, Brown knew he was making a dramatic decision but remarked, "I don't care if he is striped, polka dot, or plaid, Boston takes Chuck Cooper of Duquesne University." That same day, Brown also secured the services of "Easy" Ed Macauley, one of the great big men of the early NBA. Passed over in the draft was a local star from Holy Cross named Bob Cousy.

Chuck Cooper, Boston Celtics 1950–54

The drafting of Cooper by the Celtics broke open the floodgates. Soon the New York Knicks secured Nat "Sweetwater" Clifton, and the NBA, long deferential to Abe Saperstein and the Harlem Globetrotters regarding African American players, gradually became the most integrated of all major leagues.

Boston's other professional teams were slow to follow the Celtics' lead. The Bruins integrated nearly eight years later when swift-skating forward Willie O'Ree made his NHL debut on January 18, 1958. At a time when the league comprised only one hundred players, O'Ree dazzled fans with his skating ability and proved a worthy addition to the Bruins, despite his near blindness in one eye.

Elijah Jerry "Pumpsie" Green arrived in Boston a full twelve seasons after Jackie Robinson had broken the major league color barrier with the Brooklyn Dodgers. Green had the honor of making the Red Sox the last major league team to integrate. As a reserve infielder, Green batted .244 and hit twelve home runs in his four seasons with Boston.

Elijah Jerry "Pumpsie" Green, Boston Red Sox 1959–62

Though his NHL career consisted of only forty-five games over two seasons, Willie O'Ree will always be remembered as the first black player in the NHL. His historic debut took place at the Montreal Forum. O'Ree played the next night at the Boston Garden and was later sent down to the minors. Called up in the 1960–61 season (from Hull-Ottawa of the Eastern Pro League) to give the Bruins some speed and power, he scored two goals in forty-three games that season.

Chuck Cooper never considered himself to be basketball's "Jackie Robinson," despite having broken a now-unimaginable color barrier. During his four seasons as a Celtic, Cooper endured countless incidents of racism. In cities such as St. Louis and Washington, D.C., Cooper was allowed to stay in the same hotels as his teammates as long as he didn't eat in the dining room. So Red Auerbach allowed Cooper to use room service, and the entire team joined him for meals. Celtic Pride was born with such gestures and soon manifested itself on the court.

By 1959 the subject of race had become an embarrassment to the Red Sox. While major league baseball had blossomed with the postwar inclusion of African American and Latin American players, the Red Sox stood alone as the last major league team to integrate. Team owner Tom Yawkey, at the urging of servants on his South Carolina farm, directed his scouts to secure African American prospects. He was hopeful that Earl Wilson, a catcher-turned-pitcher, might make the team as its first African American player. However, it was infielder Pumpsie Green who earned the nod with a promotion from the Seattle Rainiers in 1959. Later that season, Wilson joined Green and ultimately became one of the best pitchers in the American League, while Green remained a journeyman.

Gold in Melbourne: Charlie Jenkins and Harold Connolly

Greater Boston was well represented at the 1956 Summer Olympics in Melbourne, Australia, as local track and field stars Harold Connolly of Allston (and Boston College) and Rindge Tech High–graduate Charlie Jenkins competed in the hammer throw and 400-meter run, respectively. Before the games were over, both men had made their hometown proud.

Connolly, who wrestled and played football in high school, took up the hammer throw to strengthen his withered left arm. He soon discovered a talent for the event and in 1955 became the first American to break two hundred feet in the event, with a toss of 201 feet and 5 inches. At the Melbourne Olympics, Connolly wore ballet shoes for better footing and, with a throw of 207 feet and 3 inches, beat former world record-holder Mikail Krivonosov on his fifth and final toss.

Besides winning gold at Melbourne, Connolly also met his future wife, Olympic discus gold medal–winner Olga Fikotova of Czechoslovakia, at

Charlie Jenkins is welcomed home to Cambridge after his triumph in Melbourne. In 1956, Cambridge native Charlie Jenkins captured the gold medal in the 400-meter dash at the Melbourne Olympics with a time of 46.7 seconds. Following the race, he modestly told reporters that teammate Louis Jones "is still the champ," on the basis of Jones's 45.2-second time, which had earned him a victory in the U.S. Olympic trials.

the games. Fikotova went on to represent the United States in four Olympics, from 1960 to 1972, while Connolly took part in the 1960 and 1964 summer games and qualified once more in 1968. In his twenty years as a hammer thrower, Connolly broke the world record seven times.

After gaining fame at Rindge Tech High, Charlie Jenkins traveled from Cambridge to Philadelphia, where he competed for legendary coach Jumbo Elliot at Villanova. Here he built a career as one of the great quarter-milers in the nation, winning national titles in the AAU 440-yard dash in 1955 and the Intercollegiate Amateur Athletic Association of America (IC4A) outdoor 440-yard run in 1955 and 1957. He also set records in the indoor 600-yard competition.

Immediately following their Olympic triumphs in Melbourne, Harold Connolly (center) and Charlie Jenkins (right) received a hero's welcome.

But Jenkins's victory in the 400-meter dash at Melbourne took the track world completely by surprise. Teammate Louis Jones had set a world record of 45.2 seconds in the U.S. Olympic trials, and Jenkins's hope was to contend for silver or bronze. When asked about his Olympic triumph, which took 46.7 seconds, Jenkins gave credit to his teammate, pointing out that his own gold medal wasn't equal in his mind to the record-setting time by Jones. Both men earned gold medals on the victorious U.S. 4 × 400–meter relay team. Upon the return of the ever-modest Jenkins to Cambridge following the Olympics, a parade was held in his honor.

Snapshots from the Decade

Bob and Bill Cleary are shown with their parents prior to a hockey game between the U.S. National and Harvard teams in 1957. The brothers never played together at Harvard, but they eventually joined forces on the victorious 1960 U.S. Olympic hockey team. Their father was one of the best-respected hockey officials in the country, an avocation that son Bill would take up before becoming the Harvard coach.

In one of his greatest marathon performances, fifty-year-old Johnny Kelley finished in ninth place overall at the 1958 Boston Marathon, with a time of 2:52:12.

Rocky Marciano of Brockton, Massachusetts, training for his second fight against Jersey Joe Walcott. Marciano defeated Walcott in the first round to retain the heavyweight title.

Scientist in Sneakers

Former Celtics "Easy" Ed Macauley and Bob Cousy agree: "Even more than Babe Ruth," says Macauley, "Bill Russell was the most dominating athlete who ever played any team game." According to Cousy, Russell "revolutionized basketball. He changed the patterns of play, both for individuals and for teams."

Perhaps the greatest leaper in basketball history (at least until Michael Jordan came along), Bill Russell, with his unique combination of athleticism and intelligence, gave basketball wings. Before he came along, leaving the floor was an almost inexcusable basketball sin. After Russell, it was an absolute necessity.

Watch a professional basketball game today, decades after Bill Russell (as player-coach of the Boston Celtics) won the last of his eleven championship rings, and you see a game played in a style and according to a set of rules invented by Russell. In fact, one could say that the modern game dates almost precisely from December 22, 1956, his first appearance on the Garden parquet.

Bill Russell was no phenom, at least not at the beginning. As a teenager in the early fifties growing up in Oakland, California, he gave no indication that he would eventually be selected the greatest basketball player who ever lived. Russell was tall but rather thin, intelligent but too insecure to let it show, and athletic but slow to mature. He tried football in junior high school but quit, and he made the junior varsity basketball team only as the sixteenth player on a fifteen-man squad. He had to share the last uniform with another youngster.

Young Russell could run, but his coordination failed him whenever he was called upon to handle something as delicate as a basketball. Even so, he felt a sense of self-esteem on the basketball court that he never found in the social world of adolescence. He practiced tirelessly, and by the time he was a six-foot five-inch, 160-pound senior at West Oakland's McClymonds High School, at least he was playing.

Since Russell attended school on a split schedule, he graduated from McClymonds in January, missing out when the team went on to win the city championship. Yet because he was a graduate and free of academic responsibilities, he was selected to join a group of California high school all-stars for a series of exhibitions across the West.

By no stretch of the imagination was Russell an all-star. He hadn't even won an honorable mention on his own league's all-star team. But he was available, and his selection proved to be one of the most important events of his life. A man named Brick Swegle coached the California all-stars, and he subscribed to a coaching philosophy that let the young men have fun. Under those relaxed conditions, Russell's emerging athleticism flourished.

At the time, most high school and college teams played a constricted, predictable game designed to get the ball to players at the exact spot from which they would then shoot. The object of the game was to wait until a player was open at that spot. If unchallenged, the player put up a set shot. If the defense overreacted, the player could pass to a teammate or cut to the basket. Any other approach was frowned upon by coaches. The jump shot, barely ten years old, was thought to be a risky and undisciplined aberration from sound basketball practice. Even in the professional ranks it was still something of a novelty. As Russell later recalled, "The very philosophy of the game in those days would be unrecognizable to most people now. The idea was to never leave your feet except when jumping for a rebound. On defense it was even worse to leave your feet."

But Coach Swegle let his young charges play, and they responded with a freer, wide-open style rarely seen off the playground. Leaping was no longer a sin, and Russell, who was just beginning to gain control of his body, went wild. On the ground he was just another player; in the air he was something else.

Playing talented opponents, Russell improved his skills exponentially. He discovered not only that he could jump but also that he could "visualize" his opponents' moves and anticipate what they would do next. He started blocking shots. Lots of shots. Nobody had ever blocked so many shots.

During the all-star tour, Russell's teammates began to comment enviously on his leaping ability. Russell himself had become aware that

he seemed to hang above the other players when battling for a rebound, still floating as they began to descend to earth. Just after the tour, during a game in which the McClymonds alumni played the high school squad, Russell, playing for the alumni, had an epiphany. Leaping to take a short jump shot, he noticed that he was looking down at the basket. That meant he was leaping some forty-eight inches off the ground. He was almost afraid to land. Even today, such leaping ability would be considered extraordinary. Any player whose vertical leap approaches forty inches is heralded as an athletic marvel. In Russell's era it was unheard of. No basketball player had ever jumped so high.

Russell did not take this gift for granted. In the gym, he would jump again and again until he could see a sliver of light between the front and back of the rim. He continued to leap until he could see the light thirty-five times in a row. Russell wanted to go that high every time.

Although Russell returned to Oakland after the tour a much-improved basketball player, his career seemed over. Then fate intervened. On the recommendation of a far-sighted alumnus from the University of San Francisco, Russell was offered a scholarship to play basketball for the school.

When Russell entered the University of San Francisco in 1952, he was an entirely different player from the one he had been the year before. Still not much of a ball handler, he realized that he didn't need to be a great dribbler or shooter to score. He could simply go over people to score. On defense, he would block shots and rebound.

Russell's roommate at USF was K. C. Jones. Each man found in the other the perfect partner. Since each found the other a willing listener and neither was blessed with offensive skills, defense became a four-year course of study for both men.

No one had ever talked defense like Jones and Russell. Previously, defense had focused on the game on the floor, but Russell and Jones added the third dimension, the air, to their defensive philosophy. As Russell described it, "We decided that basketball is basically a game of geometry." Echoed Jones, "Somehow we both realized that basketball was a game of vertical and horizontal angles." The two men created their own language to describe their unique perceptions. They were, in Russell's words, "rocket scientists in sneakers."

At the time, freshmen at USF were not allowed to play varsity basketball, so it was not until they were sophomores that Russell and Jones had the opportunity to test their ideas in varsity competition. That year, dissension between older and younger players on the team subverted what could have been a successful season. As juniors and seniors, however, Russell's and Jones's defensive theorems reaped rewards for the University of San Francisco Dons.

Over the next two seasons, the Dons lost only once and were NCAA champions in both 1955 and 1956. With Russell now a mature six-feet 10-inches tall, the Dons' opponents had no chance. Able to block shots at will, Russell also cleaned up under the boards. The blocks and rebounds keyed the fast break. As a result, the Dons were as unstoppable on offense as they were unavoidable on defense. When they missed a shot, Russell took control. In his three years of varsity ball, Russell averaged more than twenty points and twenty rebounds per game.

Oddly enough, Russell's offense may have had a greater effect on the college game than his defense. He was nearly impossible to stop around the basket. His favorite shot was what he referred to as a "steer-in," in which Russell lingered near the basket, caught shots, and dropped them into the hoop. During the 1955 NCAA tournament, he added a backward jam. After his junior year, collegiate rule makers, in what was often described as the "Russell rule," widened the foul lane from six feet to twelve feet in order to push him further from the basket. After the 1956 season, they added a rule against goaltending that, in effect, banned the steer-in.

Celtics mythology has it that when Russell joined the team in 1956, there was some question as to whether he could make it in the pro game. No suggestion could have been further from the truth. When Russell left USF, he was the most sought-after college basketball player in history. Not only was he an All-American, but in 1956 he was named the Helms Foundation Athlete of the Year. Everyone knew that he was the best basketball player there had ever been.

But Russell was in no hurry to join the pro ranks. First, he wanted to play for the United States in the 1956 Olympics. He was named to the squad on April 5, 1956, following a round-robin tournament that included teams representing the NCAA, the Amateur Athletic Union, and the armed forces. Through no doing of his own, he immediately found himself in the middle of a controversy.

Speculation surrounding Russell's professional prospects attracted the attention of Avery Brundage, president of the International Olympic Committee. Brundage was fanatically dedicated to his own definition of amateurism and was offended that any Olympian, particularly Russell, might ever practice his craft for cash. With pressure from

The 1956–57 Boston Celtics

Brundage, the International Olympic Committee attempted to modify the Olympic pledge, in which each athlete swore to his or her amateur status, by including a phrase whereby prospective Olympians would have to swear to remain amateurs for the duration of their careers. Although the phrase would be withdrawn before the Olympics, the controversy over Russell's status was news all summer.

Russell's participation in the Olympics didn't matter to the NBA. The Rochester Royals had first pick in the 1956 draft and planned to select Russell. But when they learned he was seeking a twenty-five-thousand-dollar contract, they balked and decided instead to select Sihugo Green. The St. Louis Hawks, with the second pick, would have a shot at Russell.

But Celtics coach Red Auerbach saw an opportunity. Despite the glitzy record it had amassed over the previous few seasons, his team had been unable to win the NBA championship, primarily because they lacked an aggressive rebounder. Center Ed Macauley, while a good shooter, simply lacked the bulk to battle under the boards—particularly late in the year, when he started to wear down. Auerbach wanted Russell at any cost.

In college, Macauley had starred for St. Louis University and still made his home in that city. Always a favorite with the St. Louis crowd, he was appealing to the Hawks. And besides, Macauley's son had contracted spinal meningitis and Macauley wanted to be near him. So the Celtics dealt Macauley and Cliff Hagen to the Hawks for St. Louis's draft pick.

On April 30, 1956, Rochester selected Sihugo Green. The Celtics, picking next, chose Russell. Although the Celtics couldn't negotiate with Russell officially until after the Olympics, they were more than willing to wait. As everyone had predicted, Russell led the United States to an eight-game sweep at the Melbourne Olympics, capped by an 89–55 defeat of the Soviet Union in the final. Immediately after the Olympics, Russell returned to the United States, was married on December 9, and began to consider his professional future.

Harlem Globetrotters owner Abe Saperstein was also interested in the young Olympian. Although he told the press he was offering Russell a contract in excess of fifty thousand dollars, in reality the figure was much lower. But Russell, sensitive to racial inequality and disapproving of Saperstein's patronizing attitude toward his players, turned down the Trotters.

Earlier in the year, Russell had agreed in principle to a $22,500 Celtics contract, minus six thousand dollars for his time in the Olympics. But when he sat down to talk with owner Walter Brown on December 20, 1956, Brown said he didn't think Russell should be penalized for winning a gold medal and that the two should split the six thousand dollars. Russell agreed and became a Celtic.

No other player in NBA history had entered the league freighted with such high expectations as Bill Russell. He was expected not just to contribute to the team or to help them make the playoffs or the finals; Russell was counted upon to bring the Celtics the championship. Nothing less. And it was presumed that he would do so without benefit of training camp or any period of adjustment to professional ball.

Professional basketball, though quicker and more athletic than college hoops, was still quite a few cuts below the game we know today. Defense was undervalued and the fast break accidental. Although the jump shot was becoming more popular, more than a few players— including Celtics star Bob Cousy—still favored the earthbound set shot. Teams showed little offensive patience and regularly tossed up 120 or more shots per game. Field-goal efficiency, though on the rise, was atrocious by today's standards. The league's average was only thirty-eight percent during the 1956–57 season. Today the NBA average is forty-three percent.

After a 13–3 start in 1956, the Celtics had stumbled to 16–8 by the time Russell joined the club. Keyed by the playmaking of Bob Cousy and the shooting of Bill Sharman and rookie Tom Heinsohn, the 1956–57 Celtics were a good, but not a great, basketball club.

In the NBA's Eastern Division, there was tremendous parity. All four clubs finished the 1956–57 season with a .500 record or better. Against the Western Division, the Celtics had little trouble. But against the East, Boston's rebounding and defensive deficiencies stood out. The Celtics' reputation was good offense, no defense.

Russell worked out with the team only a couple of times before beginning his professional career on Saturday, December 22, at Boston Garden, against the St. Louis Hawks. If ever a player began a career under a microscope, it was Russell. Not only was the opponent the very team from which the Celtics had obtained the right to draft Russell, but the game was televised nationally. Fans would know immediately if Russell could cut it.

They needn't have worried. In what the *Boston Herald* described as "the most spectacular regular season victory of their eleven-year existence," the Celtics downed the Hawks 95–93. Bill Sharman netted a jumper at the buzzer and was carried off the court by the crowd. Russell's debut, by contrast, was relatively inconspicuous. In twenty-one minutes of action he hauled down sixteen rebounds and scored six points. The man whom the Celtics had traded away, Ed Macauley, scored seventeen points but allowed Heinsohn to score a key basket late in the game. He then lost track of the clock and threw up an errant shot from eighty feet with eight seconds left to give the Celtics their final opportunity. He was fined fifty dollars for the gaffe by Hawks coach Red Holzman.

After a quiet 95–87 Boston loss to Fort Wayne the next day, Celtics fans got their first glimpse of the real Russell on December 25, when the Celtics faced off against the Philadelphia Warriors as part of a basketball doubleheader in New York's Madison Square Garden. Although the Celtics lost 89–82, Russell was magnificent, playing virtually the entire contest while center Arnie Risen sat out with a sprained ankle. Russell held Warriors' sensation Neil Johnston scoreless from the field during the game's first forty-two minutes. Johnston, the league's third-leading scorer—sixth in NBA history at the time— was helpless. Russell also gathered eighteen rebounds and blocked several shots before running out of steam. Johnston scored fourteen points, most of which came with the Warriors well out in front in the game's final six minutes.

In a return match the next night, Russell proved that the job he had done on Johnston was no fluke. This time, he took the game apart and rebuilt it in his own image. The Celtics then proceeded to take apart the Warriors. Russell hauled down thirty-four rebounds in only twenty minutes of play and keyed a fast break that left Philadelphia breathless. The Celtics outshot the Warriors 134–88, and out-rebounded them

95–55. Russell added fifteen easy points and left the game to a standing ovation from the neutral New York crowd. They had just witnessed the first game of a new era in pro basketball.

The Celtics rolled through the remainder of the 1956–57 season, winning the Eastern Division and going on to face the St. Louis Hawks in the finals. Russell finished the regular season with a league-leading average of 19.6 rebounds per game, a 14.7-point scoring average that would have been good enough for sixteenth in the league had he played enough to qualify, and a team-leading field goal percentage of .427.

The finals against the Hawks proved to be perhaps the most exciting finals of all time. The series went to seven games, the last of which went into two overtimes. But with the help of Russell, the Celtics prevailed, winning their first NBA title.

In one short thirteen-month period, Russell's teams had captured NCAA, Olympic, and NBA titles. He was the difference. Basketball now belonged to Bill Russell, and he belonged to basketball.

—*Glenn Stout*

GO BRUINS

FROM PHUBAI
SOUTH VIETNAM

the
Sixties

An Unspeakable Loss

My enduring memories will be of her leaping, landing with that light touch of hers, always stroking with a lift and that unforgettable twinkle in her eye.
—Dr. Tenley Albright, 1956 Olympic figure skating gold medalist,
   remembering skater Laurence Owen

Laurence Owen won the 1956 Eastern Junior Ladies Championship, the 1958 Eastern Senior Ladies Championship, and finished third in the 1958 National Junior Championship. In 1961, she won her first national title before dying two weeks later in a plane crash.

The loss could not have been more devastating, the timing more cruel. On February 15, 1961, the entire United States Olympic figure skating team, along with officials, family, and friends, died in a plane crash outside Brussels, Belgium, on their way to the World Figure Skating Championships in Prague. Among the dead were Winchester natives Maribel Vinson Owen, a nine-time U.S. figure skating champion, and her daughters, Maribel and Laurence. Just a week prior to the crash, sixteen-year-old Laurence had been featured on the cover of *Sports Illustrated* with a headline declaring her "America's best girl skater."

Olympic gold medalist Tenley Albright remembers Maribel Vinson Owen as a woman of great intelligence and strong convictions, an outspoken critic of prejudice long before the civil rights movement. According to Albright, Owen would often leave people guessing as to her race or religion and, when asked, remark that it shouldn't matter. Albright also remembers being taken at age eleven to a skating exhibition by Owen at the ballroom of the Copley Plaza. Owen's graceful style, combined with the novelty of indoor skating, created a memory that has stayed with Albright these many years.

It was only natural that Owen's girls took to the ice, with their mother as coach. Their daily routine for many years included early-morning drives from Winchester to Boston Arena, where all three would be skating by 5:00 A.M. and continue for at least two or three hours. The hard work paid off: both girls captured national championships on January 27, 1961. Laurence captured the individual title and Maribel, with partner Dudley Richards, won the pairs crown.

At the time of the plane crash, both daughters were solid contenders for gold medals at the 1964 Winter Olympics. It would take the National Figure Skating Federation years to recover from the unspeakable loss.

Like most who knew Laurence Owen and her family, Tenley Albright pauses ever so slightly when discussing their deaths. The pain is still immediate, the unfairness and scope of the loss so overwhelming. It was left to Tenley's father, Dr. Hollis Albright, to travel to Winchester to deliver the news of the crash to the only surviving family member, Mrs. Vinson. Albright remembers learning of the tragedy while at Harvard Medical School and pondering the loss to both the Vinson family and the family of American figure skaters itself. Remembering the memorial service for the team, she tells of the haunting mantra of one gentleman, who kept repeating, "I lost my whole family."

 ## *The Fiftieth Reunion of the 1914 Harvard Second Varsity Crew*

Fulfill me this and plant upon my gravemound my oar, wherewith I rowed in the days of my life, while yet I was among my comrades.
—Homer, Odyssey XI 77

The 1914 Harvard Second Varsity Crew

	Age	Height	Weight (1914)	Weight (1964)
Bow: Leverett Saltonstall	21	6-0	165	176
2: James Talcott	20	6-0	168	172
3: Henry Hixon Meyer	20	6-1	176	176
4: Henry Stump Middendorf	19	6-1	182	188
5: John William Middendorf, Jr	19	6-1	183	199
6: David Percy Morgan	19	5-11	173	173
7: Louis Curtis	22	6-3	178	200
Stroke: Charles Carroll Lund	19	6-0	169	182
Cox: Henry L. F. Kreger	21	5-6	106	145

Amateur Coach: Robert F. Herrick

Professional Coach: James Wray

The Harvard Second Varsity Crew celebrates its victory, July 4, 1914.

On July 4, 1914, Harvard University marked what the British tabloid press labeled "A Dark Day for British Sport" by scoring one of the greatest triumphs in American rowing history. On that day, Harvard's second

crew, essentially the junior varsity, defeated the Union Boat Club of Boston to become the first American eight ever to capture the Grand Challenge Cup at the Royal Henley Regatta. Harvard's victory came on the eve of World War I, in the last great festival of British amateur sport before the flower of western civilization's manhood was lost to the carnage of "the war to end all wars." Far beyond their considerable rowing skills, the 1914 Henley champions were marked by exceptional patriotism, professional achievement, and longevity.

Shortly after their victory, all but one member of the Harvard crew served in World War I, with six members stationed in France. Of their number, John W. Middendorf, Jr., was awarded a Silver Star and Croix du Guerre, while assistant manager Samuel M. Felton received a citation from General Pershing, along with the Purple Heart and Etoile Noire. Leverett Saltonstall and Henry Meyer later lost sons in World War II.

Following their Harvard days, the crew members enjoyed extraordinary successes. Three earned law degrees at Harvard, three others became investment bankers, with a Ph.D. and an M.D. added to the mix by two other rowers. Once more they were led by their captain, Leverett Saltonstall, who would serve Massachusetts as House Speaker, Governor, and U.S. Senator. Among his countless achievements, he was proudest of his efforts toward the passage of the landmark Civil Rights Act of 1964.

Over the years, the crew remained close and in relative competitive trim while vowing to reunite at Henley on the fiftieth anniversary of their triumph. And each member remained true to his word. Fifty years after they had scored their historic Fourth of July victory in the Grand Challenge Cup at the Royal Henley Regatta, the 1914 Harvard Second Varsity Crew returned to Henley and rowed the Thames once more. Greeted by Queen Elizabeth, they pulled their oars to the applause of spectators who recalled witnessing the first triumph by an American eight in the storied competition.

HENLEY, JULY 4: 1914–1964

Fair stands the wind again
For nine brave Harvard men,
Sung by both tongue and pen,
        Sailing for Henley
Won the great rowing fray
On Independence Day,
        Boyish and manly.

On Independence Day,
Fifty light-years away,
They took the victors' bay
        From mighty Britain.
They were a city joke
Till they put up a stroke
And their strong foreman broke,
As it is written.

Leverett Saltonstall
is the first name of all
That noble roll we call,
        That band of brothers;
Curtis, Talcott and Meyer,
Morgan, and Lund set fire
To England's funeral pyre,
        They and three others.

That young and puissant crew
Quickened their beat and flew
Past all opponents, who
        Watched them in wonder.
Fifty years later, we
See them across the sea
Echo that memory
        Like summer thunder.

Fair stands the wind again;
Thames bear them softly then.
        In every weather.
What though their stroke has
slowed?
        (How long they all have
rowed!)
Oarsman, accept our ode,
        Blades of a feather.

—L. E. Sissman

The Monster: Dick Radatz

Known as "The Monster" during his brief but brilliant career with the Red Sox, Dick Radatz was one of the most dominant relief pitchers in baseball history. Standing an imposing six-feet six-inches, the 250-pound right-hander saved one hundred games in a four-season period (1962–65). During that time he also won forty-nine games for teams that averaged ninety losses per season.

As a rookie in 1962, Radatz captured the American League Fireman of the Year award for best relief pitcher as he led the league with sixty-two appearances, nine relief wins, and twenty-four saves. The following season would be even better, with Radatz winning ten consecutive decisions on his way to compiling a 15–6 record with twenty-five saves and an impressive 1.97 ERA. Such a record prompted then Yankee manager Ralph Houk to remark, "Radatz is the greatest reliever I have ever seen." Houk also selected him for the 1963 All-Star Game, in which Radatz struck out Willie Mays, Dick Groat, Duke Snider, Willie McCovey, and Julian Javier while working the eighth and ninth innings.

The 1964 season saw the legend of "The Monster" grow as Radatz recorded a win or save in forty-five of Boston's seventy-two victories that year. In a particularly memorable appearance against the Yankees at Fenway Park, Radatz recorded a save on just ten pitches as he struck out Mickey Mantle, Roger Maris, and Elston Howard.

Arm trouble would eventually end Radatz's career in 1969, but for four seasons Red Sox fans were treated to a reliever who may have been the best ever.

Dick Radatz displays his victory gesture at Fenway Park in 1963.

Julius Boros Captures the 1963 U.S. Open

The 1963 U.S. Open returned to The Country Club in Brookline in honor of the fiftieth anniversary of Francis Ouimet's groundbreaking victory on the same course. In a fashion similar to the 1913 tournament, a three-way playoff was required to decide the championship. Tied at 293 on the final day were Julius Boros, Jackie Cupit, and Arnold Palmer. The high scores, a full nine over par, were the highest since the 1935 U.S. Open and were caused by some of the worst weather in Open history. Strong winds buffeted the course during all four rounds.

Fairfield, Connecticut, native Julius Boros (center) is presented the U.S. Open trophy by Francis Ouimet (left), and U.S.G.A. president John Winter.

In the playoff, calm winds aided Julius Boros, helping him shoot a 70 and seal his second U.S. Open title. His round proved to be one of only 14 of the 409 rounds shot in the tournament to fall under par. Cupit was runner up with a 73, while Palmer finished at 76. At age forty-three, Boros became the oldest American to win the prestigious title. At the award ceremony he was greeted by Francis Ouimet, who assisted in awarding the champion's trophy and a check for $17,500, plus a $1,500 bonus for having appeared in the playoff.

John Thomas:
A Photo Album

Cambridge native John Thomas was one of the greatest high jumpers of his time, first at Rindge Tech High and later at Boston University. He was among the first jumpers to surpass seven feet, and won bronze and silver medals at the 1960 and 1964 Olympic Games, respectively.

John Thomas approaching the bar at Madison Square Garden (left) and chatting with a young fan (below).

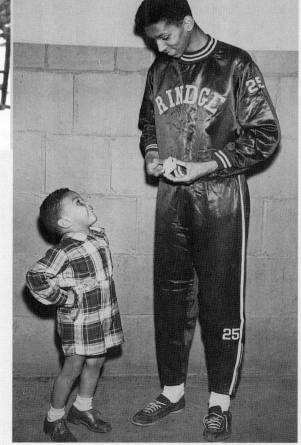

Thomas was one of the last great "straddle style" high jumpers. At the age of nineteen in 1959, as a Boston University freshman, he set a world record of 7 feet 1 1/4 inches and immediately became the popular favorite to win the event at the 1960 Olympics. Then, on February 1, 1960, Thomas made a dramatic return from a foot injury suffered in an elevator accident, winning the high jump and setting a world record of 7 feet 1 1/2 inches. His bronze medal effort at the 1960 games, for which he was criticized both by fans and the media, was not truly reflective of his great talent.

Pioneer: Roberta Gibb and the 1966 BAA Marathon

Hub Bride First Gal to Run Marathon

"Next time I'll wear a heavier pair of shoes and I won't eat cheese for breakfast." So spoke a long-distance runner who exhibited by far the best form in the grinding Boston Marathon yesterday. It was only natural for the long distance runner to have the best form because she's a blonde 23-year-old beauty from Winchester who accomplished the unprecedented feat of a woman completing the 26-mile run well ahead of about half the male competitors who staggered to the finish line.

Mrs. Roberta Bingay of 27 Sargent Road, who was married only last February to a sailor now stationed in San Diego, Cal., at first startled the runners and spectators as she joined the plodding throng, then amazed everyone when she went all the way.

She said she made up her mind last year to enter the race and "I plan to run again." It was her first competitive race but she "didn't consider today's running as competition."

Mrs. Bingay explained her shoes bothered her a little as she was used to running in a heavier pair.

Also she said that for breakfast she had an eggnog and bacon and cheese. "The cheese was too heavy and made me a little logy."

She said she came home from San Diego by bus, a three-and-a-half-day trip. She left last Friday at noon and didn't get into Boston until 6:30 P.M. Monday.

"I ate very little on the bus, just fruit, and I tried to sleep a lot," she said. "When I got to Winchester I ate everything in sight and I don't think that was such a good idea, either."

Mrs. Bingay is the daughter of Mr. and Mrs. Thomas R. P. Gibb, Jr., a professor of chemistry at Tufts College.

Last night at her parents' home she planned to "relax in a hot tub and get a good night's sleep."

The Boston Athletic Association, which sponsors the Hopkinton to Boston race, does not accept woman entries.

"I had never been over the course before," she said. "I even got lost going to Hopkinton. There I was dressed in a black bathing suit, khaki bermuda shorts and leather track shoes.

"Nobody gave me a number because I wasn't supposed to be running, but at the same time the officials were very decent—they just ignored me."

Many spectators along the way thought she was just some college girl who joined the race for a short distance, but some runners she accompanied all the way knew better and shouted encouragement to her as they gasped their way up hill and down dale.

Her run wasn't any spur-of-the-moment affair. It was the culmination of long training and a carefully thought-out plan.

After she finished, surprisingly fresh and still full of bounce, she told a Record American reporter that she first developed an interest in running while attending Tufts with her husband, William, 24, who was a member of the track team. "I liked to be near him when he was practicing," she said, "so I took up running myself."

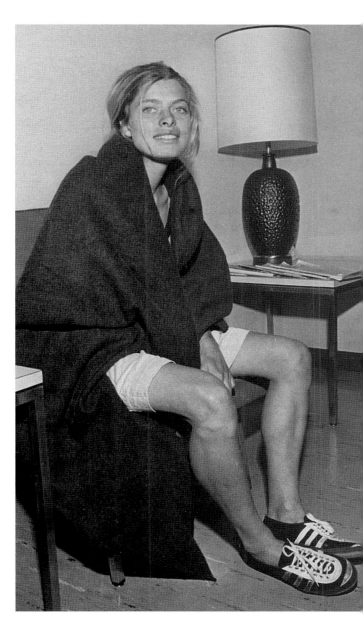

She said that she did most of her training for the Marathon in the hills around San Diego and that she used to run from her home in Winchester to the Back Bay when she was attending the Museum of Fine Arts School in Boston last year.

"I had it in the back of my mind for a long time that I'd like to try the Marathon," she said. "but I didn't definitely make up my mind until I knew that I would be coming home this week to visit my parents."

She said she went to Hopkinton Tuesday morning and hid in some bushes a couple of hundred yards from the starting line, wearing a black hood

Roberta Gibb became the first woman ever to run the Boston Marathon. Leaving her hiding place behind a tree at the race's start, she slipped into the pack of men runners. She is shown here following her finish.

over her head so she would not be immediately recognized as a girl (the officials won't allow girls to start).

The rest of her running costume consisted of a black bathing suit, tan shorts and black-and-white running shoes.

When about half the pack of 400 contestants had passed, she recounted, she jumped out of the bushes and set out for the Prudential Tower. She said she discarded the hood shortly after she started to run.

She said that she discussed the venture with her husband and that he fully approved. "He even said that maybe next year if I did well we could enter as a husband and wife team," she said. She said that she told her father about her intentions Monday night and that "he told me I was nuts."
—Boston Record American, *April 20, 1966*

 ## *Tony C: In Sunshine and Shadow*

Anthony "Tony C" Conigliaro
Boston, A.L. 1964–1985

Outfielder/designated hitter who hit 522 career home runs. Four-time American League home run champion. 1974 American League Most Valuable Player. Led Red Sox to world championships in 1967, 1974, and 1975. With teammates Carl Yastrzemski, Jim Rice, Fred Lynn, and Dwight Evans, formed one of the most potent batting orders in the modern era.
(Inscription on the plaque that should be hanging in the National Baseball Hall of Fame, Cooperstown, New York.)

Tony Conigliaro was one of baseball's great prodigies. In his first major league game, at Yankee Stadium on Opening Day 1964, Conigliaro stroked his first base hit off future Hall of Famer Whitey Ford, made a spectacular running catch at the 407-foot sign in right-center field, and was written up in national wire stories for accusing Ford of throwing spitballs in the 4–3 Red Sox victory.

Conigliaro's first home opener, on April 17, 1964, was even more auspicious. Not only was the game played as a benefit for the planned John F. Kennedy Library, but the crowd of 20,123 included such figures as former world heavyweight champions Jack Dempsey and Gene Tunney, actress Carol Channing, Hall of Famer Stan Musial, and most of the Kennedy clan. The game was also broadcast throughout New England on WHDH-TV.

Even veteran play-by-play announcer Curt Gowdy was stunned as the nineteen-year-old Conigliaro connected for a home run off White Sox starter Joel Horlen's first pitch. As the hometown hero glided around the bases, Gowdy exclaimed, "Look at that boy, just look at him. He was playing at St. Mary's High School in Lynn just a year ago."

By late June, Conigliaro had already hit twenty home runs and was batting .280 when a pitch from Pedro Ramos of the Cleveland Indians broke his arm and sidelined him until September. There is little doubt that he would have surpassed many rookie slugging records had he not been injured.

Over the next three seasons, Conigliaro continued to realize his tremendous potential by slugging home runs at a steady clip despite suffering a series of injuries. In 1965 he became the youngest slugger to lead the league in home runs, with thirty-two. But in 1966, despite playing his first injury-free season, he slumped to twenty-eight homers and a .286 batting average. The 1967 season promised to be Conigliaro's greatest ever. By mid-August he had helped lead the team into contention in the best pennant race in a generation. However, the events of Friday, August 18, would haunt the franchise for years to come.

In the fourth inning of a scoreless game against the California Angels, Reggie Smith approached the batter's box as a smoke bomb billowed and sparked in the outfield, delaying the game for ten minutes. The next batter was Tony Conigliaro. At exactly 8:42 P.M., the career of the most promising young slugger in baseball was sent into free fall by a high fastball delivered by Angels pitcher Jack Hamilton that exploded into the twenty-two-year-old's face. Red Sox physician Dr. Thomas Tierney recalled a hissing noise emanating from the slugger's skull as he remained conscious throughout his agonizing ordeal. Manager Dick Williams and trainer Buddy LeRoux helped lift Conigliaro onto a stretcher and carried him off the field to the team clubhouse, where he received treatment before being sent to Santa Maria Hospital.

Although the Red Sox would go on to win one of the greatest and most improbable pennant races in 1967, it was a bittersweet experience for many. On the final day of the regular season, Conigliaro sat in the dugout as the team clinched it's remarkable pennant victory. He later wept openly at his locker while teammates celebrated a trip to the World Series now denied Conigliaro.

Tony Conigliaro lies unconscious after being hit by a pitch from California Angels' pitcher Jack Hamilton.

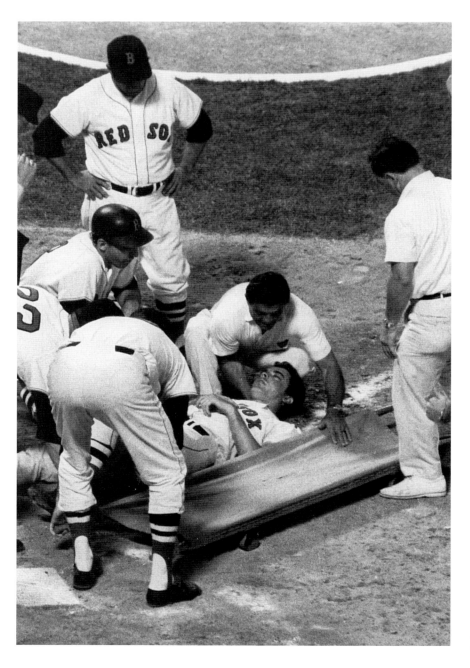

Playing without Conigliaro, the Red Sox lost the 1967 World Series to the St. Louis Cardinals. Red Sox fans will forever speculate as to whether Conigliaro's beaning cost them their first world championship since 1918. One can only imagine the dream confrontation of Conigliaro and St. Louis pitcher Bob Gibson, with all the proverbial marbles on the table. The spectre of a Red Sox mini–murderers row of Yastrzemski, Petrocelli, and Conigliaro would have intimidated most pitchers in the majors.

For one full season after the beaning, Conigliaro visited Massachusetts General Hospital on a regular basis, prayed, and plotted his return to the majors as a pitcher. Only when an eye examination showed marked improvement could he even begin thinking of taking batting practice and rebuilding his career as a hitter.

On Opening Day 1969, Conigliaro made one of the most emotional comebacks in sports history when he socked a dramatic tenth-inning home run to put the Sox ahead of Baltimore at Memorial Stadium. He finished the year with twenty home runs and a .255 batting average, and his comeback seemed assured. In recognition of his heroism, Conigliaro received the Hutch Award during the off-season. The award—named for former Cincinnati Reds manager Fred Hutchinson, who died of cancer—is given to baseball's most courageous player. Conigliaro prized this trophy above all others.

In 1970, Conigliaro continued his comeback with a spectacular season that saw him hit thirty-six homers and drive in 116 runs. Despite his remarkable achievement, the Red Sox traded him on October 11 in a deal that also sent Gerry Moses and Ray Jarvis to the California Angels for Doug Griffin, Ken Tatum, and Jarvis Tatum. In his time on the West Coast, not only was Conigliaro homesick, but he also felt that his eyesight was failing. Halfway through the 1971 season, he announced his retirement.

But Tony Conigliaro wasn't finished yet. In 1975, he convinced the Red Sox to invite him to spring training, where he beat out a rookie named Jim Rice for the designated hitter's job (the American League had introduced the dh position in 1973). In another memorable opening-day performance, Conigliaro started as designated hitter opposite Hank Aaron, who played the same role for the Milwaukee Brewers. In dramatic fashion, he lined a base hit in his first at-bat, receiving a tremendous ovation. He would get only six more hits in fifty-six at-bats before finally retiring for the last time at age thirty.

In 1982, Conigliaro, having just completed a successful audition for the position of Red Sox TV color announcer, suffered a heart attack while being driven to the airport by his brother. Brain damage resulting from this attack nearly killed Conigliaro, but he fought gamely against huge odds to survive. His family devoted the next eight years to his around-the-clock care, with the hope that if anyone deserved a miracle, it was the former slugger. But there were no more "Impossible Dreams" for the Conigliaros, and Tony died from complications of kidney failure on February 24, 1990, at age forty-five.

It is not hard to imagine that, had Conigliaro not been beaned, his career might have changed Red Sox history. By any reasonable estimate he would have been planning his Hall of Fame induction in February 1990, rather than leaving the world all too soon.

Rivermen: Ernie Arlett & Harry Parker

The Charles River boasts four major rowing programs and one famous regatta. Ernie Arlett is responsible for two of these.

Ernie Arlett was the last of that breed of English "watermen" who rowed for prize money. His grandfather had been one, his father had been one of the best, and until the money ran out, Ernie had been one. In World War II, trapped along with a half-million British soldiers on the beaches of Dunkirk, he commandeered a boat and rowed his fellow Tommies to waiting destroyers during the famous evacuation. At war's end he turned his talents to coaching. Among his students was the famous American sculler, John B. Kelly, who recognized Arlett's talents while studying under him in England and sponsored his emigration to the United States. Arlett coached at rowing clubs and high schools along the Schuylkill River in Philadelphia, then at Rutgers and Harvard before arriving at Northeastern.

Northeastern crew coach Ernie Arlett

In the spring of 1964, when Arlett was introduced to the media as the Northeastern Huskies' first-ever coach of crew, the university had no boathouse and not a single shell, rower, or oar. But after six months of training and teaching a hoard of novice rowers, Ernie had his shells ready to challenge the collegiate world when spring unlocked the river. And challenge they did. They defeated thirty-three of thirty-four shells to win the Dad Vail Regatta in Philadelphia, one of the premier small-college rowing championships.

Northeastern honored the fledgling rowers by sending them to the mecca of rowing, the Henley Royal Regatta in Ernie's hometown, Henley-on-Thames, England. There they defeated Queens College, Belfast, before bowing to Cornell University. Northeastern's success was, in the words of the *Boston Globe,* "a shining chapter in sports history."

In the fall of 1964, armed with his first shells and nearly one hundred eager crew candidates, Arlett was ready to capitalize on the success of the previous spring. But he discovered that months of autumnal toiling gave a collegiate oarsman only one thing to look forward to: months more toil in the rowing tanks. He harkened back to his days on the Thames, when Head races were held to keep the oarsmen active during the fall. "A little carrot before the stick," Arlett would say. And so, in 1965, Ernie Arlett created the Head of the Charles Regatta, a three-mile race held every October on the Charles River.

When Arlett retired from Northeastern in 1978, its rowing program was one of the nation's strongest, and the Head of the Charles had become the world's largest one-day regatta.
—*Jack Grinold*

If the Newell Boathouse is the Vatican of American collegiate rowing, then Harry Parker is its pope. Now in his fifth decade as Harvard rowing coach, Parker is the greatest collegiate rowing coach of the second half of the twentieth century. His teams have remained consistently excellent, losing only one season during his long-standing tenure. During his first twenty years, Parker's crews lost only seven races. The roster of Olympians who have emerged from his program reads like a Who's Who of American rowing.

Since 1963, when Parker took over the varsity program at age twenty-seven, his crews have completely dominated Yale in the season-ending regatta on Connecticut's Thames River—America's oldest intercollegiate sporting event, dating back to 1852. Winning is simply the only acceptable result for a man who has been called by many of his oarsmen the most competitive man that they have ever met. Strong words from students at one of the most overwhelmingly competitive institutions on the planet.

Harvard crew coach Harry Parker

For many years, Parker would impart his competitivness to his rowers by working out with them as they ran the steps at Harvard Stadium and lifted weights. In most cases, the former Olympic sculler would leave them in the dust. As much an innovator as a competitor, he also introduced new training methods, such as German intervals and the use of rowing ergometers, to Harvard years before any rival program caught on.

Parker is the unequaled master of selecting crews from the 125 athletes who make up the largest of Harvard's intercollegiate teams. He constantly tinkers with seat assignments, making sure that nobody is complacent. He can view a boat from forty feet and tell if the rigging needs adjustment or if a rower needs instruction or encouragement. He is the master of making boats move as fast as their equipment and human engines can make them go.

The Harvard rowing program was already one of the nation's greatest at the time of Parker's arrival, and because of him, it now stands alone as possibly the greatest intercollegiate program in any sport in American history.

Papa Bear: Milt Schmidt

Milt Schmidt typifies everything a hockey player should be. He has heart, courage, speed, ability, color, and provides inspiration to his team.
—*Clarence Campbell, NHL president, 1947–78*

From left to right: Milt Schmidt, Tom Johnson, Bobby Orr, and Harry Sinden with the Stanley Cup on May 10, 1970

Milton Conrad Schmidt is the only Boston Bruin to have his name inscribed on the Stanley Cup as many as four times. As a center from the thirties to the fifties, Schmidt earned a reputation as the toughest playmaker in the league. His game was a mixture of speed and skill combined with an innate ability to dish out and absorb enormous amounts of punishment in equal measure. Longtime observers compare his game to that of fellow center Mark Messier, with the qualifier that Schmidt played in a tougher era against better players.

Schmidt won the first of his four Stanley Cups in 1939, when the Bruins defeated both the Rangers and Maple Leafs to capture the franchise's second cup in eleven seasons. Just two seasons later, Schmidt again sipped from the cup as the Bruins survived a tough seven-game semifinal series with Toronto before they beat the Detroit Red Wings in four straight to win the title. It took World War II to break up what surely was a Bruins dynasty, as Schmidt and many of his teammates enlisted in the armed forces.

Following his retirement in 1954, Schmidt took over the coaching reins of the Bruins and led them to the Stanley Cup Finals in both 1957 and 1958. Molded in the image of Schmidt, they scrapped their way to heart-breaking losses to Montreal in each appearance.

However, after the two Stanley Cup losses, it would take nine seasons of abject frustration for Schmidt to lead Boston back to the threshold of hockey's greatest prize. Serving the team as assistant general manager, Schmidt turned his focus toward finding players to complement defensive phenom Bobby Orr. Having won two cups as a player, Schmidt knew the ingredients and sought to obtain them.

On May 15, 1967, Schmidt made the most one-sided trade in Bruins—perhaps all hockey—history, when he shipped Gilles Marotte, Doug Mohns, and Jack Norris to Chicago in exchange for Phil Esposito, Ken Hodge, and Fred Stanfield. In one day, he provided the team with the extra scoring punch and character it needed to improve to the point where it could win the prize that had eluded the franchise for nearly three decades. Schmidt described the events of the fifteenth as follows:

First of all you make a deal to help your team, not just to change a face, and you never know how it will turn out. During the winter of 1967 Hap Emms, the Bruins general manager, and I tried without luck to make a deal to shake up the team. We continued our efforts to no avail during the off-season and Hap finally decided that it was no use and told me that we should concentrate our efforts on working with the talent on our minor league clubs.

I told him that I thought he was giving up too soon and he granted me the authority to pursue a trade. On May 15, 1967, the last day before the trading deadline, I was sitting in my office when I received a call at 3:00 P.M. from Sarasota, Florida. It was from Tommy Ivan of the Chicago Black-hawks and he was interested in making a deal. I called Emms and Mr. Adams [team president Weston Adams, Sr.] and we discussed the names of the players and by nine o'clock that evening we had received permission to make the trade.

Also that same night, after I came home, I got on the phone and wanted to try to get Eddie Shack from Toronto. The Bruins were floundering at the time and among other things I changed the uniforms and wanted something different for the club. Well, I reached Punch Imlach and King Clancy of the Maple Leafs and made my first offer of Murray Oliver and $25,000 and after a while made my final offer of Oliver and $100,000. I could hear Clancy in the background telling Imlach he would be crazy not to accept the offer. We reached an agreement at five minutes to midnight, just under the trading deadline.

The players acquired in the trade became the core of two Stanley Cup champions. For nearly a decade Phil Esposito and Ken Hodge formed two-thirds of the Bruins' top scoring line, while Fred Stanfield helped anchor the second line with John Bucyk and Don McKenzie. The subsequent firing of Milt Schmidt has haunted the team for years, as they have not won the Stanley Cup since.

 ## *Band of Brothers:*
The 1968 Boston Bruins

Never has a team captured the hearts of Boston fans as did the Orr/Esposito–era Boston Bruins. Sparked by the arrival in 1966 of a leading man named Bobby Orr, the Bruins shook off a decade of also-ran status to contend for the Stanley Cup in just two short seasons. Bruins fans were finally rewarded for years of selling out the Boston Garden. Tickets for the 13,909 seats that had remained full during years of dreadful hockey were now the toughest to obtain in the history of Boston sports. Like their counterparts in Montreal, Boston fans were so loyal as to leave their season tickets as a part of their estates. Only death would part any serious fan from the team.

The Bruins were nothing less than a phenomenon as fans found them to be the toughest ticket in town. Their broadcasts on Channel 38 caused a run on hardware stores by customers seeking to purchase the proper antenna with which to view the games. In short, it was Bruins mania. There has been nothing like it before or since. Bruins fans sensed that their heroes were very much a throwback to the era of the Kraut Line and Eddie Shore. The team played with flash and swagger, yet included

a lineup of men who will carry the description of "Bruins-type player" to their graves. Such players played physically at both ends of the ice and did anything neccessary to win.

The prototype of the Bruin ideal was winger Eddie Westfall. Invariably Westfall was given the assigment of shadowing the opponent's best winger while also being expected to kill penalties and score the occasional goal. He routinely sparred with the likes of Bobby Hull and Frank Mahovolich while taking his own game to new heights. Never was there a more selfless player to wear the black and gold. Such men are often called "player's players," which in Boston meant that they received ovations of a decibel value almost equal to those given superstars like Orr and Esposito. Their contributions, which defied statistical analysis, were measured in team victories.

In the accompanying photo the Bruins are shown as fans from this era best remember them. They were, and are to this day, a band of brothers who played hard both on and off the ice. Many of them still can say

The 1968 Bruins display greetings from Vietnam. Top row, left to right: Fred Stanfield, Don Awrey, Ken Hodge, Ron Murphy, Don McKenzie, John Forristall, Dan Canney. Bottom row, left to right: Wayne Cashman, Bobby Orr, Glen Sather, Ed Westfall, Phil Esposito, John Bucyk.

that they haven't had to pay for a beer in Boston for over thirty years. Their selfless excellence and radiant enjoyment of their work endeared these players to fans and nonfans alike.

When CBS began producing national telecasts of the NHL in the late sixties, it was this Bruins team that captured the imagination of the American public. They were also the favorite of millions of Canadians, from Vancouver to the Maritimes, as Hockey Night in Canada beamed their swashbuckling exploits throughout the northland.

This was the team that launched a thousand hockey rinks and sparked the explosion of the game in the United States. Whether you called them the Big Bad Bruins or simply the B's, the rebirth of the Boston franchise marked the advent of the greatest period of growth in the history of the game. They are still the standard by which all Bruins teams will be measured. They endure as the most unforgettable team of their generation.

 "The Game," November 23, 1968

I come back to the Game, year after year, not so much for the sport as for a feeling of renewal. It has become a rite, and its capacity to move me does not have much to do with the final score or even the pleasures of meeting old friends there, before the kickoff and after. It has something to do with the turn of the seasons: winter begins here, every year, when the gun goes off and the last cries and songs are exchanged across the field. The Game picks us up each November and holds us for two hours and then releases us into the early darkness of winter, and all of us, homeward bound, sense that we are different yet still the same. It is magic.
—Roger Angell, Harvard Class of 1948

Gentlemen, you are now going out to play football against Harvard. Never again in your whole life will you do anything so important.
—Tad Jones, Yale head football coach, 1916–17, 1920–27

The 1968 Harvard-Yale football game really was *The* Game. Played against the backdrop of the turmoil of America's most divisive year since the end of the Civil War, the game seemed a throwback to the days when Harvard and Yale fielded the best teams in the nation. This was a contest that mattered to more than just the legions of well-heeled alumni clustered around the Ivy League elegance of Harvard. It was a game that such long-past heroes as Huntington "Tack" Hardwick, Barry Wood, and Albie Booth would have recognized as similar to those in which they had starred.

Pete Varney's catch seals the 29–29 Harvard-Yale tie.

Entering the contest, both teams were undefeated and untied, with Yale ranked in the Associated Press top twenty for the first time in more than a generation. Unranked Harvard had enjoyed a Cinderella season and was eager to avenge its heartbreaking loss to Yale in 1967. Tickets to the game were nearly impossible to obtain and were judged by area scalpers as tougher to score than those for the Red Sox World Series the previous year. More than one diplomat and captain of industry had to make due with endzone seats or vertigo-inducing perches under the guano-smeared columns of the oldest concrete stadium in America.

For nearly four quarters, the Harvard side of the stadium sat in stoic silence while Yale built a 29–13 lead. With only minutes remaining and darkness descending on the floodlight-bereft stadium, many in the crowd began to exit, their brake lights twinkling in the "parking lots" of the muddied adjacent practice fields. With just three minutes and thirty-one seconds remaining, Harvard appeared to be dead. The chill air resounded with the cries of Cole Porter's Yale anthem, "Bulldog, Bulldog, Bow Wow Wow . . . Eli Yale," as ten thousand men of Harvard searched pockets of tweed topcoats for their car keys.

Had the play-by-play drama of the climax of the game been scripted and submitted to Hollywood, the authors would have been placed on their own blacklist. For with just three-and-a-half minutes remaining, Harvard entered a fifth dimension to pull off the miracle of football miracles. With the ball on the Harvard fourteen-yard line, substitute quarterback Frank Champi drove the Crimson to both a touchdown (on a pass to Bruce Freeman) and a two point conversion (on a Gus Crim run) in twelve plays to cut the Yale lead to eight points with just forty-two seconds left to play.

Fans who paused at the exit ramps as Harvard prepared for an onsides kick hastily returned to their seats when Bill Kelly recovered for the Crimson on the Yale forty-nine-yard line. On the Yale sideline, All-American quarterback Brian Dowling pleaded with head coach Carm Cozza to allow him to enter the game as a defensive back. Cozza calmly explained that it would be unfair to deny any starter the opportunity to finish the most important game of his college career.

The remaining thirty-five thousand fans squinted through the murky twilight as Harvard drove to the six-yard line with a run by Champi (aided by a fifteen-yard face-mask penalty) and a plunging draw play by Crim. As time expired, Champi scrambled desperately before drilling a touchdown pass to halfback Vic Gatto in the corner of the endzone. For an instant Harvard Stadium became chapel silent, as if its ghosts would deem the impossible possible. Champi, set behind a line that included future Oscar-winner Tommy Lee Jones, made the final play of his collegiate career unforgettable as he hit tight end Pete Varney just over the goal line for a two-point conversion and a 29–29 tie.

Perhaps the *Harvard Crimson* best captured the essence of the contest in a headline that read "Harvard Wins 29–29."

Snapshots from the Decade

Arthur Ashe, seen here at Long-wood Cricket Club in Brookline, was undoubtedly one of the best players ever to play the game of tennis. He was the first African American to win the U.S. Open (1968), the Australian Open (1970), and Wimbledon (1975). He was also the first African American to be included on the U.S. Davis Cup Team. Ashe was a longtime supporter of Sportsman's Tennis Club in Dorchester.

In the ninety-fourth running of the Kentucky Derby, Dancer's Image finished first but was disqualified from the purse money because of the appearance of the anti-inflammatory drug Bute in his bloodstream. To this day, owner Peter Fuller (center) of Boston is adamant that the horse was clean. He felt one reason for the disqualification was that the Kentucky Derby racing establishment considered him an outsider.

Kathrine Switzer (#261) became an international celebrity in 1967 when she was accosted by Boston Marathon directors Will Cloney and Jock Semple. At the time, race regulations forbade women competitors, and the pair objected to Switzer's use of an official race number, which she obtained by entering under the name "K. Switzer." This photograph was picked up by news agencies all over the world.

In the 1966–67 off-season, Carl Yastrzemski embarked on an ambitious exercise routine with trainer Gene Berde of the Colonial Health Club. He emerged a new man and in 1967 seemed like a combination of fictional baseball heroes Roy Hobbs and "Shoeless Joe from Hannible Mo." He won baseball's Triple Crown by leading the American League in home runs, batting average, and RBIs, and led the Red Sox to the 1967 World Series.

the Seventies

Looie-Looie: The Magic of Luis Tiant

Luis used to give me one of his looks and simply say to me . . . Just give me the ball . . . it was his way of letting me know he was ready for anything.
—Dick O'Connell, Red Sox general manager, 1965–79

Statistics reveal only a sliver of the magic that characterized Luis Tiant's major league career. In fact, Tiant enjoyed two careers, the first as the fireballing ace of the Cleveland Indians and the second as the cagey pitching version of a Cuisinart for the Red Sox of the seventies.

Red Sox fans are asked periodically which pitcher they'd select to pitch a big game, such as the seventh game of the World Series. Anybody over the age of thirty-five who answers anyone but Luis Tiant (Pedro Martinez is approaching this status) wasn't paying attention. Luis Tiant is as much the standard for big games as was Joe Wood in his day and Cy Young before him.

Luis Tiant owned Fenway Park in a manner previously achieved only by Ted Williams and Tris Speaker. With chants of "Loo-ie, Loo-ie" greeting his every start, Tiant won 122 games in eight seasons with the Red Sox. Included in those victories were three seasons with twenty or more victories and a succession of clutch victories rivaled only by those of Cy Young.

Tiant not only won the opening game of the 1975 American League playoffs with a three-hit victory over the three-time World Champion Oakland Athletics, but followed up his win with two more in the World Series. An international television audience watched as Luis Tiant, Sr., flown in from Cuba, tossed the ceremonial first pitch of the 1975 World Series at Fenway Park. His son then took over to hurl a 6–0 shutout, followed by a complete-game win in game four. Although hard hit in game six, Tiant kept the Red Sox in the game long enough for Bernie Carbo and Carlton Fisk to save the day.

Tiant's big-game heroics didn't end in 1975. Three seasons later, in his final appearance for the Red Sox on September 30, 1978, Tiant shut out the Blue Jays 7–0, in the game that set up the Red Sox playoff game with the Yankees.

Although he didn't do much at the plate, Luis Tiant's pitching kept the Red Sox in the 1975 World Series.

The Catcher Next Door: Carlton Fisk

New England has always been a hotbed for catchers. Among the receivers produced by the region have been the likes of "Rough" Bill Carrigan, Mickey "Black Mike" Cochrane, Birdie Tebbets, Gabby Hartnett, and Jim Hegan. In the mold of these greats came Carlton Fisk, a native of Bellows Falls, Vermont, and resident of Charlestown, New Hampshire. Movie-star handsome and large enough to be a power forward or tight end, Fisk became the greatest catcher in Red Sox history and one of the greatest in baseball history.

Fisk burst upon the scene in 1972 and captured American League Rookie-of-the-Year honors while batting .293 and hitting twenty-two home runs. In eleven seasons with the Red Sox, he battled a succession of injuries to bat .284 and hit 162 home runs. His tenure in Boston was characterized by his stern control of the pitching staff and his intense competitiveness. In particular, Fisk's rivalry with Yankee catcher Thurman Munson underscored the tribal animosity between the two teams and made each and every game between the two an event.

Baseball fans will forever remember Fisk as the hero of the most replayed baseball moment in history. His home run off Pat Darcy of the Cincinnati Reds in the twelfth inning of the sixth game of the 1975 World Series gave the world the "reaction shot," now a standard component of all sports television. And although Boston would lose the series, Fisk's blast gave Red Sox fans a moment to savor forever. Fisk was the first catcher selected for the Red Sox Hall of Fame. He was inducted into the National Baseball Hall of Fame in July 2000.

Three-shot sequence of Carlton Fisk's game-winning home run in game six of the 1975 World Series

Living Large at Left Guard: John Hannah

John Hannah is the greatest offensive lineman I have ever coached.
—Paul "Bear" Bryant, University of Alabama head football coach,
1958–82

John Hannah is the only member of the Pro Football Hall of Fame to date to have played his entire career with the New England Patriots. Many football experts consider him to be the greatest offensive lineman in pro football history.

The native of Albertville, Alabama, was hardly a one-sport wonder in high school and college. He won national prep honors in wrestling in high school and set a school record in the shot put while earning three letters in track at the University of Alabama. His brother Charlie, a lineman with the Oakland Raiders, once remarked to *Sports Illustrated,* "He didn't even work at track. He'd just show up for the meets. There were so many things he could do. At that time he might have been the greatest large athlete in the world." NFL scouts agreed after witnessing Hannah churn his way through a 40-yard sprint in 4.8 seconds.

The New England Patriots used their first-round draft pick in 1973 to snare John Hannah, considered by many to be the greatest offensive lineman ever to put on a uniform. In 1991, he became the first member of the Patriots ever to be elected to the Pro Football Hall of Fame.

The Patriots selected Hannah with the fourth overall pick in the 1973 draft, and the six-foot two-inch, 265-pound guard quickly made his mark as the first offensive lineman in team history to start in his first game as a rookie. He later earned nine Pro Bowl appearances and missed only five of the 188 games the Patriots played during his career.

For much of his career, Hannah was grossly underpaid. In protest, he and linemate Leon Gray held out for three games during the 1977 season. The next season, armed with the services of agent Howard Slusher, Hannah signed a four-year contract comparable to those of other top-rated linemen.

Hannah more than earned his money. He excelled despite playing for teams that never met his personal standard of excellence—save for his final season of 1985. It was then that he helped lead the Patriots to their first-ever Super Bowl appearance and the first-ever by a wild card team. Following the Patriots' blowout loss to the Chicago Bears in the 1986 Super Bowl in New Orleans, Hannah underwent surgery on his left knee and both shoulders. He announced his retirement shortly thereafter. After selling his Alabama farm, Hannah went into the financial services business in Boston. In 1991, the successful businessman and adopted Bostonian was elected to the Pro Football Hall of Fame in Canton, Ohio.

 ## *The Best There Ever Was: Bobby Orr*

As a child I watched Hobey Baker at the old arena. I played against Howie Morenz when I played for the Bruins during which time I was paired on defense with Eddie Shore. I also watched the likes of Syl Apps, Gordie Howe, and Wayne Gretzky. However, I must say that there has never been a greater hockey player than Bobby Orr. He did things that players have never done, before or since.
—George Owen, Boston Bruins, 1928–31

If a player better than Bobby Orr ever comes along I pray that the good Lord allows me to live long enough to see him play.
—Milt Schmidt, Boston Bruins player, head coach, and general manager, 1936–42, 1945–54, 1955–72.

After the first period of the first game I ever played against Bobby Orr I skated over to referee Frank Udvari and suggested that he drop two pucks to start the next period . . . one for Bobby Orr and one for the rest of us. I knew that was the only way we'd ever see it.
—*Bobby Hull, Chicago Blackhawks, 1957–72*

To have watched Bobby Orr at the height of his talents was the closest many Boston hockey fans will ever get to witnessing the practice of pure genius. It is no exaggeration to compare his prodigious skills to those of performers such as Vaslav Nijinsky, Babe Ruth, Pele, Charlie Parker, Elvis, or Isadora Duncan. Like them, he not only changed the art of his craft but also burned an indelible image on the minds of all who watched him. When I think of perfection I recall the birth of my children, Breughel's painting of the hunters in the snow, the final movement of Beethoven's Fifth Symphony, and any one of Bobby Orr's multitude of breathtaking rink-length rushes.

Bobby Orr not only changed the manner in which hockey was played but also opened the game up to millions of fans and players who otherwise would have never enjoyed the game. When the National Hockey League went from six to twelve teams in 1967–68, it coincided with the start of the Bobby Orr era. The game had never seen a player as talented and charismatic. He was the player everyone wanted to be, the dream date of female fans, and the boy any mother would love to have escort her daughter to the prom.

In suburban Boston, hockey became the growth industry of the seventies as hockey rinks sprouted like crabgrass and players felt lucky to get ice time at 4:30 A.M. When CBS began broadcasting NHL games across America in the late sixties, the Bruins went from being local heroes to national cult figures. Soon, books such as *Bobby Orr and the Big Bad Bruins* and *We Love You Bruins* appeared on bookstore shelves from coast to coast. By the spring of 1970, all the Bruins and Bobby Orr needed to do to assure their immortality was win the Stanley Cup.

The 1970 season for the Bruins was a year marked by trauma and triumph. The team suffered a terrible loss during the preseason when veteran defenseman Teddy Green suffered a fractured skull in a vicious stick fight with Wayne Maki of the Vancouver Canucks. As a result of the fight, the popular assistant captain narrowly escaped death and faced the certain loss of one season and possibly the remainder of his career.

But the team regrouped and rebounded following the loss of Green and all but swaggered though the regular season, playing with a combination of brilliance and typical Bruins grit. This was a team that meshed as well as any of Art Ross's three Stanley Cup winners. Leading the way were center Phil Esposito, veteran captain John Bucyk, goalie Gerry Cheevers, and Bobby Orr.

During the 1970 season Orr captured the Norris Trophy as best defenseman and at the same time led the league in scoring, an unheard-of achievement for a defenseman. It was an exploit similar to Babe Ruth's breaking the all-time single-season home run record in 1919 while also pitching for the Red Sox. Orr's unprecedented feat also won him the Hart Trophy as league MVP and *Sports Illustrated*'s "Sportsman of the Year" award. Almost lost in his trophy case were the honors that may have been the most significant of them all: namely, the miniature Stanley Cup awarded all players on the winning team and the Conn Smythe Award for playoff MVP.

Most Bostonians and all Bruins fans know where they were at the moment Bobby Orr scored in overtime on the afternoon of May 10, 1970, to give the Bruins their first Stanley Cup in twenty-nine years. This image of Orr being upended by Noel Picard after having just beaten goalie Glenn Hall is one of the most enduring photographs in Boston sports history.

The engraving of these gems commenced soon after the events that took place at Boston Garden on the afternoon of Mothers Day, 1970. As the broadcast crews from CBS prepared to televise the fourth and possible final game of the Stanley Cup Finals between the Bruins and St. Louis Blues, scalpers reaped hundreds of dollars for prime seats. It had been twenty-nine years since then-Bruins captain Dit Clapper had hoisted the Cup, and Boston was poised to party.

Sometimes a moment in time is so perfect that, when captured on film, it is worth more than a thousand words. Thus was the case when the perfect player scored the perfect goal in a setting of near perfection. When Bobby Orr scored the deciding goal of the Stanley Cup in overtime, his triumphant celebration was captured at the precise apex of flight by *Boston Herald* photographer Ray Lussier. It is an image whose brilliance both captures and reflects upon the genius of its subject. It is one of the great sports photographs of all time and a near icon to Bruins fans.

 ## The 1972–73 New England Whalers: Boston's Other Champions

By 1970, the Boston Bruins could have easily sold out the Boston Garden three or four times over as the hockey boom reached incredible heights. Hockey quickly became a cottage industry in the region, with parents spending hundreds of dollars to outfit their kids and send them to hockey camps. The Bruins capitalized on the boom by placing their top minor league affiliate in the Boston Garden and naming them the Boston Braves. Boston was primed to receive a second major league hockey team.

The economic potential of the game was not lost on the founders of the fledgling World Hockey Association (WHA). They wisely planted one of the charter franchises in Boston. Paying a nominal league entry fee of only twenty-five thousand dollars, team president Howard Baldwin and four partners founded the New England Whalers and secured home ice at both Boston Arena and Boston Garden. They then invested their money in former Boston University coach Jack Kelley and top-flight players such as former Bruins Ted Green and Tommy Williams.

Former Bruins defenseman Ted Green (right) was captain of the Whalers when they won the first championship in WHA history, defeating Bobby Hull and the Winnipeg Jets in a hard-fought five-game series. Green skated for the Whalers until 1975, when he was traded to Winnipeg for future considerations.

The franchise's first home game on October 12, 1972, drew a capacity crowd of 14,552 to Boston Garden as the Whalers faced off against the Philadelphia Blazers. Fans were treated to a celebration of the Bruins' past and hockey's future when former teammates Ted Green and Derek Sanderson took part in a ceremonial face-off. Few fans would have expected that they were watching the start of a hockey revolution while paying homage to two stars of what turned out to be the last Bruins Stanley Cup team of the century.

Following an inspiring 4–3 opening night victory over a Philadelphia Blazers team that featured Bernie Parent in goal, the Whalers went on to enjoy a superb record of 46–30–2 and lead the league with ninety-four points. In the playoffs, they opened against the Ottawa Nationals, whom they dispatched in five games. Next they faced the Cleveland Crusaders, led by former Bruins goalie Gerry Cheevers. Again they captured the series in five games and prepared for a showdown with Bobby Hull and the Winnepeg Jets in the finals.

After forging a three-games-to-one lead over Winnipeg, the Whalers faced a national TV audience on Sunday, May 6, as they prepared for the fifth and possibly decisive game of the WHA Avco Cup series.

Former Montreal Canadien and Weymouth native Larry Pleau scored a hat trick to help lead the Whalers to a wide open 9–6 victory and the first cup title in WHA history. Because their victory came a month after the reigning Stanley Cup champion Bruins had relinquished their crown with a first-round playoff loss to the New York Rangers, the Whalers would stake their claim as the last Boston-based professional hockey team to claim the title of "world champions" in the twentieth century.

The Lunch Pail Athletic Club, Don Cherry, Prop.

Donald Stewart "Grapes" Cherry exemplified the Boston Bruins work ethic and toughness in a manner similar to that of team builder Art Ross. Although Cherry, a moderately talented blue-collar player, played only one game for the franchise in the fifties, he paid his dues by spending sixteen winters as a minor league player and coach. His return to Boston as head coach in 1974 came at a crucial time for a franchise in transition.

Don Cherry and Blue in 1978. Cherry, a former minor league journeyman, made the big time as coach of the Bruins, serving the team from 1974 to 1979. His teams were known as the "Lunch Pail A.C.," reflecting both their work ethic and style of play.

Cherry inherited a team that not only had lost a heartbreaking Stanley Cup Final that spring to the Philadelphia Flyers but had also been decimated by defections to the World Hockey Association. Likewise, the team was beset with injuries, particularly the recurring knee ailments of Bobby Orr. Many predicted the Bruins' glory days had come and gone.

Cherry immediately captured the imagination of the fans and press corps alike, displaying a sharp wit in the manner of former Red Sox manager Dick Williams. He also qualified as a genuine eccentric, bringing Blue, his bull terrier, to most practices. Blue would often be the coach's point of reference while he discussed the courage of favorite players like Terry O'Reilly or John Wensink.

With the support of General Manager Harry Sinden, Cherry retooled the team from a precision instrument to an all-terrain vehicle built of various and sundry parts. Cherry's teams had a knack for playing over their heads and with a rough style that helped fans recover from the premature departure of Bobby Orr in 1976.

Cherry's Bruins made the Stanley Cup Finals in 1977 and 1978, only to lose to the vaunted Montreal Canadiens. The following season, Cherry's last in Boston, proved truly heartbreaking as the Bruins were eliminated from the playoffs by the Canadiens in an infamous seventh game at the Montreal Forum. In this pivotal game, the Bruins were penalized for having an extra player on the ice with several minutes remaining in the third period, which led to a game-tying power-play goal by Montreal's Guy Lafleur. Montreal went on to win the game. Most observers feel that this semifinal series was the de facto final, since both clubs were tabbed favorites to defeat the New York Rangers in the Stanley Cup Finals.

Cherry's departure from the Bruins came as the result of a rift with Harry Sinden, which both men termed "unfortunate and regrettable." Writer Clark Booth summed it up best when he commented that their irretrievable breakdown arose primarily because they were so much alike.

After a coaching stint with the Colorado Rockies, Cherry returned to his native Canada, where he has enjoyed a career as both a restaurateur and sports commentator extraordinaire. To this day he refers to himself as "a Bruin for life."

 ## *Boston Billy*

I dropped running after an 8:52 two mile, quit, just like that. I began smoking half a pack of cigarettes a day and when I moved to Boston and got a job at Peter Bent Brigham Hospital, I got myself a motorcycle for transportation. After somebody stole the motorcycle, I had to run to work.
—*Bill Rodgers*

Bill Squires knew. Perhaps several members of the Greater Boston Track Club also knew that Bill Rodgers, in a perfect setting, would turn the marathon world on its ear. Rodgers had run the race once before in 1973 but had been forced to drop out, which led him to quit running altogether. But after picking up the sport again, Rodgers was more determined than ever to conquer the tricky course, as well as the distance. His small frame and compact stride were the perfect combination for the hilly course.

For most of 1973 and 1974, Rodgers worked with Squires on restoring a running career that had led him to Wesleyan University, where he competed with teammates Amby Burfoot and Jeff Galloway, both world-class marathoners. By April 1975, Rodgers was ready to join his college friends at the pinnacle of the running world. He selected Boston for his coming-out party.

The weather conditions for the 1975 Boston Marathon were ideal: windy and fifty-five degrees, with prevailing tailwinds leading to Boston. Rodgers had returned recently from the World Cross-Country Championships in Rabat, Morocco, where he'd won a bronze medal. Because of that surprisingly good finish, he was hoping for a time of 2:12 at Boston.

In 1975, Bill Rodgers became a fan favorite at the marathon. Along with Frank Shorter, Rodgers was responsible for the running boom that hit America in the early eighties.

As Rodgers waited for the race to start, his brother Charlie brought him some gardening gloves to ward off the chill. These joined a homemade uniform comprising a hand-lettered mesh shirt, which read BOSTON GBTC, and a New Balance headband. The Nike running flats worn by Rodgers were among the first marathon competition shoes produced by the then fledgling company.

Rodgers hung with the lead pack for the first half of the race but soon focused on race leader Jerome Drayton of Canada. After hearing a spectator cheer Drayton, Rodgers was consumed with a desire to run the Canadian into the ground. As soon as Rodgers passed Drayton, he surged toward the Newton hills, where he figured to win the race.

So relaxed was Rodgers on the hills that he stopped four times to drink water and once to tie his shoe. This last gesture so agitated race official and legend Jock Semple that he clambered off the press truck to plead with Rodgers, "You can set the record if ya get going, you've got to get going, lad." Rodgers soon returned to his running groove and set an American marathon record, clocking an impressive 2:09:55 to break his personal best by nearly ten minutes. The running revolution that Frank Shorter had begun in 1972 with his Olympic Marathon triumph now had a new commanding general.

In the span of a year, Bill Rodgers left the ranks of the amateur runner and helped establish running as a paid profession for himself and his colleagues. Rodgers's subsequent marathon victories in New York and Boston would further establish him as Shorter's natural successor in American running dominance.

His 1975 Boston Marathon victory will forever be Bill Rodgers's favorite. "That marathon, in terms of racing and how I did, was a big surprise to me. I broke Shorter's record with a 2:09:55 and it came out of the blue," he recalls. It was also the race that established Rodgers as the spokesperson for the sport, heralding a new era of sponsorship since embraced by the race. No one has run Boston with as much seeming insouciance or with as great an effect, before or since.

 ## *Twelve Angry Men: The 1975–76 Boston Celtics*

The triple-overtime game is what people most remember, and why not? A quarter-century later, Boston's 128–126 victory over the Phoenix Suns in game five of the 1976 NBA Finals still has many who witnessed it insisting that it was the greatest NBA game ever played.

There was a lot to savor. Gar Heard's buzzer-beating, eighteen-foot jump shot, which created the third overtime; John Havlicek's leaner a few seconds before, which had given the Celtics an apparent victory; Jo Jo White's heroic fifteen points in the overtimes; a fan coming out of the stands to attack referee Richie Powers; coach Tom Heinsohn fainting after the game; the Celtics leading by twenty-two points early in the second quarter, but Phoenix refusing to fold; individual pyrotechnics supplied by the likes of Paul Westphal, Ricky Sobers, and Curtis Perry; referee Powers refusing to acknowledge Paul Silas's plea for a time-out he didn't have, which would have given Phoenix a chance to win via a technical foul; five men fouling out; and finally, Glenn McDonald's Warholian minute and eight seconds of third overtime glory (six vital points while playing for a fouled-out Silas).

But what those on the inside will remember most is the titanic emotional struggle endured by the Celtics, a team that all season long had battled age (both Havlicek and Don Nelson were thirty-six, while Silas, the team's conscience, was thirty-three), injury, and an inevitable strain between veteran players and a coach to whom they had grown weary of listening. The Celtics peaked at 35–13 on February 13, lurched

The 1975–76 Boston Celtics celebrate their championship at City Hall. Top row, left to right: Dave Cowens, Paul Silas, Jo Jo White, John Havlicek, Don Nelson, Charlie Scott, Steve Kuberski, Tom Boswell. Bottom row, left to right: Jim Ard, Glenn McDonald, Jerome Anderson, Kevin Stacom.

home at a 19–15 pace, and entered the playoffs as anything but a solid favorite.

Things had looked very gloomy when Havlicek emerged from a victory in the first playoff game against the Buffalo Braves with a torn plantar fascia in his left foot, an injury that hobbled him thereafter. But with Charlie Scott coming up big in the deciding sixth games against both Buffalo (31 points, 8 assists) and the Cleveland Cavaliers (20 points), the Celtics got into the finals against a surprise foe in the Phoenix Suns.

A foul-plagued Scott contributed little in the triple-overtime epic, but he turned out to be the only principal with fresh legs when everyone reconvened thirty-six hours later in Phoenix. Dave Cowens, with 21 points, 17 rebounds, and one particularly huge hoop emanating from a midcourt steal from Alvan Adams, came up big, while Scott played his third consecutive monster game six (25 points, 11 rebounds) in Boston's clinching 87–80 victory, which gave them championship number thirteen.

There were better Celtics championship teams, to be sure, but none ever had to conquer so many internal demons.

—*Bob Ryan*

the *Eighties*

Overtime Overdue: The 1980 Beanpot Tournament

Would you believe that in 1979 some Northeastern University hockey fans were lobbying for the Huskies to withdraw from the popular Bean-pot Tournament? Their reason: too much suffering. In twenty-seven years the Huskies had won only two semifinal contests, only to have their dreams of hockey nirvana squashed by Boston University in the finals; first in 1958, by a score of 9–3, and then in 1967, 4–0. If you had been a true Husky fan during this time you would have witnessed two second-place finishes, seven third-place finishes, eighteen last-place finishes, and, of course, zero championships. You were frustrated.

Wayne Turner celebrates his game-winning goal against Boston College in the 1980 Beanpot Tournament.

Beanpot 1980 did not look any more encouraging than had the past twenty-seven. The semifinal opponent was the Boston University Terriers, who were the defending champs but sported only a 9–8 record. However, the Huskies were a God-awful 3–11 and were at the bottom of the twelve-team ECAC. But this time things would be different. The game slid into overtime when Northeastern captain Wayne Turner tied the game at five with three minutes remaining. The overtime was all Northeastern, as the born-again Huskies attacked the Terriers' net. After four good North-eastern shots were turned aside, a John Montgomery slapshot from forty-five feet snuck in at 5:09 and rid Northeastern of the "Consolation Kids" moniker they had suffered with for thirteen straight years.

Meanwhile, in the other semifinal, Boston College dispatched Harvard by a score of 4–3 to run their record to 19–4–1, keep their number-one ECAC ranking secure, and move to number two in the national polls. Lots of hockey followers were disappointed. The final appeared to be a mismatch. And it started as such. Boston College raced out to a 3–1 lead in the first period. The Huskies then brought it to 3–3 after two periods,but Boston College scored six minutes into the third to reclaim the lead. Northeastern hopes were low until sophomore Paul McDougal tied the score with less than four minutes remaining.

Of the 14,456 fans attending the game, it appeared that 14,455 were for Northeastern as overtime started. After the teams traded shots, North-eastern's Dale Fernandi stole the puck, split two Boston College defend-ers, and slid the puck forward as he was tripped from behind. Captain Turner picked up the loose puck and fired it past the Boston College goalie. Pandemonium broke loose. Husky hockey hell was over.

—*Jack Grinold*

Do You Believe in Miracles?
The 1980 U.S. Olympic Hockey Team

They were the generation of American hockey players raised in an era when Bobby Orr and the Bruins were the staple of CBS national hockey telecasts on Sunday afternoons. They were the bleary-eyed kids glad to get ice time at five A.M. Their basements and garages were impromptu street hockey rinks where everyone wanted to take a slapper with a blade curved on the heat of mom's gas stove.

Hockey was as much a part of the seventies as the Brady Bunch and Peter Frampton. In metropolitan Boston alone there was an explosion in the construction of hockey rinks. The generation of American players that grew up during this era had much to celebrate, except for the fact that there were few Americans in the National Hockey League. Until the hockey boom erupted, the game had lived on the fringes of American sport, with the nation's best players coming exclusively from hotbeds such as Minnesota and New England. Even these players emerged from but a handful of schools and colleges. However, by the mid-seventies the game had started to widen its appeal, as thousands of youth players graduated to scholastic and collegiate programs.

Mike Eruzione, Jack O'Callahan, and Dave Silk are welcomed back to Boston in a ceremony at Walter Brown Arena at Boston University.

The 1980 United States Olympic hockey team was a perfect blend of old-school values and the enthusiasm of the new generation of players. Coach Herb Brooks of Minnesota had been the last player cut from the gold medal–winning 1960 U.S. Olympic hockey team, and nobody was hungrier than he to orchestrate a repeat of that improbable feat. Included on his roster were four Boston University Terriers, all from

Massachusetts, and all members of the generation that had skated in pre-dawn practices with visions of Orr in their heads. All would play key roles in the incredible U.S. victory at Lake Placid.

Captain Mike Eruzione was the veteran of the team. A native of Winthrop and former captain at Boston University, Eruzione was selected as captain both for his leadership skills and because many felt that Brooks had filled his lineup with too few Eastern players. Selecting Eruzione as captain was Brooks's way of easing tension on the team. Defenseman Jack O'Callahan, a Charlestown native out of Boston Latin and Boston University, helped shape the team's personality. His gap-toothed jack-o'-lantern smile and tough checking lent the team a swaggering attitude not unlike that of his hometown Bruins. Goalie Jim Craig of North Easton had recently led Boston University to an NCAA title. Teammate Dave Silk, a winger out of Thayer Academy and BU, skated as smoothly as his name. All were in for the fight of their lives.

The Olympic tournament started well for the U.S. team as they opened with a 2–2 tie against Sweden. The first glimmer of greatness came with a 7–3 trouncing of a heavily favored Czech team, after which Brooks's men beat West Germany, Romania, and Norway to set up a medal round game with the Soviet Union.

The context of the game included much drama, not the least of which being the announcement that the United States would boycott the 1980 Summer Olympics, to be held in Moscow. Not only were the Soviets unbeaten in Olympic competition since 1968 but they had just recently defeated the United States in an exhibition game at Madison Square Garden by a score of 10–3. The odds were stacked against the U.S. team.

The game was played in the afternoon and taped by ABC for future broadcast. Only a few radio outlets in the country picked it up, as even the most dedicated fans of the Americans expected their medal hopes to die hard against the best team in the world.

But at Lake Placid the Americans forged a miracle, fighting back to tie the game three times. The Hollywood ending was more than perfect, with Captain Mike Eruzione scoring the eventual game-winning goal halfway through the third period. The ten minutes that ensued proved to be the toughest skate in the Americans' young lives, as they staved off attack after attack. The final siren brought an eruption of joy unlike any celebration at an Olympics. The American players flung their sticks into the air and piled onto the ice to hug goalie Jim Craig and Eruzione. Jack O'Callahan's toothless smile would soon grace sports pages around the world.

The gold medal game against Finland, broadcast live, attracted a huge national audience. People in non-hockey outposts such as Texarkana and Key West stopped what they were doing, transfixed by their new heroes. Goalie Jim Craig had a great game, leading the team to a come-from-behind 4–2 victory. The Americans had to fight off three power plays in the third period and score three goals to seal the victory. The indelible images from the victory celebration were those of Craig, draped in an American flag, searching for his father in the stands, and Eruzione calling the entire team up to the podium for the gold medal presentation.

Not only did the U.S. victory signal the arrival of American hockey, but it also proved that sport still possessed the power to captivate and inspire an entire nation. Do you remember where you were when you learned we had beaten the Soviets?

The Big Three: Bird, Parish, and McHale

By the finish of the 1978–79 season, the Celtics Dynasty had been declared dead by most of the Boston media. The team had finished out of the playoffs the previous two seasons, and the organization was in almost complete disarray following a bizarre franchise swap between Irv Levin of the Celtics and John Y. Brown of the Buffalo Braves. Under terms of the arrangement, the Celtics were to remain in Boston under the direction of Brown's partner, Harry Mangurian, while the Braves were to move to San Diego—renamed the Clippers. All Celtics fans cared about was that John Havlicek had retired and the only two remaining links to their storied past—team president Red Auerbach and player-coach Dave Cowens—couldn't restore the team to glory by themselves.

The Big Three at Boston Garden. From left to right: Kevin McHale, Robert Parrish, and Larry Bird.

Red Auerbach, the man responsible for much of the Celtics' longtime success, had never faced a bigger challenge than rebuilding what was the worst team in franchise history. But a move that Auerbach had made prior to the 1978–79 season was about to pay off. After conferring with his assistant, Jan Volk, Auerbach had decided that the team would use its sixth pick in the 1978 NBA draft to select Larry Bird, a fourth-year junior at Indiana State University. Per NBA rules, the team was allowed to select Bird in the draft year in which he would have graduated had he not dropped out of college briefly. The Celtics exploited this technicality in their quest for the best available player. Auerbach felt Bird was well worth the wait.

In a short time Bird proved to be a savior for the Celtics. In the 1979–80 season, the Celtics—now coached by Bill Fitch—experienced the greatest single-season turnaround in league history. Celtics home attendance increased over forty-five percent, with most games sold out in advance. Although the team lost the Eastern Conference finals to Philadelphia by a margin of four games to one, it was clear that the team was only one or two players away from being championship-caliber.

Red Auerbach held the number-one pick in the NBA draft that summer and once again made a move that added to his legend. This time, he dealt the pick to the Golden State Warriors for center Robert Parish and the Warriors' number-three pick. Golden State was pleased to use their pick to select center Joe Barry Carroll of Purdue, while the Celtics plucked University of Minnesota forward Kevin McHale with the third pick.

Within a year, the Celtics were celebrating their thirteenth NBA title, with veteran forward Cedric Maxwell capturing playoff MVP honors. McHale secured his place on the season's all-rookie team, while Parish proved a worthy successor to Dave Cowens at center. Bird was simply the best Celtics player since Havlicek, and his presence assured the first-ever season of sellouts in franchise history.

If Larry Bird was the Celtics' Babe Ruth, then Parish and McHale took turns playing Lou Gehrig. Never has the league witnessed a more dominant front line. In their eleven seasons together, the Big Three of Bird, Parish, and McHale helped lead the Celtics to three NBA world championships and five finals appearances. During this time, Bird captured three NBA Most Valuable Player awards and appeared in eleven NBA All-Star Games, while Parish appeared in nine All-Star Games and McHale seven.

Doug Flutie: Winner

He will always be the finest athlete in his class. Doug Flutie can still dunk a basketball at Boston College alumni games and skate with the best of them in hockey scrimmages. Nearing forty, he still possesses the same enthusiasm that he brought to the Heights when he arrived as an untouted prospect in 1980.

Flutie arrived at Boston College from Natick , after receiving the last scholarship on Jack Bicknell's football team. At five-feet nine-inches, the young quarterback had to battle just to get recognized in practice. But after a dazzling performance as a substitute against Penn State, the freshman began to turn heads. Soon he was starting for Bicknell.

Doug Flutie not only brought new respect to the Boston College football program but also made the school nationally famous on the afternoon of November 23, 1984. His forty-six-yard "Hail Mary" touchdown pass to Gerard Phelan, on the final play of a nationally televised game against the University of Miami, captured the Heisman Trophy for Flutie as the Eagles won by a score of 47–45. He would later lead the Eagles to a 45–28 drubbing of the University of Houston in the Cotton Bowl.

Doug Flutie's heroics put Boston College football back on the national sports scene for the first time since Frank Leahy led the Eagles to the 1941 Sugar Bowl. To this day, many credit Flutie with generating millions of dollars of television income for the school through televised regular season games and bowl game appearances.

Following his college career, Flutie made headlines with his mega-contract from the New Jersey Generals of the short-lived USFL. Then, after

Doug Flutie embraces brother Darren following the "Miracle in Miami," November 1984.

brief stints with the Chicago Bears and the New England Patriots, in 1990 Flutie moved to the Canadian Football League, where he flourished as no other player had in the history of the league. He captured the league's MVP award six times, led the league in passing five times, and won Gray Cup titles with the Calgary Stampeders in 1992 and the Toronto Argonauts in 1996 and 1997.

In 1998, Flutie rejoined the NFL as a member of the Buffalo Bills and received a new lease on his professional career when first-string quarterback Rob Johnson was injured. Taking over the team five games into the season, Flutie directed the Bills to a 7–3 record and a playoff berth in ten starts. His performance earned him the NFL Comeback Player of the Year award and a trip to the Pro Bowl.

Off the field, Flutie continues to work out up to four hours a day and devotes much of his time to generating donations for the Doug Flutie Jr. Foundation for Autism. In 1997, Flutie's hometown of Natick named a street in his honor. It is appropriately called "Flutie Pass" and runs through the heavily traveled Natick Mall.

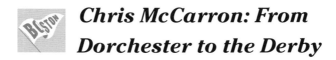 Chris McCarron: From Dorchester to the Derby

Like other kids who grew up in Dorchester in the late sixties and early seventies, Chris McCarron wanted to play for the Boston Bruins. McCarron idolized Orr, Esposito, Cheevers, and company and dreamed that he too might possibly get as far as Boston Garden. Little did he know that the dreams he would realize would be just as significant, however unimaginable.

As it turned out, McCarron was too small for the Bruins. Instead, he worked his way to fame as a jockey. In the process, he traveled as far from Dorchester as one can while remaining in the continental United States. Riding mostly out of southern California's Del Mar track, McCarron became one of the most successful jockeys of his time. He has won each of the Triple Crown races on two occasions, most notably aboard Alysheba in 1987, when he won the Kentucky Derby and the Preakness before falling in the Belmont Stakes. He also has captured seven Breeder's Cup races in a variety of classes. He led all jockeys in money won in 1980, 1981, 1984, and 1991 and continues to place in the top ten for money earned.

As of January 1, 1998, McCarron was the leading all-time money winner among thoroughbred jockeys, with purses totaling $213,851,293. Not bad for a Dorchester boy too small for the Bruins and too big for the local racing scene.

Joan Benoit's
Run for the Record

In 1979, Joan Benoit arrived from Maine as a long shot to win the Boston Marathon and proceeded to outrun favorite Patti Catalano. In the process she not only won the race but also captured the imagination of the crowd by wearing her Bowdoin College singlet and an askew Red Sox cap, which she donned for the final four miles of the race. Barely a dozen years after pioneers such as Roberta Gibb and Kathrine Switzer had proved that women could run the event, Benoit was clocking times that would have bested the likes of former male champions such as Clarence DeMar.

Among Chris McCarron's legendary mounts have been John Henry and 1987 Kentucky Derby and Preakness winner Alysheba.

Like her friend and New England counterpart Bill Rodgers, Benoit was the product of a running community that had produced world-class marathoners for most of the twentieth century. Training with runners such as Judi St. Hilaire, Lynn Jennings, and Jacqui Gareau did much to hone her technique and stoke her competitive fires.

In 1982, Benoit moved to Boston to coach the Boston University women's track team. She also underwent an operation on both heels and wondered if she would ever again run competitively. However, by April 1983, she was fully recovered and fresh from competing at the World Cross-Country Championships in Gateshead, England. While in England she decided to run the Boston Marathon again, motivated by an arduous training run with sportswriter and former Olympic marathoner Kenny Moore.

By 1983, women's marathoning had experienced an enormous surge in popularity. The International Olympic Committee had just sanctioned the event for the 1984 Los Angeles Summer Games, and many women runners were considering a step up to the event from shorter track events. Joan Benoit, with as diverse an athletic background as any marathon runner, was poised for a breakthrough.

Benoit's judgment could not have been better. It took her only ten thousand meters to shred the women's field at the 1983 Boston Marathon. For twenty miles she competed solely with the clock in the company of world-class marathoner Kevin Ryan, who was reporting on the race for WBZ radio. She set records at each race checkpoint and clearly was enjoying her greatest race to date.

Cape Elizabeth, Maine, native Joan Benoit won her second Boston Marathon in 1983, shattering the women's course and world records with a time of 2:22:43. With her Olympic win at Los Angeles in 1984, Benoit capped perhaps the most prestigious double in distance running, becoming the first runner ever to capture both the Boston and Olympic marathons.

As Benoit strode down Commonwealth Avenue, the hometown crowd brought her home with a world record of 2:22:43. Benoit's time took over two minutes off the existing record. It was a time that would have captured fifty-four of the previous eighty-six men's Boston Marathons. Benoit's victory established her as the favorite for the inaugural women's Olympic Marathon a year later.

Roger Clemens Fans Twenty

In the 110-year history of major league baseball, few individual achievements haven't been reached in a single game, much less duplicated. Achievements such as four homers or seven hits in a game, while rare, have been accomplished several times. But in the 306,616 major league games leading up to April 29, 1986, no pitcher had ever recorded as many as twenty strikeouts in a nine-inning game.

The game between the Red Sox and the Seattle Mariners that evening had a bizarre feeling from the start. Attendance was well below capacity, as only 13,414 hearty souls braved the cold and chose to forgo a Celtics playoff game against the Atlanta Hawks to see Clemens go for his fourth straight win. The game had also been bumped from its normal place on AM radio to a more obscure FM station so that the Celtics game could be showcased to a larger audience. Furthermore, the game was televised only on New England Sports Network, whose cable-borne signal wasn't even available in most Boston neighborhoods. Unless you bought a ticket, chances are you neither saw nor heard the game until after the fact.

The chilly weather was perfect for power pitcher Roger Clemens, who thrived in such conditions. He struck out six batters through three innings and was just hitting his stride. In the fourth, after Spike Owen singled to right, Clemens struck out Phil Bradley and Ken Phelps before Gorman Thomas chipped a foul toward Don Baylor, which the first baseman dropped. Clemens proceeded to strike out Thomas, then learned in the dugout that Baylor had dropped the ball on purpose, knowing that the pitcher would record yet another strikeout.

By the seventh inning, Clemens had struck out sixteen Mariner batters. But Gorman Thomas homered off a cross-seam fastball to give the Mariners a short-lived 1–0 lead. By the end of eight, Clemens had struck out two more Mariners and was within sight of a new major league strikeout record. Dwight Evans socked a three-run homer off Mike Moore to give Clemens the cushion he needed to finish his job.

In the top of the ninth, Clemens got shortstop Spike Owen to chase a high fastball for the record-tying nineteenth strikeout. With one out, he broke the record by getting Mariner left fielder Phil Bradley to stare at a called third strike on a pitch that reached ninety-seven miles per hour on the radar gun. After catcher Rich Gedman gunned the ball to Wade Boggs at third base, Boggs walked over to Clemens, handed him the ball and said, "Awesome." Clemens's pitching line for the night was an amazing twenty strikeouts, zero walks, and one earned run.

Roger Clemens had made history before slightly more spectators than had watched Ted Williams hit a home run in his final at-bat. A meager radio audience listened as Ken Coleman and Joe Castiglione relayed

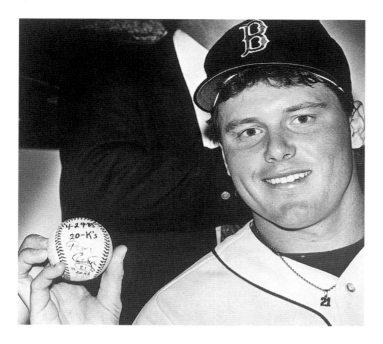

Roger Clemens with twentieth-strikeout ball, April 29, 1986

the action via the FM airwaves in Boston. And fewer still watched on NESN.

For the first time since the Dead Ball era, pitching was preeminent at Fenway Park, and Roger Clemens was nothing short of a modern-day Smoky Joe Wood. His twenty-strikeout performance was his fourth straight win. Clemens would go on to win another ten straight games as the Red Sox staked their claim to a division and a league title.

In 1996, Clemens duplicated his feat at Tiger Stadium. On May 6, 1998, young Kerry Wood of the Chicago Cubs tied the mark in only his fifth major league start when he struck out twenty Houston Astros while allowing only one questionable hit and no walks. The next day Wood received a congratulatory telegram from his boyhood idol, Roger Clemens.

The Happy Warrior: Billy Sullivan

The 1986 Super Bowl was as appropriate a going-away gift as has ever been bestowed upon an owner in sports. In a year in which Billy Sullivan knew that he must surely give up the team he had founded and painstakingly built, he found himself embroiled in an Irish American family drama as familiar as any penned by Eugene O'Neill.

Billy Sullivan was forced to sell the New England Patriots because of enormous financial losses incurred by the team when his son, attorney Chuck Sullivan, co-produced a Michael Jackson concert tour along with boxing promoter Donald King. The Sullivans were lucky to emerge from the deal with their shirts and not much else. Three decades of hard work evaporated over one long summer.

Meanwhile, the 1985 Patriots hadn't been picked to do anything except maybe finish at .500 with an outside shot at a playoff spot. As the season unwound, such predictions seemed fair until the team mounted a great effort in the final regular-season home game to defeat the Cincinnati Bengals and clinch a wild-card playoff berth.

As the Sullivan family made arrangements to meet prospective buyers, the team prepared for a playoff schedule consisting entirely of road games. For three weekends, New England football fans stood enthralled as their team defied the odds to beat the New York Jets, Los Angeles Raiders, and Miami Dolphins to clinch a Super Bowl berth against the Chicago Bears. Billy Sullivan stood like Frank Skeffington in "The Last Hurrah," his lifetime dream having been achieved at the eleventh hour. Hollywood writers couldn't have written a better script unless they had researched his past and documented where he had come from to get to the pinnacle.

The Boston Patriots were born in the imagination of Billy Sullivan. Sullivan started his career as one of the first great public relations men in sports. Working for football coaching legend Frank Leahy at Notre Dame, Sullivan helped promote the legend and myth of Notre Dame football. It was Sullivan who spearheaded the groundbreaking promotional campaign to secure the Heisman Trophy for quarterback Angelo Bertelli in 1943.

Soon Sullivan's skills brought him home to work for the National League Boston Braves. Here he devised such fan-friendly innovations as a Braves team film, which was made available to community groups at no charge, and an array of promotional dates at the park that included fan appreciation day. The underdog Braves needed the promotional savvy and hustle of Sullivan, who wasted no time in promoting third baseman Bob Elliot as the successful candidate for National League MVP in 1947. Sullivan's "rookie rocket," an airplane slated to deliver Boston journalists to Braves' farm teams in 1952, allowed many a first peek at a prospect named Hank Aaron.

A lifelong sports fan, Billy Sullivan led the New England Patriots for three decades.

Perhaps his greatest achievement for the Braves was the creation of the Jimmy Fund in 1947. The cancer charity has since raised tens of millions of dollars for research and has helped drop the mortality rate for children's cancer to record lows. When the Braves pulled up stakes in

1953 after seventy-six years in Boston, Sullivan stepped out of sports and into a business career. It would last but a few years until the lure of sports struck once more with the Patriots.

In 1959, Sullivan had to borrow money from relatives and even raid his children's piggy banks to secure the twenty-five thousand dollar rights for the fledgling American Football League franchise. Sullivan felt he could accomplish what countless others had tried and failed to do in sports-mad Boston: successfully launch a pro football team—the Patriots.

Sullivan was everyman as team owner. The opportunity presented by the Patriots represented a once-in-a-lifetime chance for the former public relations executive to sell both himself and what he saw as a most possible dream. The American Football League was starting in the wake of the most stirring championship football game of all time, the 1959 title game between the New York Giants and Baltimore Colts. For years Boston had been Giants country, and Sullivan viewed it as largely unplowed territory for a sport that had captivated the rest of the nation.

Everything about the Boston Patriots was grass roots. They practiced on a glorified median strip leading to Logan Airport named White Stadium, where they viewed game films on a bedsheet stretched across a blackboard. Their logo, taken from a sports cartoon by artist Phil Bissell, was selected by Billy's son Patrick, who broke the stalemate in a late-night meeting by answering his dad's query as to which logo he preferred. Sullivan possessed enough stubbornness and faith to prevail in straits that would have tried the endurance of most men.

The team was not only undercapitalized but also unwanted. The Patriots lived in nomadic fashion for their first eleven seasons, going from Boston University's Nickerson Field to Fenway Park to Boston College's Alumni Stadium to Harvard Stadium and finally to their present home at Foxboro Stadium. And, until 1986, the team saw little success, perpetually finishing near the bottom of their division.

Although Hollywood wouldn't have scripted the Patriots' one-sided loss to Chicago in their first Super Bowl, their story and that of their owner was still fairy tale material. Pro football's happy warrior died in 1998, having seen his team ascend to the status of the region's second favorite franchise behind the Red Sox.

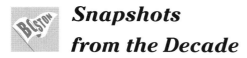

Snapshots
from the Decade

Red Sox pitcher Dennis "Oil Can" Boyd was a throwback to the spirit of the Negro Leagues, a player who was both colorful and doggedly competitive. Not only did he wear his uniform in an old-fashioned style, but he often commented that he felt "old-timey." He aspired to pitch like his hero, Satchel Paige.

"Marvelous" Marvin Hagler with daughter Charelle Monique and Goody and Pat Petronelli following Hagler's victory over Thomas Hearns in April 1985. Hagler renewed the Brockton tradition of championship boxing when he ruled the eighties as middleweight champion of the world. The Hearns bout has been called one of the great title fights of all time.

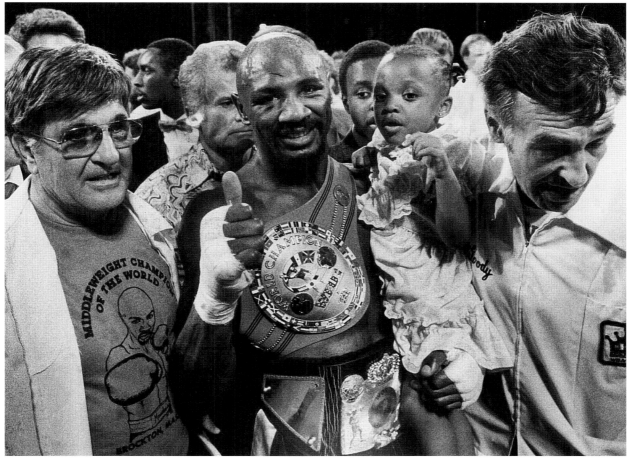

Red Sox Clinch the Division: A Photo Album

On Sunday, September 28, 1986, the Boston Red Sox clinched their first Eastern Division title since 1975 as Dennis "Oil Can" Boyd pitched a superb 12–3 victory over the Toronto Blue Jays to record a career-high sixteenth win. Following the game, Roger Clemens rode around Fenway Park on a police horse, while other players savored their unexpected victory. Little did they know what lay in wait for them: an incredible comeback victory over the California Angels in the American League Championship Series, followed by devastating losses to the New York Mets in the sixth and seventh games of the World Series.

Bruce Hurst at his locker

However, for one perfect afternoon in late September, there was no talk of curses, blisters, or wild pitches. There was only a division title and the possibility of greater glory to consider.

Bruce Hurst continued to grin through a postseason that saw the left-hander compile a combined 3–0 record in both the league championship series and World Series. In twenty-three World Series innings, Hurst struck out seventeen Mets and allowed but five runs while winning two games.

Calvin Schiraldi

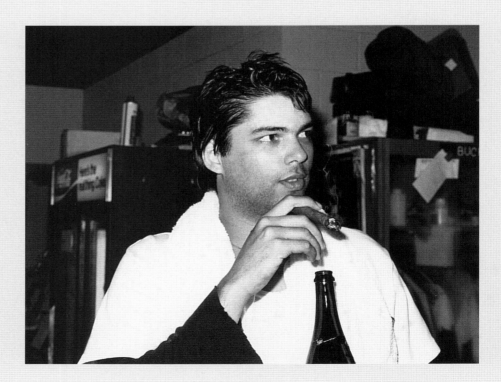

Right-handed reliever Calvin Schiraldi was the third member of the 1983 University of Texas NCAA champions to play for the 1986 Red Sox, along with pitcher Roger Clemens and shortstop Spike Owen. Schiraldi was superb in his first run through the American League, before hitters began timing his fastball to devastating effect. In postseason play in 1986, Schiraldi was a combined 0–3 against the Angels and the Mets. Among Schiraldi's losses was the infamous sixth game of the World Series, in which his wild pitch and first-baseman Bill Buckner's untimely error gave the Mets a victory.

Coming off a subpar performance in the American League Championship Series, Dwight Evans batted .308 with a team-leading nine RBI in the 1986 World Series. Evans is shown following the division-clinching game beside the locker he inherited from Carl Yastrzemski.

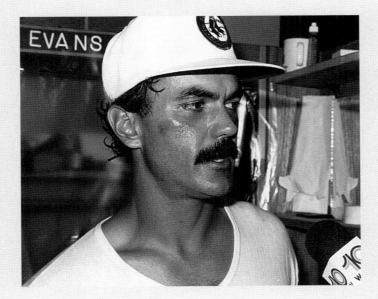

Dwight Evans

 # The Glory of the Boston Marathon: Pioneers, Champions, and Legends

On April 15, 1996, more than fifty thousand runners crowded the roads in and around Hopkinton, Massachusetts, for the 100th running of America's greatest foot race, the Boston Athletic Association Marathon. This unprecedented throng equaled the total number of runners who had toed the starting line from 1897 through 1979. And even that mob could have easily been doubled had the Boston Athletic Association allowed every runner who wanted to compete in the centennial race to take part. No other sporting event in the world can compare with it in terms of size, appeal, and tradition.

Born in the aftermath of the first modern Olympiad in 1896, the Boston Marathon, or American Marathon as it was called at the time, remained an amateur event from 1897 to 1986. And despite the addition of prize money, the race is still run mostly by amateur competitors, who compose roughly 99.9 percent of the field. What has made Boston so special all these years is that it is the one elite marathon that allows every man and every woman the opportunity to compete with the best athletes in the world on the same course and on the same day. It affords workaday athletes the ultimate Walter Mitty experience; not only do they conquer the same physical challenges as the champions, but they are cheered by the same teeming crowds—estimated at well over a million—from Hopkinton to Boston.

Running the Boston Marathon is the real-life version of any number of sports fantasies. Imagine playing at the Augusta National Golf Club the same afternoon as the final round of the Masters and you get an idea of what it is like to run Boston. Imagine stepping up to bat at Fenway Park before an overflow Opening Day crowd and you come close. But there is no sports experience quite like running the Boston Marathon. It is simply Boston's gift to the sporting world.

PIONEERS

John Graham   When Harvard and Boston Athletic Association trainer and manager John Graham led the Boston contingent of athletes to the first modern Olympiad in Athens in 1896, little did he know that roughly a year later he would help create another great sporting tradition. Graham was so moved by the Olympic Marathon that he set about convincing the BAA to establish their own race.

At first the BAA was reluctant to sponsor the race, and so the first marathon held in the United States was in suburban New York in the autumn of 1896. However, in time the BAA agreed to organize the Boston race. Then, on April 19, 1897, runners starting at Ashland embarked on a twenty-four-mile journey to Boston. The tradition was launched. Graham not only suggested that the April date coincide with the celebration on Patriot's Day but also surveyed and set the course. It was thus largely through his efforts that the Boston Marathon was born.

Roberta Gibb   It was the sheer joy of running, not sexual politics, that led Roberta Gibb, the race's first-ever female competitor, to the 1966 Boston Marathon. The Winchester native first began running in the late 1950s with her dogs and later while she was a student at the School of the Museum of Fine Arts. In 1965, she witnessed her first Boston Marathon, loved the race, and decided to run the next year. Following a three-day cross-country bus trip from San Diego, where she lived with her husband, Gibb (then known as Roberta Bingay) arrived in Boston the day before the race. In due time she swapped the nurse's shoes she had planned to wear in the race for a pair of men's size-six running shoes. She combined them with a black one-piece bathing suit, a pair of khaki shorts, and a hooded sweatshirt for her uniform.

Emerging from a hedgerow, to escape detection, Gibb started the race to cheers from her fellow competitors and an especially enthusiastic crowd at Wellesley College. She completed the race in 3:20:00 and shook hands with Governor Volpe, only to be denied the traditional postrace cup of beef stew at the Prudential Center cafeteria. Her male competitors had fully accepted her, but it would be six years before the BAA would officially allow women competitors in the Marathon.

Bob Hall

Bob Hall   In 1975, Bob Hall of Belmont received permission from race director Will Cloney to enter the race and went on to become the first official wheelchair winner of the Boston Marathon, with a time of 2:58:00. Five years earlier, Eugene Roberts, a native of Baltimore who had lost his legs to a Viet Cong landmine, had competed unofficially in the race. Like Roberts, Hall competed in a hospital chair, which was ill-suited to the rugged terrain of the course.

Hall, a Boston State College graduate, had always been active in a variety of sports as a wheelchair competitor. At Boston State he hooked up with coach Bill Squires, who assisted him with his training and recruited him for the Greater Boston Track Club. In 1977, Hall defended his Boston crown while besting a field of six competitors and setting a new course record of 2:40:10. Today, Hall is one of the world's top manufacturers of marathon and sports wheelchairs. He returned to competition for the centennial race in 1996, as an homage to the race that changed his life.

THE GREAT CHAMPIONS

Clarence DeMar   Seven-time winner Clarence DeMar was the Babe
Ruth of his sport. In the glory days of athletics in the roaring twenties,
the press viewed DeMar on a par not only with Ruth but also with athletes like Jack Dempsey, Bill Tilden, Helen Wills, and Red Grange. However, such fame belied a man whose achievements were matched by
his modesty.

A printer by trade, DeMar trained for the marathon by running back
and forth from his Melrose home to his typesetter's job at the *Boston
Herald.* Legend has it that, on more than one occasion, DeMar would
return to work following one of his Boston Marathon victories and set
the type that proclaimed his victory in the next day's paper. DeMar's
career is especially amazing when one learns that he quit marathon
running for nearly a decade at the height of his career on the advice of
a cardiologist. Eleven years elapsed between DeMar's first victory in
1911 and his second in 1922. Five more victories followed, with his last
coming at age forty.

Les Pawson   Les Pawson, a pattern weaver in Pawtucket, Rhode
Island, was another working-class hero of the Boston Marathon. In running circles he was known primarily as a speedy distance runner who
specialized in races of two to ten miles in length. But in 1933, he
changed the Boston Marathon forever when he blazed to a course-
record time of 2:31:01, while coping with the worst headwinds in the
race's history. So strong were the headwinds that Pawson's face, arms,
and legs were visibly chapped and burned.

Pawson's superb form and loping stride carried him to a whopping five-
and-a-half minute margin of victory over future winner Dave Komonen.
In the process, Pawson shaved an incredible two minutes and seven
seconds off the course record.

In 1938, Pawson repeated his feat in seventy-five-degree heat by beating Johnny A. Kelley and Pat Dengis with a time of 2:35:34. In 1941, at
age thirty-six, he won for a third and final time, with a personal best
time of 2:30:38.

Eino Oksanen   Eino Oksanen will always be remembered, both for his
three victories at Boston and for his epic duels with local hero John J.
Kelley. Oksanen, a detective in the Helsinki police department, was

Eino Oksanen

nicknamed "the Ox" because of his muscular 144-pound frame and strength as a runner. In 1959, he won Boston in 2:22:42, a time that women's champion Joan Benoit nearly duplicated in 1983. However, it was Oksanen's second win that was most noteworthy.

In 1961, Oksanen dueled John J. Kelley and Fred Norris for much of the race, only to see a stray dog knock down Kelley in the Newton hills. While the gallant Norris forsook his bid for victory by helping Kelley to his feet, Oksanen took the opportunity to surge toward the finish line. Following the race, Kelley was effusive in his praise of the sportsmanlike Norris; Oksanen would only comment that the dog should be shot. Oksanen captured his third Boston marathon in 1962 with a time of 2:23:48.

Bill Rodgers   Bill Rodgers became the most successful in a long line of interconnected, New England–bred marathon champions that began with Johnny A. Kelley and Jock Semple. Rodgers, a four-time winner, had roomed with 1968 winner Amby Burfoot at Wesleyan. Burfoot, in turn, had been coached by John J. Kelley, who had been inspired by his namesake, John A. Kelley, and coached by Jock Semple. Rodgers's route to fame was unusual, as the former collegiate track star returned to the sport after forsaking cigarettes and other bad habits. His international breakthrough came in the 1975 Boston Marathon, when he broke the course and American records in almost nonchalant fashion. He was the last champion to compete in both the amateur era and professional era and was instrumental in bringing about the latter.

When I first won Boston I was more shocked than anything. I do remember thinking that this was something I could share with Amby Burfoot because we were so close and because it hadn't been that long since he won the race. However, later on I did think about it, and felt that each year I just had to win another—much in the same manner that Johnny Kelley went about preparing for the race. In fact, I sense that Johnny felt even more this way than myself and still does. After all, he has run more than sixty Bostons, and

put simply, no one loves the Boston Marathon more than Johnny Kelley.
Who could possibly love the Boston Marathon more than Johnny?
—Bill Rodgers

Toshihiko Seko   If Bill Rodgers was the marathon's Peter Pan, forever young and enthusiastic, Toshihiko Seko was Boston's Mr. Spock—focused, businesslike, and humorless. Seko was the protégé of the legendary Japanese coach and sports philosopher Kiyoshi Nakamura. Nakamura, an independently wealthy running enthusiast, trained a stable of runners who lived, ran, and studied with him. He designed his workouts and a training regimen to create the best runners in the world. Of Seko he said, "God gave me Seko and I want to thank God by making Seko the best marathon runner in the world."

In 1981, Seko achieved his coach's goal by capturing the first of his two Boston Marathon victories with a course-record time of 2:09:26, which bested Bill Rodgers's record by one second. He returned to Boston in 1987 to post his second victory, in a time of 2:11:50. This victory was in memory of Nakamura, who had died only months before the race. Seko's first act after crossing the finish line was to turn toward Nakamura's widow and bow in respect.

Joan Benoit Samuelson   On meeting Joan Benoit Samuelson, one would not suspect that the petite, soft-spoken mother of two is still, in her forties, one of the best marathoners in America and one of the toughest athletes ever to wear Boston's laurel. Her record-setting victory in 1983 was the prelude to greater glory the following year, when she captured the Olympic-trials marathon just seventeen days after having arthroscopic knee surgery. In Los Angeles, she destroyed the greatest field of women distance runners ever assembled, winning the inaugural women's Olympic Marathon. In addition to raising her family, Samuelson has written two books, given lectures, and conducted clinics around the world.

At mile twenty-three or so somebody came out of the crowd and ran along with me for a few seconds. He said he was a Bowdoin DKE; I didn't catch the name or the class. In one hand he held a beer, in the other, a Red Sox cap. He said, "Either wear the cap or chug the beer," so I grabbed the cap and put it on backward. From then on the Boston people were with me. Patti [Lyons, formerly Catalano] was a local and I'm sure most of the

spectators wanted her to win, but I had a long lead by then. Seeing Bow-
doin written across my chest and the Red Sox cap on my head, the specta-
tors took my victory with grace, even enthusiasm. They've since made
Boston feel like my second home.
—Joan Benoit Samuelson

Jim Knaub

Jim Knaub Jim Knaub has been a pole vaulter and an actor, and both
disciplines have helped him become one of the most prominent athletes in marathon history. His incredible upper-body strength, combined with superb coordination, helped him win five Boston Marathon
titles between 1982 and 1993. His personable nature has made him the
perfect goodwill ambassador for wheelchair athletes. Like Clarence
DeMar before him, Knaub has remained an elite competitor over an
extended period and shows no signs of slowing down. He is one of the
few competitors who have won the wheelchair division both before
and after it was given official status and prize money by the BAA.

Cosmas Ndeti In 1995, Kenyan Cosmas Ndeti became only the third
runner (and the first non-American runner) in marathon history, after
Clarence DeMar and Bill Rodgers, to capture three consecutive races.
Only twenty-nine at century's end, Ndeti is the most likely candidate to

equal or surpass DeMar's total of seven Boston men's titles. Ndeti already owns the course record of 2:07:15, which he set in 1994. He celebrated the second birthday of his son, Gideon Boston Ndeti, on April 17, 1995, with a victory in honor of the boy whom he had named after the race. Ndeti has stated on many occasions that he hopes to run as many Boston Marathons as his hero and role model, Johnny A. Kelley.

LOCAL LEGENDS

John A. Kelley ("The Elder")   It should come as no surprise to learn that the grandparents of the man most singularly associated with the Boston Marathon arrived on these shores from Ireland on April 10, 1870, aboard the S.S. *Marathon.* With such a portent, Johnny A. Kelley was bound to become a Boston Marathon legend.

Johnny A. Kelley may be the most amazing American athlete of the twentieth century. Consider these facts: when Kelley first ran the Boston Marathon in 1928, a young first baseman named Lou Gehrig was just beginning his legendary consecutive-game streak for the New York Yankees. In 1992, on the same day that Kelley finished his sixty-first and final Boston Marathon, a veteran Baltimore Oriole shortstop named Cal Ripken, Jr., was already three-quarters of the way toward breaking Gehrig's streak. Unlike baseball, running is a daily activity that requires a marathoner to train constantly. In the context of streaks and endurance, Kelley is the truest Iron Man of them all.

Of Kelley's sixty-one Boston Marathons, eighteen included top-ten finishes, one of which was an astonishing ninth-place finish at the age of fifty. His two victories, in 1935 and 1945, were separated by a decade, during which he finished as runner-up seven times. To this day, Kelley claims he should have won at least three of those races.

John J. Kelley ("The Younger")   Where but Boston would two elite athletes in the same sport and the same event share the same name yet not be related? The younger Kelley was once quoted as saying, "By fillip of teasing fate I bore the monarch's name." The similarities between the two men are incredible, especially when you consider that the seventy-year-old Kelley is still running marathons like his older namesake, and that his record of one victory and five second-place finishes is remarkably similar to the elder Kelley's record of two victories and seven second-place finishes.

Kelley made history in 1957 when he became the first American to win the Boston Marathon since his namesake had done so in 1945. In later years he engaged in some of the race's great duels, against the likes of Anti Viskari and Eino Oksanen. A teacher and writer by profession, Kelley the Younger is also rapidly approaching his namesake in marathon starts.

John "Jock" Semple   Jock Semple brought a fierce integrity and passion to his work for the Boston Athletic Association. He was also a gentle soul with an enormous generosity of spirit. Simply put, Jock was the heart and soul of the marathon for six decades. As a competitor, the Glasgow-born runner was among the top marathoners in America and finished seventh at Boston in 1930. In later years, he served as an unpaid race coordinator while operating his famed physical therapy clinic (aka "salon de rubdown") from the Boston Athletic Association's offices at Boston Garden. His death in 1988 prompted many runners at that year's marathon to pin plaid ribbons on their singlets in honor of their friend.

Some of the most memorable moments of my life have been at the Boston Marathon. I must list two as the most memorable because it is hard to separate them. In 1930, a year after the Depression started, I was in Philadelphia and out of work, so I hitchhiked to Boston. I came to run the marathon, and also meet my mother, who was visiting from Scotland. I was up with the leaders most of the way, and then started picking them off. In those days it was a solid-gold medal for the first eight, elaborate ones with the unicorns and crossed U.S. flags on them. When I got to eighth, with two miles to go, I had a lump in my throat. I picked up one more place and my mother was there at the finish line. Believe me, that was a thrill. The other, of course, was young John Kelley's win in 1957. He ran the legs off the Finns and everyone else. That was great. I'd had Johnny since he was a sixteen-year-old schoolboy. He had never run for any other club than the Boston Athletic Association.
—Jock Semple

Jerry Nason   Perhaps the greatest nonrunner in Boston Marathon history was a writer who once received a letter, postmarked from Japan, addressed simply to "Most Famous Marathon Writer, Greatest Newspaper, Boston." Needless to say, the letter was delivered to the *Boston Globe*'s Jerry Nason quicker than if it had included his middle name and office number.

Jerry Nason covered fifty Boston Marathons for the *Globe* from 1934 to 1984. Among his lasting contributions to the race was his naming of Heartbreak Hill following the 1936 race and his establishment of the marathon's checkpoint system. Not only was Nason the Boswell of the Boston Marathon, he did more than any writer in America to enhance the reputation of distance running.

Dick and Rick Hoyt   If there is one universal sentiment among spectators at the marathon, it is that the most emotional moment of the race comes when the father-son duo of Dick and Rick Hoyt run by. Their partnership is based on love, both for each other and for the many events in which they compete. Needless to say, the Boston Marathon is the main event on their calendar. Father and son originally began running together when Rick, a victim of cerebral palsy, said he wanted to run Boston, and since 1980 the Holland, Massachusetts, natives have inspired millions with their courage and kinship. The competition has served to bond their family, and they've become as much a fixture of the event as Johnny A. Kelley.

Jerry Nason

THE GREAT RACES

1926   On the day that promised the greatest showdown in marathon history, a wiry outsider from Nova Scotia pulled off an incredible upset. All ten Boston newspapers had devoted considerable space promoting the anticipated duel between reigning Olympic Marathon champion Albin Stenroos and four-time Boston winner Clarence DeMar. Little did they know that a twenty-year-old lad named John Miles had visited the offices of the Boston Athletic Association and proclaimed to the race manager, "You won't be disappointed if I win this race." Such pluck seemed unwarranted as Miles, outfitted in ninety-eight-cent sneakers, lined up against his heroes on Patriot's Day. But Miles dogged Stenroos through the Newton hills and surged to a course record of 2:25:40. The next day's headlines trumpeted the saga of the "unknown runner," and a Boston Marathon legend was born.

1936   The 1936 Boston Marathon turned out to be one of the great all-time showdowns, featuring defending champion Johnny A. Kelley and a running prodigy named Ellison "Tarzan" Brown. Running hard from the gun, Brown set course records at every checkpoint. Lying in wait for Brown to falter, Johnny A. Kelley ultimately abandoned his strategy and gave pursuit through the Newton hills. After making up a substantial deficit of a half-mile, Kelley approached Brown and gave him a friendly tap on the shoulder, which in turn propelled the startled Brown toward the first of his two Boston Marathon titles. Kelley finished in fifth place, with his failed attempt to overtake Brown prompting Jerry Nason of the *Boston Globe* to christen that section of the course "Heartbreak Hill."

1954 In what sportswriters dubbed "The Race of Champions," the 1954 marathon featured a world record holder, champions from America, Europe, and Japan, and the 1948 Olympic Marathon champion. It was the deepest field in the history of the race. The Olympic champion, Delfo Cabrera of Argentina, followed a time-honored Boston tradition by becoming the sixth Olympic champion to fail to win the Boston Marathon. World record holder Jim Peters made the mistake of arriving

Veikka Karvonen (#2) and Jim Peters (#1) during the 1954 marathon

the day before the race and finished second, unable to shake his fatigue. It was left to Veikko Karvonen, a postal clerk from Finland and reigning European champion, to win the race in a time of 2:20:39.

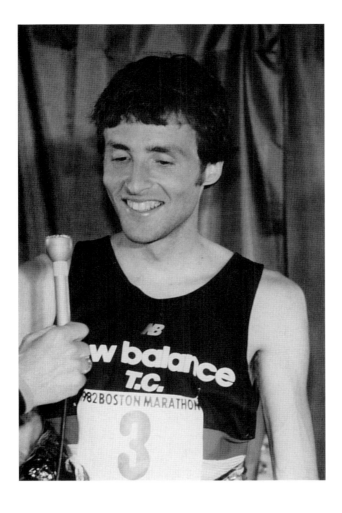

Dick Beardsley

1982   In 1982, Wayland native Alberto Salazar defeated Dick Beardsley in a race characterized by countless lead changes over the last eight miles. It is still considered one of the great duels in Boston Marathon history. Both runners shattered the course record by thirty-three and thirty-five seconds, respectively, while clocking the fourth- and fifth-fastest marathon performances of all time.

Beardsley remarked, "The sun was such that I could see Alberto's shadow, so whenever he tried to come up on me, I would make a move myself." Salazar used his track speed to win in a final desperate sprint. Beardsley summed up his feelings and those of the crowd when he said at the finish line, "It's too bad anybody had to lose."

1988 In one of the closest finishes in Boston Marathon history, two African runners, Juma Ikanga of Tanzania and Ibrahim Hussein of neighboring Kenya, battled down Boylston Street on April 18, 1988. Hussein utilized his forty-seven-second 400-meter speed to edge Ikanga in a race that has come to symbolize the era of African domination of the men's open division.

With his victory, Hussein became the first African to win both the Boston and New York City marathons. He also began an era of African dominance in the men's division. Hussein, who had grown up idolizing Kenyan Olympic hero Kip Keino, has become a national hero himself.

the
Nineties

Lynn Jennings: World Class

Lynn Jennings is ever the individualist. As the greatest American cross-country runner ever, male or female, she has won three world championships and nine American titles. Always reserved and focused, Jennings, along with Joan Benoit Samuelson, has carried high the torch of an honored local long-distance running heritage created by the likes of Clarence DeMar, John A. and John J. Kelley, Les Pawson, Tarzan Brown, Roberta Gibb, and Bill Rodgers. However, unlike any of them, her success has come while running on road and track as well as cross-country. Such versatility makes her the greatest all-around runner in New England history. Much of the drama surrounding her career has unfolded on the roads and trails of Boston.

In the mid-seventies, Jennings was every bit as much a running prodigy as her Bay State counterpart Alberto Salazar, with one major exception. Unlike Salazar, who retired to raise a family after less than a decade in the spotlight, Jennings has competed at the top levels of track and field and road racing for twenty-four years. In this regard she is closer to another local legend, namely Johnny A. Kelley.

As a student at the Bromfield School in Harvard, Massachusetts, Jennings emerged as the best American female distance runner of her generation. Because her school didn't have a girls' track or cross-country team, she was able to experiment as a runner—even running the Boston Marathon at age seventeen. Her time of 2:46 in the 1977 race was world class, and it came on the heels of her having set national records in both the mile and two-mile run.

Jennings matriculated at Princeton in the autumn of 1979. She soon lost her zeal for running and, in her words, became "overweight and confused." Instead of focusing on running, she dedicated herself to studying and finding herself outside the narrow context of running. Following her graduation in 1983, Jennings returned to Massachusetts, where she worked as a legislative aide to Massachusetts state senator John McGovern.

It was soon after her return that Jennings contemplated resurrecting her track career. After consulting with longtime coach and confidante

John Babington, she realized there was running yet to do and set about working her way back to the top. Within five years she had qualified for the 1988 Olympic team in the 10,000 meters, ultimately finishing sixth in the event and vowing to do better the next time.

While preparing for the Barcelona Olympics, Jennings trained at her New Hampshire home as well as in Colorado and California. She soon emerged as the best cross-country runner of her generation and the best American woman since Doris Brown Heritage in the sixties and seventies. Jennings captured three world cross-country titles, one of which was a gem in the snow at Franklin Park in March 1992.

The Franklin Park win was an incredible Boston homecoming that came nearly fifteen years after her triumph in the first Bonne Bell (now Tufts 10K) road race. She would need to launch a devastating kick from nearly five hundred yards out to edge Catherine McKiernan of Ireland before a worldwide TV audience and a roaring crowd of fans and friends who braved unseasonable snow and cold.

Jennings's success carried over to the Barcelona Olympics, where she captured a bronze medal in the 10,000 meters. Her time of 31:19:89 stood as the American record at the end of the century. In 1996, the unpredictable champion dropped down to the 5000 meters competition, at an age when most runners would have contemplated a move up to the marathon. She would finish ninth in the sweltering heat of the Atlanta Olympics.

Lynn Jennings winning the 1992 Tufts 10K road race.

Prior to her start in the 1999 Boston Marathon, Jennings had run in 243 career races and finished in the top three 205 times—an astonishing podium ratio of 84.4 percent. She also had captured at least one national running title, either on the roads or on the track, for fifteen consecutive years—a total of thirty-nine. Of her twelfth-place finish at the 1999 Boston Marathon, Jennings said, "It was a learning experience, just to keep putting one foot in front of the other." But she refused to quit and nailed a qualifying time for the 2000 Olympic trials in the marathon.

 ## *For the Defense: Ray Bourque*

Playing defense for the Boston Bruins has similarities to patrolling left field for the Red Sox. First and foremost is the link to history and the men who played the position in years past. The Red Sox boast of a picket line of left fielders that includes Duffy Lewis, Ted Williams, Carl Yastrzemski, and Jim Rice. Likewise, the Bruins present an equally formidable lineup of defenseman with Lionel Hitchman, Eddie Shore, Dit Clapper, Fernie Flaman, Bobby Orr, Brad Park, and Ray Bourque.

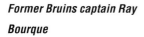
Former Bruins captain Ray Bourque

Ray Bourque has never been concerned with comparisons to other players. While he wisely acknowledges the genius of Bobby Orr, Bourque deflects the inevitable comparisons by noting only their differences. It was a distinct pleasure for Bruins fans to note both the differences and similarities of the two. In fact, Bruins fans have been downright spoiled, getting to watch the two best defensemen ever to wear the black and gold.

In an era obsessed with sports statistics, Ray Bourque stands out as one of the few great athletes whose reputation transcends mere numbers. So it is ironic that, in the twilight of his career, statistics are finally being connected with his name. On December 19, 1998, Bourque moved past Gordie Howe into third place on the all-time NHL assist list. He also leads the league in such career statistics as lifetime goals by a defenseman, while sitting second in assists and points.

Bourque's defensive prowess has helped him capture the Norris Award as the league's best defenseman five times, and he has been a first-team NHL all-star twelve times—which is not to be confused with his record-tying eighteen All-Star Game appearances. The only trophies he has richly deserved but that have eluded him are the Hart Trophy (for league MVP) and the Stanley Cup.

Ray Bourque arrived in Boston as the highly touted eighth choice in the 1979 NHL draft. His selection came on the heels of the most devastating Bruins playoff loss in modern memory, the infamous "too many men on the ice" overtime loss to the Montreal Canadiens in the Stanley Cup semifinals. Bourque, who grew up only a few miles away from the Montreal Forum, was viewed as the player who could help the Bruins break the Montreal jinx and return to the Stanley Cup Finals.

Bourque's rookie season gave every indication of a bright future, as he won the Calder Trophy for being the NHL's best rookie. He became an NHL first-team all-star immediately and allowed Bruins fans to believe that, while he was not Bobby Orr reincarnate, he was the best player they had seen wearing a Bruins uniform since Orr. In his first twenty-one seasons, Bourque helped lead the team to twenty playoff appearances, topped by finals berths in 1988 and 1990.

Bourque's star was forever placed in the galaxy of local sports heroes on the night of December 3, 1987. On a night in which the Bruins were to retire the number 7 in honor of Bruins center Phil Esposito, Bourque stole the show while paying homage to the former star. In an unforgettable moment prior to the raising of Esposito's retirement banner, Bourque took off his number 7 jersey to reveal a new number 77 shirt. Esposito brushed back a tear, and Boston Garden rocked with an emotional ovation directed at both men. It was a gesture as memorable as any Stanley Cup ceremony and one that men such as Hitchman, Shore, Clapper, Flaman, Orr, and Park could applaud both in person and in spirit.

Like Orr and Shore before him, Bourque departed Boston after establishing his Hall of Fame credentials. The trade that sent Bourque to the Colorado Avalanche in March 2000 concluded an era of Bruins' history that lasted nearly a generation.

 ## The 1991 Sports Museum Challenge Cup

The Challenge Cup Tournament in Boston was a major boost towards helping us win the World Cup. That competition raised the bar for the treatment of our program overall.
—Anson Dorrance, U.S. women's soccer head coach, 1985–94

In the spring of 1991, the U.S. women's soccer team was traveling in Europe to play a series of friendly international matches. At one point, they happened to be in Paris at the same time as their male counterparts from the States. The U.S. men's team, longtime also-rans, had qualified for only one World Cup (1990) since their improbable upset victory over England in the 1950 World Cup. However, while the men and their traveling party of soccer officials were housed in a three-star hotel, the women made do in a youth hostel. In seven months, the women would play for the first ever Women's World Cup in China.

1991 was a significant year for soccer in Boston, with Jack Charlton's Irish National Team visiting Foxboro Stadium for a match against the U.S. men in June. Tickets were still being sold at halftime as over fifty-one thousand fans filled Foxboro Stadium and cheered the one-all draw. It was the first ever match for the U.S. Men's National Team in Massachusetts, and it left many wondering why they hadn't visited long before.

Among those who had pushed for the men's visit to Boston was a committee composed of soccer players and fans representing the Sports Museum of New England. Their original vision was to invite both the U.S. men's and women's teams to Boston and stage a doubleheader at either Harvard or Foxboro Stadium, with a portion of the games' proceeds to benefit the educational outreach programs of the museum.

During preliminary discussions related to the match, one prominent official from the United States Soccer Federation indicated that he felt the women might attract an additional five spectators to the match. After a stunned pause, during which committee member Michael LaVigne asked the official to repeat himself, the discussion continued and a deal was struck for the women to appear in Boston exclusive of the men. The U.S. women would meet World Cup contender Norway in a two-match series to be played on a Friday night and Sunday afternoon, with the first match played in New Britain, Connecticut, and the second at the Ellis Oval at Tufts University. Both teams viewed the match as invaluable preparation for the competition to come in China. Few would have predicted it as a preview of the championship match.

Despite the fact the United States lost both games by an aggregate score of 4–2, it played well without the services of striker Michelle Akers-Stahl. The two games also proved popular with Boston fans. The Sunday match was broadcast on SportsChannel, in the first-ever telecast of a U.S. Women's National Team international game on American soil. Fans were treated to a sold-out match that showcased the talents of young superstars such as Kristine Lilly and teenager Mia Hamm.

Karen Jennings in action versus Norway at Tufts University, September 1, 1991.

Three months later in China, the U.S. women turned the tables on Norway as Michelle Akers-Stahl converted an errant Norwegian backpass into the winning goal for a 2–1 victory in the World Cup final. Coach Anson Dorrance, reflecting upon the first-class hotel accommodation, training facilities, and hospitality provided his team in Boston, remarked, "Boston and the [Sports Museum] Challenge Cup has set a new standard for the women's program. There is no doubt that you helped us win the World Cup in China."

In subsequent years, the U.S. women returned to Boston and New England many times. In 1999, they faced North Korea in a World Cup match at a sold-out Foxboro Stadium and came away with a resounding victory on their way to their second World Cup triumph of the decade.

 ## *The Journey of Calvin Davis*

Y'all kids take notice, something good can come out of Franklin Field.
—Helen Davis, mother of Calvin Davis, addressing Boston schoolchildren at a 1996 rally honoring her son.

Calvin Davis signs autographs at Franklin Park following a ceremony in his honor.

In 1896, the odds against a Harvard dropout from South Boston winning a gold medal in the broad jump in the first Olympics were about as great as the odds against a kid from Dorchester High School winning an Olympic medal one hundred years later in only his thirteenth race as a hurdler. But like James Brendan Connolly, who made history and brought glory to Boston and Southie in 1896, Calvin Davis beat the odds to bring glory to the Franklin Field projects in 1996.

In his journey to the victor's podium at Atlanta, Davis cleared a variety of figurative and literal hurdles to achieve his goal. As a kid in Dorchester, Davis was the fastest runner in his class at the Grover Cleveland Middle School. At Dorchester High he was recruited for the track team by coach Charley Hayes, who saw his potential to become a champion runner. Soon he was nationally ranked in the 400 meters and slated to attend Auburn University on a track scholarship following his graduation from high school in 1990.

However, Davis's plans went awry when Auburn claimed they had run out of scholarships for Proposition 48 students. Adrift for several months, Davis moved into his grandfather's house in Eutaw, Alabama, before attending Wallace State Junior College. In a town that Davis has described as "having no place to go with nothing to do," it was easy to focus on studying and running. Before long he had raised his grades and captured the National Junior College outdoor championship in the 400 meters. Soon, a raft of four-year schools were at his door, begging him to attend. Among them were Auburn and the school he always wished to attend, the University of Arkansas.

In selecting Arkansas, Davis entered what was the premiere track school in America during the nineties. Among the trophies he'd capture while a Razorback were the "best newcomer" award for the track squad and an NCAA championship in the 400 meters in 1993. His performance could well have earned him the best newcomer award in all of collegiate track had such an award existed.

Olympic dreams lay ahead, but not in the 400 meters. Aware of the depth in his event, Davis switched to the 400-meter hurdles. In his words, "there were nine guys better than me in the United States [in the 400 meters] even when I won the NCAA's." It would prove a wise move. He qualified for the Atlanta Olympics after competing in the 400-meter hurdles for only the seventh time, a remarkable feat.

In Atlanta Davis blossomed, winning his qualifying heat to earn a spot in the final. In the final he ran a less than flawless race, hitting the first hurdle and scrambling the entire race to make up lost ground. But he recovered enough to earn a bronze medal. In the stands Calvin's mother, watching only the second track meet of her life, screamed with joy when his third-place finish was listed on the scoreboard. Calvin realized the dream that had seemed so distant just six years earlier.

Following the games, Boston mayor Tom Menino feted Davis with a day in his honor. At the ceremony, Roxbury Community College athletic director John Thomas, a two-time Olympic medalist in the high jump, remarked, "It's a great feeling to see a local kid like this do so well, it proves you can work within the system to succeed. You don't have to be from Texas or California. Calvin is a Boston kid, Boston's Champion."

 ## *Jack Parker: Hockey's Mr. Chips*

When Jack Parker became the head hockey coach at Boston University in 1973, Bobby Orr had just won the seventh of his eight Norris Trophies, and a certain Watergate matter had just started making headlines. By the end of the century, Parker had reached his twenty-seventh season, in an age when Terrier alumni could catch the Beanpot broadcast via the Internet from anywhere in the world. The only place where time stood still was Parker's icy domain at Walter Brown arena.

Jack Parker's accomplishments are legendary: two NCAA championships, eighteen Beanpot trophies, and enough graduates who have made it to the NHL to stock an entire alumni team. Four of his players were key members of the 1980 United States Olympic hockey team, including team captain Mike Eruzione. He is the premier college hockey coach of his generation.

Growing up in basketball-mad Somerville in the late fifties and early sixties, Parker played basketball before making the switch to hockey in the eighth grade. It was here that he emulated his twin brother, Bob, following his sibling to hockey power Malden Catholic. But his stay there was short, as the school expelled him for having lied about writing a sick note as a cover-up for skipping school and going to the movies. Luckily, he ended up at Catholic Memorial High in West Roxbury, where he blossomed as a hockey player.

Boston University became Parker's next stop. Here he played under the legendary Jack Kelley. Parker was named captain his senior year and graduated with a finance degree in 1968. But after trying his hand at banking and insurance, Parker decided to follow his heart and seek a position in coaching and teaching. His first breaks came at Medford High School and then Avon High School, where he coached for a few years before Kelley brought him back to Boston University as an assistant.

Jack Parker conducting practice at Walter Brown Arena.

Parker was scarcely older than many of his players when he assumed the head job in 1973. But he proved up to the challenge. Within five seasons he had won an NCAA championship against crosstown rivals Boston College and was directing the most feared team in the ECAC.

Parker's greatest skill has always been a knack for assembling the right blend of players. He often looks for a player with a tremendous work ethic and a varied background, such as a city kid with a prep-school education or the son of a hockey player bent on besting the reputation of his old man. And his teams have remained loyal to him, with relatively few players departing without a degree to turn pro.

Likewise, Parker has remained loyal to Boston University. He has rejected two lucrative offers to coach the Bruins in the past decade. He even once held the title of Athletic Director at Boston University for less than a day before resigning. His reasoning, as with his rejection of the Bruins' offers, was that he felt he was best suited to being Boston University's hockey coach. Period.

In January 1998, Parker faced one of his biggest challenges when he was told an artery to his heart was clogged by a blockage of ninety percent. Following successful surgery, he missed only one game and was back behind the Terriers' bench for the eventual (and some would say inevitable) Beanpot victory.

Over the past few years, Parker has grown especially close to Travis Roy, the young Boston University player who was paralyzed just eleven seconds into his college career. Parker has remained as loyal a friend to Roy as he has to the university and the game itself. This is not surprising for a man who exhorts his players with the same statement before every game: "Let's have some fun."

Mo Vaughn: An MVP Reflects on His Game

Bridgeport, Connecticut, native Mo Vaughn was the greatest local star to play for the Red Sox since Carlton Fisk. He was also a larger than life figure in the mold of Jimmie Foxx and Babe Ruth. Like Ruth, Vaughn was a kid magnet who could do no wrong with young fans. On the field, his bat did the talking, with the booming authority expected of Red Sox heroes. Off the field, Vaughn lived just as large (much to the chagrin of Red Sox management), frequenting local night clubs and strip joints—even if only for breakfast.

The stormy relationship between Vaughn and Red Sox management led to the slugger's departure to the Anaheim Angels as a free agent following the 1998 season. His 1995 MVP season and children's foundation remain his lasting legacy in Boston.

On the 1995 MVP award: *It's not like I'm going to go out and say,
"That's the best year I've ever had." It might look like that on the stat
sheet. But in my mind, I had some flaws, though I'm not going to tell
everybody what those are. But I still had some parts of my game that still
had to come up. Man, you can never rest in this game. You can play as
long as you want now, with expansion and all the different teams. So now,
it's just a competition with yourself to go out and produce. And that's what
I'm going to do.*

*I'm a young guy, I'm still learning this game. Who knows what I can do if I
put it all together? A complete year? I don't know what type of honors that
brings. But I do know I can go out there and play the game the way it's supposed to be played. And if I do that, good things will happen.*

Mo Vaughn

*I'm not going to make a lot of brash
changes and I'm not going to change my
concepts or change my ideas about how
I play the game. I'm going to do what
made me an MVP. I just want to do it a
little better, try to do more. It's a will to
excel.*

On his game and values: *There's no
time in the off-season to think negative
thoughts, to think what I could have,
should have, would have done. I've got
some fine-tuning to do, and I have all
this time in the off-season to think about
what I will do.*

*It doesn't matter if I'm making one dollar
or twenty-five million dollars. I'm going
to continue to go out there and compete.
My first goal is to try to help my club get
back into the playoffs and to do a better
job in the playoffs to help us to win. We
have a great team. We know we're going
to win and that's all you can ask for, to
be in that position. I'll be ready to go
because my pride and name on my bat
mean more to me than anything.*
—Mo Vaughn

Reggie Lewis 1965–1993: Rest in Peace

I'll remember him as a great son. I am proudest that he always cared for everybody else before himself. He was loyal to his family and his friends and he'd do anything for us.
—*Irvin "Butch" Lewis, Reggie's father*

With the life he lived as a celebrity, this community belonged to him, but he also allowed it that he belonged to the community. He did more, in his short life, for race relations in this city than anyone else. It wasn't by design. It was just Reggie.
—*M. L. Carr, Boston Celtics*

I once read a quote that applies more to Reggie Lewis than any other professional athlete I've known: "It's nice to be important, but it's more important to be nice." That sums up Reggie to a T.
—*Dave Gavitt, Boston Celtics vice chairman*

Reggie was an unselfish team player. He wanted to win. I thought the future of the Celtics was in good hands with him and our other young players.
—*Larry Bird, Boston Celtics, 1979–92*

I'll always remember that big smile on his face. He was a very kind person, a good guy to be around. He always tried to see the good things in people, the silver lining in the black cloud.
—*Kevin McHale, Boston Celtics, 1980–93*

He was very caring, very soft, very warm, very friendly. Reggie chose the quiet way to lead. He just went out and did whatever he needed to do.
—*Dennis Johnson, Boston Celtics, 1983–90*

Despite the exposure and attention he received in college, and the superstar status he achieved as a professional, he remained essentially a shy, unaffected, concerned person. He was fully aware of his responsibilities to his family, his teammates, and the community he lived in.
—*Bob Cousy, Boston Celtics, 1950–63*

I'll remember Reggie as a very self-disciplined athlete. He was very quick. He could shoot the ball extremely well. He was team-oriented and one of those guys who is a pleasure to coach. He epitomized being a Celtic.
—*Red Auerbach, Boston Celtics vice-chairman of the board*

When he was with the Celtics, he would come back to Northeastern all the time. Sometimes he would go to the gym to play ball, and he might come over and play with old-timers, like me, or he might play with some students—who obviously weren't in his league.

Reggie Lewis, c. 1992

But Reggie wouldn't try to embarrass you or devastate you. One of the things that always amazed me was that these students would come running back to me and they'd tell me they'd played basketball with Reggie. And in the next breath they'd say, 'Hey, Dean Motley, I was killing him in the gym!' Yeah, right. And he was fronting Michael Jordan last night. The thing is, Reggie wasn't in the business of taking away dreams, because he understood what dreams were about and how he had had one of his own dreams fulfilled.
—Dean Keith Motley, Northeastern University

The Celtics' first-round pick in the 1987 NBA draft, Reggie Lewis was a four-year starter at Northeastern University, where he led the Huskies to four straight NCAA tournament appearances. Reggie was named captain of the Celtics after the retirement of Larry Bird, and he kept the team playing playoff-caliber basketball after Bird's departure.

In 1992, Lewis was named to the all-star team, the only Celtic to earn the honor that year. During the 1991–92 season, he became the first player to lead the Celtics in scoring (20.8 ppg), steals (125), and blocked shots (105) in the same season.

The Country Club:
The 1999 Ryder Cup

Overhyped. Overwrought. Boorish. Noble. Inspiring. Excessive. Heroic. All aptly describe the 1999 Ryder Cup, a tradition-bound golf tournament between the United States and Europe that transformed the lush surroundings of The Country Club in Brookline into a corporate Woodstock. Rumor has it that so garish were one pair of slacks, worn near the mammoth Fidelity Corporate Hospitality Tent, that their offending pigment was spotted by an Interpol surveillance tracking satellite.

Justin Leonard celebrates "The Putt" on the seventeenth green.

The 1999 Ryder Cup was the perfect event for the end of a decade defined by the Standard and Poor index. It was also a time when anyone with standards probably was poor and certainly not anywhere near Brookline, Massachusetts, on the weekend of September 24–26. Tickets to the event and even passes to practice rounds were routinely traded earlier in the summer on a one-to-two basis for tickets to the All-Star Game at Fenway Park. Boston had never experienced a sporting event with as sheer a magnitude of money and hype as the Ryder Cup.

Leafy fairways and corporate tents aside, all talk before the tournament had centered around money and the demand by American players that a larger share of the prize money be allocated to them and/or their designated charities. Before a single drive had rocketed from a tee, the United States team was already the object of ridicule both here and abroad for its financial demands. Team captain Ben Crenshaw did all he could do to keep from exploding while reminding his charges that they carried a mantle previously toted by the likes of Bobby Jones, Walter Hagen, Ben Hogan, Arnold Palmer, and Jack Nicklaus.

The Country Club was the perfect setting for golf's de facto Olympics. It was here that Francis Ouimet had scored the first monumental victory in American golf history when he defeated Harry Vardon and Ted Ray in a playoff to win the 1913 U.S. Open. Ouimet's victory almost instantaneously opened the game up to the public. Only in America could a former caddie, with a ten-year-old caddie guiding him through the most prestigious tournament in the nation, achieve such an improbable victory.

At the end of the century, Brookline would again lend itself as a backdrop for the seemingly impossible, this time on the final day of the 1999 Ryder Cup. As a stunning early autumn Sunday morning dawned, the tournament, on its final day, seemed to have sunk beneath the weight of its own expectations. Not only had the U.S. team fallen into a nearly insurmountable four-point deficit, but the galleries had even grown testy and vocal. It would take a miracle finish for the Americans to regain a trophy they had not won since 1993.

Ouimet himself would have appreciated the grit with which the American players approached their Sunday matches. Team captain Ben Crenshaw wept openly as his men captured the first six matches of the day and eight of the twelve singles matches to win the cup. It was almost as if Ouimet's spirit had appeared at the seventeenth green to help guide Justin Leonard's monumental forty-five-foot putt homeward. For it was also on the seventeenth green that Ouimet had made crucial putts in both the final round and playoff to win his historic open. Leonard's gem was the culmination of a stretch in which the Texan won five straight holes to overtake Masters champion José Maria Olazábal. Their resulting draw proved crucial, as the half point gained by Leonard contributed mightily to the U.S. victory.

The celebration on the seventeenth green following Leonard's epic putt delayed Olazábal's twenty-foot putt and momentarily diminished the spirit of the competition. However, the achievement of the American team cannot be diminished or underestimated. It was a comeback to rank with the greatest in sports, much less golf, history.

The 1999 Ryder Cup was an event for the ages hosted by the best sports city in America, if not the world. And, in keeping with the corporate identity of the tournament, even the score sounded like a Dow Jones listing: U.S.A. 14½, Europe 13½. How sweet it was.

The victorious 1999 United States Ryder Cup Team celebrates its victory at The Country Club.

The 1999 Red Sox

The first Red Sox century ended with a surprisingly satisfying season, considering its beginnings. The 1999 campaign opened under the cloud of talk-show dissatisfaction and pessimism about the prospects for the new season. This pessimism was fueled by a number of factors, including the Yankees' 114-win season in 1998; the media blitz for a new Fenway Park; the defection of Mo Vaughn to the Anaheim Angels after an extraordinarily acrimonious public debate over his value to the team and the community; the willingness and ability of the club to pay big money for players given the shadowy financial dealings of the Yawkey Trust; and General Manager Dan Duquette's apparent inability to get along with the massive egos of stars like Vaughn and Roger Clemens.

The acquisition of free agent Jose Offerman after the departure of Vaughn seemed to epitomize the fate of the Red Sox. Management had replaced a slugger with a second baseman who was not known for defense and couldn't hit homers but might steal bases, when the club needed power, defense, and pitching. Coming into the season, the Red Sox were pinning their hopes on Pedro Martinez and Nomar Garciaparra—both superb and charismatic players, but not enough to carry this team much higher than fourth place.

The team's lack of stars was compounded by the loss of Tom Gordon (the American League's best reliever in 1998), who entered the 1999 season with a streak of forty-three consecutive saves. Gordon managed to run the streak to fifty-four before going on the disabled list until the end of September with a bad elbow. Without their best slugger and closer, 1999 should have been a lost year.

It wasn't. The 1999 season turned out to be a vindication of Dan Duquette's general managing and Jimy Williams's field managing. The club got off to a hot start, as the Sox won their first five games and Jose Offerman hit .341 in April. Furthermore, Mo Vaughn was injured in the opening game of the season, which silenced the inevitable comparisons between the two players and the volcanic negativity poised to erupt from the press, sports radio, and the bleachers.

The club finished April 11–11, tied for third place. The pitching staff consisted of Pedro Martinez (off to his usual brilliant start), wily Bret

Saberhagen and his rebuilt right shoulder, unpredictable knuckleballer Tim Wakefield, well-traveled veterans Pat Rapp and Mark Portugal, and youngster Brian Rose, with a bullpen that included an ailing Gordon, ever-promising Derek Lowe, ever-hopeful John Wasdin, rotund Rich Garces, and solid Rheal Cormier. The offense paralleled the pitching with a superstar in Nomar Garciaparra, a solid veteran in Mike Stanley, a questionable veteran in John Valentin, and a good-but-not-great hitter in Troy O'Leary. But there were serious doubts about catcher, first base, and right field. Jason Varitek had yet to hit, Brian Daubach was unknown to all but Dan Duquette, and right fielder Trot Nixon was a slow-developing prospect from the Lou Gorman era. After Pedro and Nomar, the club looked like spare parts, castoffs, and waiver-wire bargains.

In May, the Red Sox won twenty of twenty-eight games, and were in first place on Memorial Day, setting the tone for a remarkable year. Pedro Martinez, 10–1 on June first, went on to have one of the very greatest seasons in the live ball era. Pedro was virtually unbeatable and, at times, unhittable. He would finish the season with a record of 23–4, compiling 313 strikeouts in 213 innings while walking only 37. His ERA of 2.04 was almost a run-and-a-half better than the next best. The high point came on September 10 in Yankee Stadium, when Pedro pitched a one-hitter, walking none and fanning seventeen—the most ever against the Yankees. Observers agreed it was the most dominating game ever pitched against the Yankees at the Stadium. Yankee hitters looked like they'd given up.

Meanwhile, Nomar Garciaparra led a surprisingly balanced offense, leading the American League in hitting with a .357 average, despite missing twenty-seven games. On May 10 against Seattle, Nomar hit three home runs (two were grand slams), and drove in ten runs. The rest of the lineup, shrewdly manipulated by Jimy Williams, was a surprise. Four players, including the unknown Daubach and unproven Varitek, hit twenty or more homers. Mike Stanley hit nineteen, and Trot Nixon, after a horrendous spring, hit fifteen.

The pitching, after Pedro, was a clever patchwork of veterans, pick-ups, good middle-inning relievers (especially Derek Lowe) and a carefully juggled combination of Tim Wakefield, Lowe, Wasdin, and Rod Beck at closer. Eight pitchers won six or more games. Only Pedro and Bret Saberhagen won ten or more. Like the offense, the pitching was a well-managed team effort.

After winning ninety-three games and clinching the American League wild card, the Red Sox met the Cleveland Indians in the first round of the playoffs. Disaster struck twice in the first game. Pedro pulled a muscle in his back in the fourth inning and had to leave the game, and the Indians scored in the ninth inning to win 3–2. It was unclear if Martinez could pitch again in the postseason. Cleveland then bombed Bret Saberhagen in game two, winning 11–1. The Indians, needing only one win, faced Ramón Martinez in game three. Martinez had pitched only 20.2 innings all year, and the Boston lineup was without Nomar Garciaparra, whose wrist was bothering him again after a late-season beaning. But Ramón pitched well, and the Sox scored six runs in the seventh inning to win 9–3. In game four, Boston started late-season pick-up Kent Mercker, which seemed like a gamble. The Red Sox, however, scored eighteen runs in the first five innings and set playoff

Pedro Martinez enjoyed one of the greatest seasons ever for a pitcher in 1999.

THE NINETIES

records by scoring twenty-three runs on twenty-four hits (including two homers and seven RBIs by John Valentin), to force a fifth and deciding game.

The last game was the stuff of legend. Saberhagen was hit hard and the Sox trailed 5–2 after two innings, but the team went ahead 7–5 in the third on a Troy O'Leary grand slam. Then, after Cleveland rallied to close the gap, Jimy Williams brought in Pedro. No one, including the manager, expected Martinez to be able to pitch more than an inning or two. Incredibly, Pedro pitched six no-hit innings, and Boston won 12–8 on another O'Leary homer. Pedro could not throw as hard as usual, but he adjusted his motion and destroyed the Indians with breaking balls and an indomitable will.

The American League Championship Series against the Yankees was a frustrating anticlimax with another moment of Pedro Martinez glory. Bad umpiring and Yankee depth did in the Sox. Boston led in game one 3–0, but the Yankees scored two runs in the second inning and tied it in the seventh. In the top of the tenth inning, with Jose Offerman on first, Brian Daubach hit a hard shot to third, and Yankee Chuck Knoblauch dropped the relay throw at second base. But umpire Rick Reed called Offerman out (he later admitted he made a mistake) and the inning eventually ended on a double play. Bernie Williams, the first Yankee batter in the tenth, homered to end it.

The Red Sox also led the next night 2–0, but lost 3–2. Game three marked the return of Roger Clemens to Fenway Park, in a match-up with Pedro. The game was heralded as the biggest meeting of aces at Fenway since Joe Wood dueled Walter Johnson in 1912. Pedro lived up to expectations, pitching seven shutout innings. Meanwhile, Boston hammered Clemens for five runs in two innings and won 13–1. But New York won the next two games, 9–2 and 6–1, to take the series. Another bad call against the Red Sox in the ninth inning of game five led to a near riot, as fans pelted the field with paper cups and showered Yankees and umpires with invective.

Although the loss was hard to swallow, there was much for Boston fans to be proud of. The 1999 Red Sox will be remembered for far surpassing expectations, for returning from the dead against the Indians, and for the deadly competitiveness and lethal stuff of Pedro Martinez.
—*Luke Salisbury*

 ## *Snapshots from the Decade*

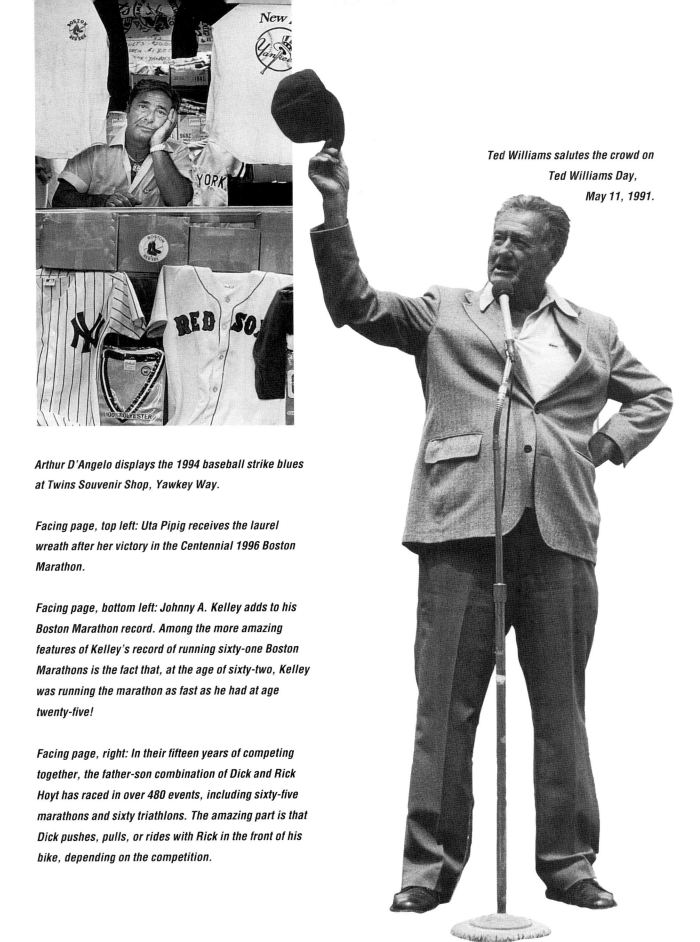

Arthur D'Angelo displays the 1994 baseball strike blues at Twins Souvenir Shop, Yawkey Way.

Facing page, top left: Uta Pipig receives the laurel wreath after her victory in the Centennial 1996 Boston Marathon.

Facing page, bottom left: Johnny A. Kelley adds to his Boston Marathon record. Among the more amazing features of Kelley's record of running sixty-one Boston Marathons is the fact that, at the age of sixty-two, Kelley was running the marathon as fast as he had at age twenty-five!

Facing page, right: In their fifteen years of competing together, the father-son combination of Dick and Rick Hoyt has raced in over 480 events, including sixty-five marathons and sixty triathlons. The amazing part is that Dick pushes, pulls, or rides with Rick in the front of his bike, depending on the competition.

Ted Williams salutes the crowd on Ted Williams Day, May 11, 1991.

Index

Credits

Photography

Unless otherwise indicated, the photographs in this book are from the collection of the Sports Museum of New England (SMNE).

Page xi (top): Courtesy Northeastern University

2: Courtesy Keeper of the Prints, Boston Public Library

3: SMNE/Sam Foulds Donation

4–5: Courtesy John Sears

9: SMNE/Tim Leone Donation

10–11: Courtesy Northeastern University

12: Courtesy Stanley Museum

19: Courtesy Richard Johnson

20: Courtesy National Baseball Hall of Fame

21: Courtesy Michael Andersen Collection

23: Courtesy Richard Johnson

25: Courtesy *Boston Herald*

28: Courtesy Harvard University Sports Information Department

31: Courtesy Baseball Antiquities

33 (top): Courtesy National Baseball Hall of Fame

33 (bottom): SMNE/Frank Bradley Donation

41: Courtesy Richard Johnson

46–47: SMNE/Sam Foulds Donation

51: Courtesy Boston Athletic Association

56: Courtesy *Boston Herald*

57 (top): Courtesy *Boston Herald*

59: Courtesy *Boston Herald*

61: Courtesy Boston Athletic Association

63: Courtesy Pro Football Hall of Fame

66, 71: Courtesy *Boston Globe*

78: Courtesy Pro Football Hall of Fame

84, 86: Courtesy George Altison

90: Courtesy Boston Athletic Association

93: Courtesy Keeper of the Prints, Boston Public Library

99, 101–102: Courtesy *Boston Herald*

107: Courtesy Frank MacDonald

109: Courtesy *Boston Herald*

112–114: SMNE/Dick Thompson Collection

116: Courtesy George Sullivan

118: Courtesy Boston Athletic Association

121: Courtesy New Boston Garden Corporation

125: Courtesy Frank MacDonald

127: Courtesy Maxwell Collection

130: Courtesy John Brooks

134: Courtesy Boston University

136 (top): Courtesy *Boston Globe*

136 (bottom): Courtesy *Boston Herald*

139: Courtesy *Boston Herald*

144 (bottom): Courtesy George Sullivan

147: Courtesy *Boston Herald*

148 (top): SMNE/Bill Cleary Donation

148 (bottom left): Courtesy Brearley Collection of Rare Negatives

159: Courtesy Brearley Collection of Rare Negatives

160: Courtesy *Boston Herald*

162–163: Courtesy Harvard University Sports Information Department

167 (top and bottom): SMNE/John Thomas Donation

169: Courtesy Boston Athletic Association

174: Courtesy Northeastern University

176: Courtesy Al Ruelle, Photographer

179: Courtesy Brearley Collection of Rare Negatives

181: Courtesy *Sports Illustrated,* photograph by Dick Raphael

183: Courtesy *Boston Herald*

184 (top): Courtesy Boston Athletic Association

185–188: Photographs by Michael Andersen

189: Courtesy John Sandhaus, photographer

192: Photograph by Ray Lussier

194: Photograph by Michael Andersen

195: Courtesy Al Ruelle, photographer

197: Courtesy Jeff Johnson, photographer

199: SMNE/Dave Cowens Donation

201: Courtesy Tom Miller, photographer

202: Courtesy Northeastern University

204–205: Courtesy *Boston Herald*

207: Courtesy Tom Miller, photographer

211: Courtesy *Boston Herald*

212: Courtesy Fay Foto, Inc.

214: Courtesy Boston Red Sox

215, 217: Courtesy *Boston Herald*

218–219: Photographs by Richard Johnson

220–226: Courtesy Boston Athletic Association

230–232: Courtesy Boston Athletic Association

235–236: Courtesy *Boston Herald*

239: Courtesy Tom Miller, photographer

240–250: Courtesy *Boston Herald*

253–254: Courtesy Boston Baseball and Michael Rutstein, Photographer/Publisher

256 (top left): Courtesy *Boston Herald*

257 (left): Courtesy *Boston Herald*

257 (right): Photograph by Richard Johnson

Text

Pages 14–18: Passage excerpted from Francis Ouimet, *A Game of Golf.* Friends of Francis Ouimet and Francis Ouimet Caddie Scholarship Fund, 1963.

29: Harry Hooper quote excerpted from Lawrence S. Ritter, *The Glory of Their Times: The Story of the Early Days of Baseball Told by the Men Who Played It.* New York: Morrow, 1984.

50–52: Passages excerpted from Clarence DeMar, *Marathon.* Brattleboro, Vt.: Stephen Daye Press, 1937.